Collins
Spanish
Phrasebook
and Dictionary

KU-492-353

Spanish Phrasebook and Dictionary

Other languages in the
Collins Phrasebook and Dictionary series:
French, German, Greek, Italian, Japanese,
Mandarin, Polish, Portuguese, Turkish.

HarperCollins Publishers
Westerhill Road, Bishopbriggs,
Glasgow G64 2QT

www.collinslanguage.com

First published 2004
This edition published 2008

Reprint 10 9 8 7 6 5 4 3 2

© HarperCollins Publishers 2004, 2008

ISBN 978-0-00-726456-8

Typeset by Davidson Pre-Press Graphics Ltd,
Glasgow

Printed in Malaysia for Imago

Contents

Your *Collins Spanish Phrasebook and Dictionary* is a handy, quick-reference guide that will help make the most of your stay abroad. Its clear layout will save valuable time when you need that crucial word or phrase. Download free all the essential words and phrases you need to get by from www.collinslanguage.com/talk60. These hour long audio files are ideal for practising listening comprehension and pronunciation. The main sections in this book are:

Everyday Spain – photoguide
Packed full of photos, this section allows you to see all the practical visual information that will help with using cash machines, driving on motorways, reading signs, etc.

Phrases
Practical topics are arranged thematically with an opening section, Key talk containing vital phrases that should stand you in good stead in most situations. Phrases are short, useful and each one has a pronunciation guide so that there is no problem saying them.

Eating out
This section contains phrases for ordering food and drink (and special requirements) plus a photoguide showing different places to eat, menus and practical information to help choose the best options. The menu reader allows you to work out what to choose.

Grammar
There is a short Grammar section explaining how the language works.

Dictionary
And finally, the practical 5000-word English-Spanish and Spanish–English Dictionary means that you won't be stuck for words.

So, just flick through the pages to find the information you need and listen to the free audio download to improve your pronunciation.

Useful websites

Accommodation
www.abouthotel.com

www.europeanhostels.com (hostels)

www.hostels.com/es.html (Hostel accommodation)

www.venere.com

www.parador.es (Paradors)

Culture & Activities
www.cyberspain.com

www.gomadrid.com (What's on in Madrid)

www.operabase.com

www.surinenglish.com (Costa del Sol news in English)

www.webmadrid.com (Information on the capital)

Currency Converters
www.x-rates.com

Driving
www.aseta.es (Spanish motorways)

www.dgt.es

www.drivingabroad.co.uk

Facts
www.cia.gov/library/publications/the-world-factbook

Foreign Office Advice
www.fco.gov.uk/travel

www.dfat.gov.au (Australia)

www.voyage.gc.ca (Canada)

Health advice
www.dh.gov.uk/travellers

www.thetraveldoctor.com

www.smartraveller.gov.au (Australia)

www.phac-aspc.gc.ca (Canada)

Internet Cafés
www.cybercafes.com

Passport Office
www.ukpa.gov.uk

www.passports.gov.au (Australia)

www.pptc.gc.ca (Canada)

Pets
www.defra.gov.uk/animalh/quarantine

Sightseeing
www.goski.com (Skiing info for Pyrenees and Andalucia)

www.okspain.org (to Spain from US)

www.revistaiberica.com

www.tourspain.es (National Tourist Office site)

Transport
www.europeanrailguide.com

www.iberia.com (National airline)

www.metrobilbao.net

www.metromadrid.es (Madrid metro)

www.raileurope.com (info on train travel and passes)

www.renfe.es (National rail network)

www.spain-2.com/autobuses.html (Spanish coach services)

www.tmb.net (Barcelona)

Weather
www.bbc.co.uk/weather

We've tried to make the pronunciation under the phrases as clear as possible. We've broken the words up to make them easy to read, but don't pause between syllables. The syllable to be stressed is shown in **bold type**. Spanish isn't really hard to pronounce and once you learn a few basic rules, it shouldn't be too long before you can read straight from the Spanish.

Most letters are pronounced as in English: **b**, **ch**, **d**, **f**, **k**, **l**, **m**, **n**, **p**, **s**, **t**, **y** and (usually) **w** and **x**. As for the vowels, **a** is always as in 'tap' (never as in 'tape'); **e** is always as in 'pet' (never as in 'Pete'); **i** is always ee; **o** is always as in 'hop' (never as in 'hope'); **u** is always oo rather than the English sound 'hut'. They keep their sound even in combination with other letters, so au (e.g. **autobus ow**-to-boos) is like English ow, not like English 'automatic'.

6

The letter **h** is always silent, and **r** is always rolled (even more strongly when double **r**). Spanish **v** and **b** are pronounced exactly the same, something like English **b**, while **q** is like English **k**. The letter **c** before **e** or **i** and the letter **z** are pronounced like the **th** in 'thin'. The letter **g** before **e** or **i** and the letter **j** have the guttural sound you hear in the Scottish word 'loch' and which we show as **kh**.

Basic rules to remember are:

Spanish	sounds like	example	pronunciation
ll	mi**lli**on	**calle**	**kal**-ye
ñ	o**ni**on	**mañana**	ma-**nya**-na
c	**c**at	**comer**	ko-**mer**
c (before **e**/**i**)	**th**ink	**hacer**	a-**ther**
g	**g**ot	**gafas**	**ga**-fas
g (before **e**/**i**)	lo**ch**	**hijo**	**ee**-kho
z	**th**ink	**zapatos**	tha-**pa**-tos
j	lo**ch**	**hijo**	**ee**-kho
q	**k**ick	**quiero**	**kyer**-o

Everyday photoguide

Everyday Spain

ABIERTO

Open

CERRADO

Closed

Most shops close for lunch from 1.30–4.30pm and stay open till about 8.30pm.

Salida

Exit Salida is also used for 'exit' on motorways.

PROHIBIDO FUMAR

No Smoking The word for forbidden is **prohibido**.

ESTA VD.

You The polite word for 'you' is **Usted** (abbreviated to **Vd**).

USTED ESTÁ AQUÍ

Usted está aquí means 'you are here.'

FUERA DE SERVICIO

Out Of Order If something is working, you will see the words **en servicio**.

Informació

Information You will notice in Mallorca that the Spanish is slightly different. This is Mallorquín.

ENTRADA

EINGANG - ENTRANCE

Entrance Look out for **entrada libre** which means free entry (museums, etc).

CAJA

Pay Here 'Caja' is the till or cash box.

horario

Timetable Hour is **hora** ('h' is silent).

 Cash machines are known as **cajeros automáticos** and are widely available. You can carry out the transaction in English and it saves time queuing in banks. Check your bank's handling fee before you go on holiday.

 In Spanish a comma is used instead of a decimal point. This is the price per kilo (**kg**).

Euro Spain is in the euro zone.

Precios

Prices

 Most banks can be identified by the word **Banco** or **Caja** (**Caixa**). The big banks in Spain include **BBVA**, **Banco de Santander**, **Caixa de Cataluña** and **Caja España**. Banks usually open from 9am until around 2pm.

The euro is the currency of Spain. It breaks down into 100 euro cents. Notes: 5, 10, 20, 50, 100, 200, 500. Coins: 1 and 2 euros, 1, 2, 5, 10, 20 and 50 cents. Although coins are officially **cents**,

 Spanish people call them **céntimos** (**then**-tee-mos). Euro is pronounced **eoo**-ro. Euro notes are the same throughout Europe. The backs of coins carry different designs from each of the member European countries.

Some cash dispensers are accessed by swiping your card in the door. Either the green light will flash for you to enter (**acceso libre**) or the red light will flash to indicate out of service (**fuera de servicio**).

Cash Machine
Operates as at home.
Borrar = clear
Cancelar = cancel
Anotación = proceed

Tipping in Spain is usually about 5-10% of the bill. This is to cover service which is generally not included.

 Importe exacto = coins

No devuelve cambio = no change given

recibo
Receipt

billetes
Banknotes

 Friends and acquaintances greet each other with a kiss on each cheek if one of the people is female. Even if you are just being introduced to someone for the first time.

 Tobacconists are known as **estancos**, state-licensed shops which sell tobacco products, stamps, bus tickets, postcards and basic stationery. Look for the distinctive maroon sign with the yellow script and leaf logo. If you want stamps it is much easier to buy them here. Post offices are not as easy to come across.

 Police The **Policía local/municipal** deals with local bylaws and parking. Emergency no. is 092. **Guardia Civil** deals with traffic accidents and driving offences.

Museo

HORARIO
De 10:00 a 21:00.
Domingos de 10:00 a 14:30
Martes Cerrado

Museum Most close one day a week usually Monday. In this sign the museum is closed Tuesday (**Martes Cerrado**). **Domingos** = Sundays. There are 3 dates worth mentioning when admission is free. They are: May 18th (International Museum Day), Oct. 12th (Spanish National Holiday), and Dec. 6th (Constitution Day). You can sometimes get a discount with an International Student Card.

CONSERVE SU ENTRADA HASTA LA SALIDA

Keep Ticket Until Exit The word for ticket is **billete** or **tique** for bus, train, etc. and **entrada** for museum, cinema, etc.

SE VENDE 270544
se vende = for sale

SE ALQUILA
OFICINA-983-270544
se alquila = for rent

OFICINA DE TURISMO

Tourist Information The tourist office can help with accommodation, local attractions and transport, etc. There will usually be at least one English-speaker in the office.

BUEN TIEMPO
GOOD WEATHER

PRECAUCION
PRECAUTION

PELIGRO
DANGER

PLAYA
JOSELUIS
HAMACAS
2,40€

Playa = beach
Hamacas = sunshades
The orange sign indicates restricted swimming areas.

Most tourist beaches have a lifeguard and flag system. They are cleaned regularly and have shower (but not changing) facilities.

ITALIA
2ª PLANTA

Accommodation is divided into several different categories: hotels, **pensiones** and **hostales**. There is not much difference between the latter two. They are usually owned by a live-in proprietor, like very large guest-houses, and do not provide meals.

Post Office is **Correos**. Signs and postboxes are yellow.

piscina

Swimming Pool
You must wear a swimming cap at all indoor pools.

OCUPADO

Engaged

LIBRE

Vacant

Ladies

Gents

Post Box When sending normal letters or cards, find a yellow postbox. If you have a choice, use the slot marked **EXTRANJERO** (Overseas). Red boxes are for a faster service (**urgente**) for which you pay a higher rate.

Taps F = **Frio** (cold)
C = **Caliente** (hot).
The red tap will be hot and the blue will be cold.

Toilets Look out for the words **Servicios** and **Aseos**, both mean toilets.

AGUA NO POTABLE

Not Drinking Water Water is **agua ag**-wa.

Spanish people are very conscious about recycling. Most homes have 2 or 3 different rubbish bins: one for organic material, one for inorganic material and one for paper. The containers in the street are labelled: blue for paper, yellow for containers and inorganic material, grey for organic material and green for glass.

Timetables

Los Días		The Days
lunes	**loo**-nes	Monday
martes	**mar**-tes	Tuesday
miércoles	**myer**-ko-les	Wednesday
jueves	**khwe**-bes	Thursday
viernes	**byer**-nes	Friday
sábado	**sa**-ba-do	Saturday
domingo	dom-**een**-go	Sunday

In Spanish, neither months nor days start with a capital letter as they do in English.

mañana
Morning

tarde
Afternoon

| departures | arrivals | frequency | daily |

Salidas Barcelona Nord	Llegadas Madrid	Frecuencias
01:00	08:30	Diario (*)
07:00	14:30	Diario (*)
08:30	16:00	Diario (**)
09:00	16:30	Diario (*)
10:00	17:30	Diario (**)

Timetable
Horarios = times

Los Meses		The Months
enero	en-**er**-o	January
febrero	feb-**rer**-o	February
marzo	**mar**-tho	March
abril	a-**breel**	April
mayo	**ma**-yo	May
junio	**khoon**-yo	June
julio	**khool**-yo	July
agosto	a-**gos**-to	August
septiembre	sept-**yem**-bre	September
octubre	ok-**too**-bre	October
noviembre	nob-**yem**-bre	November
diciembre	deeth-**yem**-bre	December

Opening Hours
Monday to Friday

Saturdays

Horario de Apertura
Lunes a Viernes:
de 8:30 a 20:30 h.
Sábados:
de 9:30 a 14:00 h
Domingos y Festivos:
ERRADO

Sundays and holidays closed

Tickets

A 10-journey **metro-bus** ticket (10 **viajes**) can be used on the metro and buses. On a bus, you validate it in the machine beside the driver.

A 10-journey bus ticket is known as a **bono-bus**. Validate it in the machine next to the driver in the direction of the arrow. These tickets can be used by a group of you, provided it is validated for each person.

LLEGADAS
Arrivals

SALIDAS
Departures

13

RETRASADO
Delayed

a.: Laborables excepto sábados.
d.: Sábados y festivos.
x.: Efectúa parada en Seseña 5 min. después de Aranjuez.
(1): No circula del 01/08/06 al 01/09/06 ambos inclusive.
(2): Circula diario del 01/08/06 al 01/09/06 ambos inclusive.

	Aranjuez	Ciempozuelos	Valdemoro	Pinto	Getafe Central	San Cristóbal	Villaverde Alto	Sol Centro
x.	16.00	16.10	16.15	16.20	16.25	16.28	16.30	
	16.30	16.40	16.45	16.50	16.55	16.58	17.00	
	17.00	17.10	17.15	17.20	17.25	17.28	17.30	
	17.30	17.40	17.45	17.50	17.55	17.58	18.00	
a.	17.50	18.00	18.05	18.10	18.15	18.18	18.20	
a.	17.58	18.08	18.13	18.18	18.23	18.26	18.28	
a.	18.10	18.20	18.25	18.30	18.35	18.38	18.40	
	18.30	18.40	18.45	18.50	18.55	18.58	19.00	

Train Timetable Key

a. Weekdays (**laborables**) except Saturdays (**sábados**)
d. Saturdays (**sábados**) and holidays (**festivos**)
x. Stops at Seseña 5 minutes after (**después de**) Aranjuez
(1) No service (**no circula**) from ... to ... both (**ambos**) inclusive
(2) Daily (**diario**) service from ... to ... inclusive

Getting around

Paseo And Calle both mean street.

Sign on leaving town.

Tourist Information Notice the slightly different spelling in this Majorcan sign.

glorieta = roundabout

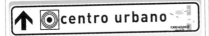

Town Centre Notice the circular pictogram for town centre which is very common.

playa = beach

You Are On The Top Floor **VD.** = **Usted** = you **planta** = floor **alta** = top

PLAZA MAYOR

Plaza Mayor = main square. **Plaza** (**pla**-tha) = square.

Town Hall Notice the different spelling on the Majorcan sign.

Abbreviation for **plaza = pza.**

Accident And Emergency (A & E)

Police Station

Market

Taxi Stand Prices are usually displayed at the taxi stand. Taxis are generally white. If a taxi is free it shows a green light and the word **libre**. If it has passengers it usually shows a red light with the word **ocupado**.

Bus Stop with the number of service and stops en route. Flag down the bus – they don't always stop automatically.

Train Notice Board

Name of the station

Metro

High-speed train

Ticket office

Long distance
Regional

Information point

Automatic Ticket Machine These are very common now.

Metro Bus Tickets for bus and underground on sale here.

Tipo de Billete
Type of ticket
sencillo = single
ida y vuelta
(**regreso**) = return

The national rail network is called RENFE.

Driving

City centre (note the circular sign). If you don't see your destination signposted, follow **todas direcciones** (all routes). To get to the town centre, follow **centro ciudad**.

Road Signs
In cities and towns note the colour-coding on road signs. White indicates a major route from a town. Yellow identifies places of local interest. Green gives names of street.

Pay And Display
Indicates that parking must be paid for in advance. Times are Monday to Friday from 9am–2pm and 5–9pm, Saturdays from 9am–2pm.

No Parking
ambos lados = both sides
reservado minusválido = disabled parking

Spanish Speed Limits In built-up areas the limit is 50 kph. On ordinary roads 90 kph, on dual carriageways (**autovías**) and on motorways (**autopistas**) 120 kph.

lavado manual
= handwash
cambio de aceite
= oil change

Spanish motorways are signposted in blue. The speed limit is 120 kph. Motorway info website is **www.aseta.es**. Some motorways (**autopistas**) are free and some carry toll charges (which can be expensive). Look out for the sign **peaje** (toll). Payment is due on completion of each sector covered. You do not receive tickets.

Exit/Junction 214
Word for exit is **salida**.

17

Petrol Colour-coded pumps: black for diesel (**gasóleo**), green for unleaded (**sin plomo**) and red for leaded (**super**). 95-octane petrol is usually fine for most cars, unless they have powerful engines or are towing a caravan.

Toll Stop At the toll stop you have a choice of payment: either cash (**Manuales**) for all vehicles (**metálico** means cash), card (**Tarjetas**) or prepaid (**Telepeaje**).
Sólo tarjetas =
cards only

SOLO TARJETAS

TALLER MECANICO
GRUA PERMANENTE 24 HORAS
SERVICIO NEUMATICOS TURISMO

Garage for repairs. This one offers 24-hour pick-up truck and tyre service for cars.

Shopping

Alimentación
General grocer's. Small shops' opening hours are 10am-2pm and 5-8.30pm.

Supermercado
Large supermarkets are found on the outskirts of towns. These include **Carrefour**, **Eroski** and **Alcampo**. Locker and present-wrapping areas are usually available. You must leave bags in a locker or with an attendant who will give you a token. Supermarket trolleys usually take 50 cents or 1 euro coins.

Caja Rápida
Quick Checkout
Maximum 10 items.

Sales Sales usually take place in January/February and again in July/August.

mercado
Market Larger towns will have a daily market and smaller ones a weekly market.

FARMACIA **Pharmacy** Sells medical items for which you often don't need a doctor's prescription. A good place for advice on minor ailments and non-prescription medicines (even some antibiotics). Each town has a 'duty chemist'. Each will list a duty rota (**Farmacia de Guardia**) in the window or posted nearby. This list is also in local newspapers, including English language ones. Now, there are so-called **Parafarmacias** who have baby food, accessories, toothbrushes, suncream, etc, at a lower price than in some Pharmacies.

SERVICIO FARMACEUTICO DE URGENCIAS
TORREMOLINOS - 24 horas
(De 9.30 Mañana a 9.30 Mañana)
LUNES 7   MES: AGOSTO
URBANIZACION LOS ALAMOS
Avda Principal (250 mts. Gasolinera)

Bread (**pan**) When asking for bread, ask for **una barra** (similar to French stick) or the number of rolls (**bollos**) you want.

For a more rounded country loaf, ask for **un pan**.

Gluten-free Singlu indicates gluten-free products. In this case gluten-free flour (**harina**) for bread and pastry.

Butcher Specialises in veal (**ternera**), pork (**cerdo**) and lamb (**cordero**).

Organic **Bio** generally indicates organic produce.

You can ask for cheese or ham by the number of slices (**lonchas**) rather than by weight. **Jamón serrano** = cured ham; **jamón de York** = cooked ham.

Milk (**leche**) Milk is almost always UHT (long-life). Here, blue is for whole milk (**leche entera**), green is semi-skimmed (**semidesnatada**) and pink is skimmed (**desnatada**) but colour coding can vary.

Fat Free

Without Sugar

Keeping in touch

Post Office

Two posting boxes, one for national mail, the other for overseas (**extranjero**).

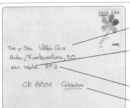

Addressing an envelope:
Avda./ = abbrev. for **avenida** street
esc. = abbrev. for **escalera** floor
izqda. = abbrev. for **izquierda** left
(**dcha.** = abbrev. for **derecha** right
3º2 3rd floor, door number 2
postcode and town

Internet Many cafés offer deals where you buy a number of hours in advance. However, check how many days you have to use up your hours – some offers are not as good as they look.

@ The Spanish word for 'at' is **arroba** ar-**rro**-ba.

www.

www dot is **tres uve dobles punto** tres **oo**-be **dob**-les **poon**-to.

Larger cities usually have a phone centre (**locutorio**) where you phone from a booth and pay afterwards (by credit card or cash).

Phonecard (tarjetas telefónicas)

Key talk

Key talk

- Spanish has two forms of address, formal and informal. You should use the informal **tú** only when you know someone well; otherwise use **usted**.
- **Hola** is more informal than **buenos días** or **buenas tardes**.
- The easiest way to ask for something is to name it and add 'please', **por favor**.

yes	sí
	see
no	no
	no
that's fine	¡vale!
	¡**ba**-le!
please	por favor
	por fa-**bor**
thank you (very much)	(muchas) gracias
	(**moo**-chas) **gra**-thyas
don't mention it	de nada
	de **na**-da
hello	hola
	o-la
goodbye	adiós
	a- **dyos**
good night	buenas noches
	bwe-nas **no**-ches
good morning (until lunch)	buenos días
	bwe-nos **dee**-as

good afternoon/ evening (until dusk)	**buenas tardes** **bwe**-nas **tar**-des
excuse me! (to catch attention)	¡oiga por favor! ¡**oy**-ga por fa-**bor**!
sorry!	¡perdón! ¡per-**don**!
what?	¿cómo dice? ¿**ko**-mo **dee**-the?
a...	un... ('el' words) oon...
a coffee	un café oon ka-**fe**
2 coffees	dos cafés dos ka-**fes**
a...	una... ('la' words) **oo**-na...
a beer	una cerveza **oo**-na ther-**be**-tha
2 beers	dos cervezas dos ther-**be**-thas
a coffee and two beers, please	un café y dos cervezas, por favor oon ka-**fe** ee dos ther-**be**-thas, por fa-**bor**

• Spanish doesn't often use the words for 'I', 'you', 'he', etc., so to ask a question simply change the intonation of a statement and put a question mark in your voice: **¿tiene una habitación?** (Do you have a room?)
• To get someone's attention, you can use **por favor**, **señor/señora**.

I'd like...	quería... ke-**ree**-a...
we'd like...	queríamos... ke-**ree**-a-mos...
I'd like an ice cream	quería un helado ke-**ree**-a oon e-**la**-do

we'd like to visit Toledo	queríamos visitar Toledo
	ke-**ree**-a-mos bee-see-**tar** to-**le**-do
do you have...?	¿tiene...?
	¿**tye**-ne...?
do you have any milk/cheese?	¿tiene leche/queso?
	¿**tye**-ne **le**-che/**ke**-so?
do you have stamps?	¿tiene sellos?
	¿**tye**-ne **sel**-yos?
do you have a map?	¿tiene un mapa?
	¿**tye**-ne oon **ma**-pa?
how much is it?	¿cuánto es?
	¿**kwan**-to es?
how much does ... cost?	¿cuánto cuesta...?
	¿**kwan**-to **kwes**-ta...?
how much is the cheese?	¿cuánto cuesta el queso?
	¿**kwan**-to **kwes**-ta el **ke**-so?
how much is the ticket?	¿cuánto cuesta el billete?
	¿**kwan**-to **kwes**-ta el bee-**lye**-te?
how much is a kilo?	¿cuánto cuesta el kilo?
	¿**kwan**-to **kwes**-ta el **kee**-lo?
how much is each one?	¿cuánto cuesta cada uno?
	¿**kwan**-to **kwes**-ta **ka**-da **oo**-no?

- You often hear the expression **claro**, meaning 'of course' or 'yes'.
- **Hasta luego** (**as**-ta **lwe**-go) means 'see you later'.
- If you want to apologise for bumping into someone (and perhaps causing them to spill their drink), you say **¡perdón! lo siento** (per-**don** lo **syen**-to), 'excuse me! I'm sorry'. Ladies = **señoras**, gents = **caballeros**.

where is...?	¿dónde está...?
	¿**don**-de es-**ta**...?
where are...?	¿dónde están...?
	¿**don**-de es-**tan**...?
where is the station?	¿dónde está la estación?
	¿**don**-de es-**ta** la es-ta-**thyon**?

where are the toilets?	¿dónde están los aseos?
	¿**don**-de es-**tan** los a-**se**-os?
is there/are there...?	¿hay...?
	¿aee...?
there is no...	no hay...
	no aee...
is there a restaurant?	¿hay un restaurante?
	¿aee oon res-tow-**ran**-te?
where is there a chemist?	¿dónde hay una farmacia?
	¿**don**-de aee **oo**-na far-**ma**-thya?
are there children?	¿hay niños?
	¿aee **nee**-nyos?
is there a swimming pool?	¿hay piscina?
	¿aee pees-**thee**-na?
there is no hot water	no hay agua caliente
	no aee **a**-gwa ka-**lyen**-te
there are no towels	no hay toallas
	no aee to-**a**-lyas
I need...	necesito...
	ne-the-**see**-to...
I need a taxi	necesito un taxi
	ne-the-**see**-to oon **tak**-see
I need to send a fax	necesito mandar un fax
	ne-the-**see**-to man-**dar** oon faks

24

- 1º /**primero** = first; 2º/**segundo** = second, etc. **Primera** (which goes with feminine words) is abbreviated to 1ª (the 'o' and 'a' in 1º, 1ª are underlined).
- C/ = **calle** = street.
- s/n (or S/N) = **sin número** = no number (this is used in addresses because some places don't have a number. For example: **Calle de España s/n**).

can I...?	¿puedo...?
	¿**pwe**-do...?
can we...?	¿podemos...?
	¿po-**de**-mos...?

can I pay?	¿puedo pagar?
	¿**pwe**-do pa-**gar**?
can we go in?	¿podemos entrar?
	¿po-**de**-mos en-**trar**?
where can I...?	¿dónde puedo...?
	¿**don**-de **pwe**-do...?
where can I buy bread?	¿dónde puedo comprar pan?
	¿**don**-de **pwe**-do kom-**prar** pan?
when?	¿cuándo?
	¿**kwan**-do?
at what time...?	¿a qué hora...?
	¿a ke **o**-ra...?
when is breakfast?	¿a qué hora es el desayuno?
	¿a ke **o**-ra es el de-sa-**yoo**-no?
when is dinner?	¿a qué hora es la cena?
	¿a ke **o**-ra es la **the**-na?
when does it open/close?	¿cuándo abren/cierran?
	¿**kwan**-do **a**-bren/**thye**-rran?
when does it begin/finish?	¿cuándo empieza/termina?
	¿**kwan**-do em-**pye**-tha/ter-**mee**-na?
yesterday	ayer
	a-**yer**
today	hoy
	oy
tomorrow	mañana
	ma-**nya**-na
this morning	esta mañana
	es-ta ma-**nya**-na
this afternoon	esta tarde
	es-ta **tar**-de
tonight	esta noche
	es-ta **no**-che
is it open?	¿está abierto?
	¿**es**-ta a-**byer**-to?
is it closed?	¿está cerrado?
	¿**es**-ta the-**rra**-do?

- Mr is **Señor** (se-**nyor**), abbreviated to **Sr**.
- Mrs or Ms is **Señora** (se-**nyo**-ra), abbreviated to **Sra**.
- Miss is **Señorita** (se-nyo-**ree**-ta), abbreviated to **Srta**.
- If you are trying to get past, perhaps in a busy street, or off a crowded bus, you can use **¿me permite?** (me per-**mee**-te).

how are you?	¿cómo está?
	¿**ko**-mo es-**ta**?
fine, thanks. And you?	muy bien, gracias. ¿Y usted?
	mwee byen, **gra**-thyas. ¿ee oos-**ted**?
my name is...	me llamo...
	me **lya**-mo...
what is your name?	¿cómo se llama?
	¿**ko**-mo se **lya**-ma?
I don't understand	no entiendo
	no en-**tyen**-do
do you speak English?	¿habla inglés?
	¿**a**-bla een-**gles**?
do you understand?	¿entiende?
	¿en-**tyen**-de?
I don't speak Spanish	no hablo español
	no **a**-blo es-pa-**nyol**
this is my husband/ wife	le presento a mi marido/mujer
	le pre-**sen**-to a mee ma-**ree**-do/moo-**kher**
pleased to meet you	encantado(a)
	en-kan-**ta**-do(a)
I've enjoyed myself very much	lo he pasado muy bien
	lo e pa-**sa**-do mwee byen
the meal was delicious	la comida estaba deliciosa
	la ko-**mee**-da es-**ta**-ba de-lee-**thyo**-sa
we'd like to come back	nos gustaría volver
	nos goos-ta-**ree**-a bol-**ber**

Money

Money – changing

- Spain is in the eurozone. Euro is pronounced **eoo**-ro and cent, known as **céntimo**, is pronounced **then**-tee-mo.
- Check bank opening times as most close around 2pm. Look for the words **Banco** and **Caja** (**Caixa** in Catalan).
- **Oficinas de cambio** (bureaux de change) stay open longer than banks but charge more commission.

where can I change money?	**¿dónde se puede cambiar dinero?** ¿**don**-de se **pwe**-de kam-**byar** dee-**ne**-ro?
where is the bank?	**¿dónde está el banco?** ¿**don**-de es-**ta** el **ban**-ko?
where is the bureau de change?	**¿dónde está la oficina de cambio?** ¿**don**-de es-**ta** la o-fee-**thee**-na de kam-byo?
when does the bank open?	**¿cuándo abre el banco?** ¿**kwan**-do **a**-bre el **ban**-ko?
when does the bank close?	**¿cuándo cierra el banco?** ¿**kwan**-do **thye**-rra el **ban**-ko?
I want to cash these traveller's cheques	**quiero cambiar estos cheques de viaje** **kye**-ro kam-**byar es**-tos che-kes de **bya**-khe
what is the rate...?	**¿a cómo está el cambio...?** ¿a **ko**-mo es-**ta** el **kam**-byo...?
for pounds	**de libras** de **lee**-bras
for dollars	**de dólares** de **do**-la-res
I want to change ... pounds	**quiero cambiar ... libras** **kye**-ro kam-**byar** ... **lee**-bras

I want to change ...	**quiero cambiar ... dólares**
dollars	**kyer**-o kam-**byar** ... **do**-la-res
where is there a	**¿dónde hay un cajero?**
cash dispenser?	¿**don**-de aee oon ka-**khe**-ro?
I'd like small notes	**quería billetes pequeños**
	ke-**ree**-ya bee-**lye**-tes pe-**ke**-nyos

Money – spending

• Major credit cards are widely accepted. Usually the card is passed through a reader, but sometimes you have to enter your PIN on a keypad.
• Cash machines are widespread and you'll be able to use English instructions. **Fuera de servicio** means 'out of service'.
• Take your bank's phone number in case of problems.

how much is it?	**¿cuánto es?**
	¿**kwan**-to es?
how much will	**¿cuánto me costará?**
it be?	¿**kwan**-to me kos-ta-**ra**?
I want to pay	**quiero pagar**
	kye-ro pa-**gar**
we want to pay	**queremos pagar por separado**
separately	ke-**re**-mos pa-**gar** por se-pa-**ra**-do
can I pay by credit	**¿puedo pagar con tarjeta de crédito?**
card?	¿**pwe**-do pa-**gar** kon tar-**khe**-ta de **kre**-dee-to?
do you accept	**¿aceptan cheques de viaje?**
traveller's	¿a-**thep**-tan **che**-kes de **bya**-khe?
cheques?	
how much is it...?	**¿cuánto es...?**
	¿**kwan**-to es...?
per person	**por persona**
	por per-**so**-na
per night	**por noche**
	por **no**-che

per kilo	**por kilo**
	por **kee**-lo
are VAT and service included?	**¿incluye el IVA y el servicio?**
	¿een-**kloo**-ye el **ee**-ba ee el ser-**bee**-thyo?
can I have a receipt?	**¿puede darme un recibo?**
	¿**pwe**-de **dar**-me oon re-**thee**-bo?
do I pay a deposit?	**¿tengo que pagar un depósito?**
	¿**ten**-go ke pa-**gar** oon de-**po**-see-to?
I've nothing smaller	**no tengo cambio**
	no **ten**-go **kam**-byo
keep the change	**quédese con la vuelta**
	ke-de-se kon la **bwel**-ta

Getting around

Airport

• The word for airport is **aeropuerto**.
• Most signs will be in Spanish and English.
• The word for 'flight' is **vuelo**. The word for 'delay' is **retraso**.
• Check out airports of southern Spain on **www.andalucia.com/travel/airports/home.htm**.
• Airports in Spain **www.aena.es** (official) **www.spanish-airport-guide.com**

to the airport, please	**al aeropuerto, por favor**
	al ae-ro-**pwer**-to, por fa-**bor**
how do I get into town?	**¿cómo se va al centro?**
	¿**ko**-mo se ba al **then**-tro?
where do I get the bus to the town centre?	**¿dónde se coge el autobús para el centro?**
	¿**don**-de se **ko**-khe el ow-to-**boos pa**-ra el **then**-tro?
how much is it...?	**¿cuánto es...?**
	¿**kwan**-to es...?
to the town centre/airport	**al centro/aeropuerto**
	al **then**-tro/ae-ro-**pwer**-to
where do I check in for...?	**¿dónde se factura para...?**
	¿**don**-de se fak-**too**-ra **pa**-ra...?
which gate is it for the flight to...?	**¿cuál es la puerta del vuelo para...?**
	¿kwal es la **pwer**-ta del **bwe**-lo **pa**-ra...?
boarding will take place at gate number...	**el embarque se efectuará por la puerta número...**
	el em-**bar**-ke se e-fek-twa-**ra** por la **pwer**-ta **noo**-me-ro...

last call for passengers on flight...	**última llamada para los pasajeros del vuelo...**
	ool-tee-ma lya-**ma**-da **pa**-ra los pa-sa-**khe**-ros del **bwe**-lo...
your flight is delayed	**su vuelo sale con retraso**
	soo **bwe**-lo **sa**-le kon re-**tra**-so

Customs and passports

● EU citizens with nothing to declare can use the blue customs channels, which are subject to spot checks.
● There's no restriction by quantity or value on goods purchased by travellers in another EU country, provided they are for their own personal use (this covers gifts). For further information, check **www.hmrc.gov.uk** for guidelines.

I have nothing to declare	**no tengo nada que declarar**
	no **ten**-go **na**-da ke de-kla-**rar**
here is...	**aquí está...**
	a-**kee** es-**ta**...
my passport/ my green card	**mi pasaporte/mi carta verde**
	mee pa-sa-**por**-te/mee **kar**-ta **ber**-de
this is the baby's passport	**este es el pasaporte del bebé**
	es-te es el pa-sa-**por**-te del be-**be**
do I have to pay duty on this?	**¿tengo que pagar derechos de aduana por esto?**
	¿**ten**-go ke pa-**gar** de-**re**-chos de a-doo-**a**-na por **es**-to?
it's for my own personal use	**es para uso personal**
	es **pa**-ra **oo**-so per-so-**nal**
here is the receipt	**aquí tiene el tique**
	a-**kee** tye-ne el **tee**-ke
I'm...	**soy...**
	soy...
English (m/f)	**inglés(esa)**
	een-**gles**(**gle**-sa)

Australian (m/f)	**australiano(a)**
	ows-tra-**lya**-no(a)
I bought it/them in Spain	**lo/los compré en España**
	lo/los kom-**pre** en es-**pa**-nya

Asking the way – questions

● ●

• You can ask the way with **¿el museo, por favor?** Nothing more complicated is required.
• You can get maps free from the local Tourist Information Office, and street maps of the neighbourhood are displayed outside all Madrid's Metro stations.
• You can also attract someone's attention with **por favor** or **perdone**.

excuse me!	**¡oiga por favor!**
	¡**oy**-ga por fa-**bor**!
where is...?	**¿dónde está...?**
	¿**don**-de es-**ta**...?
where is the nearest...?	**¿dónde está el/la ... más próximo(a)/ cercano(a)?**
	¿**don**-de es-**ta** el/la ... mas **prok**-see-mo(a)/ ther-**ka**-no(a)?
how do I get to...?	**¿cómo se va a...?**
	¿**ko**-mo se ba a...?
is this the right way to...?	**¿se va por aquí a...?**
	¿se ba por a-**kee** a...?
to the station	**a la estación**
	a la es-ta-**thyon**
to the museum	**al museo**
	al moo-**se**-o
to the hotel	**al hotel**
	al o-**tel**
is it far?	**¿está lejos?**
	¿es-**ta le**-khos?
can I walk there?	**¿puedo ir andando?**
	¿**pwe**-do eer an-**dan**-do?

is there a bus that goes there?	¿hay algún autobús hasta allí?
	¿aee al-**goon** ow-to-**boos as**-ta a-**yee**?
we're looking for...	**estamos buscando...**
	es-**ta**-mos boos-**kan**-do...
we're lost	**nos hemos perdido**
	nos **e**-mos per-**dee**-do
can you show me where ... is on the map	¿puede indicarme dónde está ... en el mapa?
	¿**pwe**-de een-dee-**kar**-me **don**-de es-**ta** ... en el **ma**-pa?

Asking the way – answers

• Key words are 'right' **a la derecha** (a la de-**re**-cha), 'left' **a la izquierda** (a la eeth-**kyer**-da), and 'straight on' **recto** (**rek**-to).
• 'Street' is **calle** (**ka**-lye), or **paseo** (pa-**se**-o), 'square' is **plaza** (**pla**-tha), and 'roundabout' is **glorieta** (glo-**rye**-ta).
• In shopping centres, hotels, etc, 'floor' is **planta** (**plan**-ta); 'basement' is **sótano** (**so**-ta-no).

33

no, this is not the way to...	**no, por aquí no se va a...**
	no, por a-**kee** no se ba a...
turn left/right	**gire a la izquierda/derecha**
	khee-re a la eeth-**kyer**-da/de-**re**-cha
keep straight on until you get to...	**siga todo recto hasta llegar a...**
	see-ga **to**-do **rek**-to **as**-ta lye-**gar** a...
as far as...	**hasta...**
	as-ta...
you have to turn round	**tiene que dar la vuelta**
	tye-ne ke dar la **bwel**-ta
take...	**coja/tome...**
	ko-kha/**to**-me...
the first on the right	**la primera calle a la derecha**
	la pree-**me**-ra **ka**-lye a la de-**re**-cha
the second on the left	**la segunda calle a la izquierda**
	la se-**goon**-da **ka**-lye a la eeth-**kyer**-da

until you get to...	**hasta llegar a/al...**
	as-ta lye-**gar** a/al...
the road to...	**la carretera de...**
	la ka-rre-**te**-ra de...
follow the signs for...	**siga las señales de...**
	see-ga las se-**nya**-les de...

Bus

• •

• For long distance travel, coaches are often cheaper than the train. You can buy your ticket up to 2 months ahead – this is recommended at weekends and in the high season.

• You buy single tickets on the bus. You can get multi-journey tickets (**bonobús** or **metrobús**, valid for the metro and the bus in Madrid). All tickets have to be validated in the machine on the bus.

where is the bus station?	**¿dónde está la estación de autobuses?**
	¿**don**-de es-**ta** la es-ta-**thyon** de ow-to-**boo**-ses?
I want to go...	**quiero ir...**
	kye-ro eer...
to the station	**a la estación**
	a la es-ta-**thyon**
to the museum	**al museo**
	al moo-**se**-o
to the Prado	**al Prado**
	al **pra**-do
to Toledo	**a Toledo**
	a to-**le**-do
is there a bus that goes there?	**¿hay un autobús que vaya allí?**
	¿aee oon ow-to-**boos** ke **ba**-ya a-**yee**?
which bus do I take to go to...?	**¿qué autobús se coge para ir a...?**
	¿ke ow-to-**boos** se **ko**-khe **pa**-ra eer a...?
where do I get the bus to...?	**¿dónde se coge el autobús para...?**
	¿**don**-de se **ko**-khe el ow-to-**boos pa**-ra...?
how often are the buses?	**¿cada cuánto hay autobuses?**
	¿**ka**-da **kwan**-to aee ow-to-**boo**-ses?

when is the last bus?	¿cuándo sale el último autobús?
	¿**kwan**-do **sa**-le el **ool**-tee-mo ow-to-**boos**?
can you tell me when to get off?	¿me dice cuándo tengo que bajarme?
	¿me **dee**-the **kwan**-do **ten**-go ke ba-**khar**-me?

Metro

• Madrid, Barcelona and Bilbao have Metro systems. Maps are available from station booths. A 10-trip ticket (**metrobús**) can be used on buses as well as the metro in Madrid.
• Metrobus is a ticket that exists only in Madrid. There are different types of tickets with different names for different uses in Barcelona and Bilbao, just check the websites for further info.
• Busy times are 8.30-10am and 3.30-8pm.
• For information, check out **www.metromadrid.es**, **www.metrobilbao.net** and **www.tmb.net** (Barcelona).

where is the metro station?	¿dónde está la estación de metro?
	¿**don**-de es-**ta** la es-ta-**thyon** de **me**-tro?
are there any special discount tickets?	¿hay algún billete con descuento especial?
	¿aee al-**goon** bee-**lye**-te kon des-**kwen**-to es-pe-**thyal**?
do you have a map of the metro?	¿tiene un plano del metro?
	¿**tye**-ne oon **pla**-no del **me**-tro?
I want to go to...	quiero ir a...
	kye-ro eer a...
can I go by metro?	¿se puede ir en metro?
	¿se **pwe**-de eer en **me**-tro?
do I have to change?	¿tengo que cambiar de línea?
	¿**ten**-go ke kam-**byar** de **lee**-ne-a?
where?	¿dónde?
	¿**don**-de?
which line is it for...?	¿cuál es la línea para ir a...?
	¿kwal es la **lee**-nea **pa**-ra eer a...?
what is the next stop?	¿cuál es la próxima parada?
	¿kwal es la **prok**-see-ma pa-**ra**-da?

which is the station for the Prado?	**¿cuál es la estación de metro para el Prado?**
	¿kwal es la es-ta-**thyon** de **me**-tro **pa**-ra el **pra**-do?
please let me through	**¿me deja pasar, por favor?**
	¿me **de**-kha pa-**sar**, por fa-**bor**?

Train

• A high-speed train service called AVE links Madrid with Seville. The TALGO 200 service is as good as AVE but cheaper (journeys take 15 minutes longer). AVE network's base is at the RENFE Atocha Station in Madrid.

where is the station?	**¿dónde está la estación?**
	¿**don**-de es-**ta** la es-ta-**thyon**?
to the station, please	**a la estación, por favor**
	a la es-ta-**thyon**, por fa-**bor**
a single to...	**uno a...**
	oo-no a...
2 singles to...	**dos a...**
	dos a...
a return to...	**uno de ida y vuelta a....**
	oo-no de **ee**-da ee **bwel**-ta a...
2 returns to...	**dos de ida y vuelta a...**
	dos de **ee**-da ee **bwel**-ta a...
a child's return to...	**un billete de niño de ida y vuelta a...**
	oon bee-**lye**-te de **nee**-nyo de **ee**-da ee **bwel**-ta a...
1st class/tourist	**de clase preferente/turista**
	de **kla**-se pre-fe-**ren**-te/too-**rees**-ta
I want to book a seat on the AVE/Talgo 200 to Madrid	**quería reservar un asiento en el AVE/Talgo 200 a Madrid**
	ke-**ree**-a re-ser-**bar** oon a-**syen**-to en el **a**-be/**tal**-go dos-**thyen**-tos a ma-**dreed**
when is the first/ last train to...?	**¿cuando sale el primer/último tren para...?**
	¿**kwan**-do **sa**-le el pree-**mer**/**ool**-tee-mo tren **pa**-ra...?
when does it arrive in...?	**¿cuando llega a...?**
	¿**kwan**-do **lye**-ga a...?

| is there a buffet service? | **¿hay servicio de cafetería?** |
| | ¿aee ser-**bee**-thyo de ka-fe-te-**ree**-a? |

- Reduced fares are available for certain age groups (such as students and over-60s) on certain days of the year called **días azules** ('blue days').
- Check out **www.renfe.es**.
- Children under 4 travel free; those aged 4 to 13 get a 40% discount.

---

do I have to pay a supplement?	**¿tengo que pagar suplemento?**
	¿**ten**-go ke pa-**gar** soo-ple-**men**-to?
can I have a timetable?	**¿me da un horario?**
	¿me da oon o-**ra**-ryo?
is this pass valid on this train?	**¿es válido este pase en este tren?**
	¿es **ba**-lee-do **es**-te **pa**-se en **es**-te tren?
I want to book...	**quiero reservar...**
	kye-ro re-ser-**bar**...
a seat	**un asiento**
	oon a-**syen**-to
a couchette	**una litera**
	oo-na lee-**te**-ra

- Couchettes are available in trains called 'Trenhotel' in tourist class cabins. There are also single or double first class and even grand class compartments.

---

do I need to change?	**¿tengo que hacer transbordo?**
	¿**ten**-go ke a-**ther** trans-**bor**-do?
where?	**¿dónde?**
	¿**don**-de?
which platform does it leave from?	**¿de qué andén sale?**
	¿de ke an-**den sa**-le?
does the train to ... leave from this platform?	**¿el tren para ... sale de este andén?**
	¿el tren **pa**-ra ... **sa**-le de **es**-te an-**den**?
is this the train for...?	**¿es este el tren para...?**
	¿es **es**-te el tren **pa**-ra...?

where is the left-luggage?	¿dónde está la consigna?
	¿**don**-de es-**ta** la kon-**seeg**-na?
is this seat taken?	¿**está ocupado (este asíento)?**
	¿es-**ta** o-koo-**pa**-do (**es**-te a-**syen**-to)?

Taxi

....

- You can either hail a taxi or pick one up at a taxi stand. There may be surcharges for baggage and for travelling late at night and at weekends.
- Taxis are usually white and display a green light when free, and a red light when they're not.
- Tipping isn't common, but it's usual to round up the cost.
- It's compulsory to wear seat belts in both front and back seats. There may be a sign on the taxi window asking you to fasten your seat belt.

to the airport, please	**al aeropuerto, por favor**
	al ae-ro-**pwer**-to, por fa-**bor**
to the station, please	**a la estación, por favor**
	a la es-ta-**thyon**, por fa-**bor**
take me to this address, please	**lléveme a esta dirección, por favor**
	lye-be-me a **es**-ta dee-rek-**thyon**, por fa-**bor**
how much will it cost?	¿**cuánto puede costar?**
	¿**kwan**-to **pwe**-de kos-**tar**?
how much is it to the centre?	¿**cuánto cuesta hasta el centro?**
	¿**kwan**-to **kwes**-ta **as**-ta el **then**-tro?
it's too much	**es demasiado**
	es de-ma-**sya**-do
where is the taxi stand?	¿**dónde está la parada de taxis?**
	¿**don**-de es-**ta** la pa-**ra**-da de **tak**-sees?
please order me a taxi	**por favor, ¿me pide un taxi?**
	por fa-**bor**, ¿me **pee**-de oon **tak**-see?
can I have a receipt?	¿**puede darme un recibo?**
	¿**pwe**-de **dar**-me oon re-**thee**-bo?
I've nothing smaller	**no tengo cambio**
	no **ten**-go **kam**-byo

| keep the change | **quédese con la vuelta** |
| | **ke**-de-se kon la **bwel**-ta |

Boat

. . . .

- There is a good ferry service from Valencia and Barcelona to the Balearic Islands on modern ships with excellent facilities.
- Fast ferry services link Andalucia to North Africa. The crossing from Tarifa to Tangiers takes 35 minutes.
- Boat and ferry timetables follow peak summer-season schedules.
www.ferrylines.com www.aferry.es

1 ticket/2 tickets	**un billete/dos billetes**
	oon bee-**lye**-te/dos bee-**lye**-tes
single/round trip	**de ida/de ida y vuelta**
	de **ee**-da/de **ee**-da ee **bwel**-ta
is there a tourist ticket?	**¿hay algún billete de clase turista?**
	¿aee al-**goon** beel-**lye**-te de **kla**-se too-**rees**-ta?
are there any boat trips?	**¿hay excursiones en barco?**
	¿aee eks-koor-**syo**-nes en **bar**-ko?
how long is the trip?	**¿cuánto dura el viaje?**
	¿**kwan**-to **doo**-ra el **bya**-khe?
when is the next boat/ferry?	**¿cuándo sale el próximo barco/ferry?**
	¿**kwan**-do **sa**-le el **prok**-see-mo **bar**-ko/**fe**-rree?
when is the first/ last boat?	**¿cuándo sale el primer/último barco?**
	¿**kwan**-do **sa**-le el **pree**-mer/**ool**-tee-mo **bar**-ko?
when do we arrive in?	**¿a qué hora llegamos a...?**
	¿a **ke o**-ra lye-**ga**-mos a...?
when does the boat leave?	**¿cuándo sale el barco?**
	¿**kwan**-do **sa**-le el **bar**-ko?
is there a restaurant on board?	**¿hay restaurante en el barco?**
	¿aee rest-ow-**ran**-te en el **bar**-ko?
can we hire a boat?	**¿podemos alquilar una barca?**
	¿po-**de**-mos al-kee-**lar oo**-na **bar**-ka?
do you have a timetable?	**¿tiene un horario?**
	¿**tye**-ne oon o-**ra**-ryo?

Car

Driving

- To drive in Spain you must have a valid pink EU driving licence and be at least 18 years old. Make sure you bring your licence and registration document with you.
- You pay a toll on some motorways. Look for the word **PEAJE**.
- Seatbelts are compulsory in front and rear.
- Check out **www.dgt.es** and **www.aseta.es** for road and traffic info.
- The legal blood alcohol limit is 0.05%
- The use of mobile phones, other than a hands-free, whilst driving is banned and you can be fined if caught.

can I/we park here?	¿se puede aparcar aquí?
	¿se **pwe**-de a-par-**kar** a-**kee**?
where can I park?	¿dónde puedo aparcar?
	¿**don**-de **pwe**-do a-par-**kar**?
is there a car park?	¿hay un parking?
	¿ee oon **par**-keen?
do I/we need a parking disc?	¿hace falta tique de aparcamiento?
	¿**a**-the **fal**-ta **tee**-ke de a-par-ka-**myen**-to?
where can I get a parking disc?	¿dónde puedo comprar un tique de aparcamiento?
	¿**don**-de **pwe**-do kom-**prar** oon **tee**-ke de a-par-ka-**myen**-to?
how long can I park here?	¿cuánto tiempo puedo aparcar aquí?
	¿**kwan**-to **tyem**-po **pwe**-do a-par-**kar** a-**kee**?
we're going to...	vamos a...
	ba-mos a...
what's the best route?	¿cuál es la mejor ruta?
	¿kwal es la me-**khor roo**-ta?

which exit is it for...?	¿cuál es la salida de...?
	¿**kwal** es la sa-**lee**-da de...?
how do I get onto the motorway?	¿por dónde se va a la autopista?
	¿por **don**-de se ba a la ow-to-**pees**-ta?

Petrol

. . . .

- Petrol stations often still have attendants.
- Leaded petrol has been withdrawn from most stations. Unleaded (**sin plomo**) pumps are always coloured green.
- Service stations are **áreas de servicio** – they often have cash dispensers, shops, eating places, play areas, etc. They are not common on toll motorways, but there are more of them on non-toll roads.
- Mobile phones are forbidden while refuelling. The engine and radio must both be off. It is forbidden to smoke anywhere in a petrol station.

is there a petrol station near here?	¿hay alguna gasolinera por aquí?
	¿aee al-**goo**-na ga-so-lee-**ne**-ra por a-**kee**?
fill it up, please	lleno, por favor
	lye-no, por fa-**bor**
... euros worth of unleaded	... euros de sin plomo
	... **eoo**-ros de seen **plo**-mo
pump number...	surtidor número...
	soor-tee-**dor noo**-me-ro...
that is my car	ese es mi coche
	e-se es mee **ko**-che
where is the air line/water?	¿dónde está el aire/el agua?
	¿**don**-de es-**ta** el **aee**-re/el **a**-gwa?
please check...	¿me revisa...?
	¿me re-**bee**-sa...?
the tyre pressure	la presión de los neumáticos
	la pre-**syon** de los neoo-**ma**-tee-kos
the oil/water	el aceite/el agua
	el a-**they**-te/el **a**-gwa

can I pay with this credit card?	¿puedo pagar con esta tarjeta de crédito?
	¿**pwe**-do pa-**gar** kon **es**-ta tar-**khe**-ta de **kre**-dee-to?
which pump did you use?	¿qué surtidor ha usado?
	¿ke soor-tee-**dor** a oo-**sa**-do?

Problems/breakdown

• It is compulsory for drivers to carry spare light bulbs, a warning triangle and visibility or fluorescent vests (chalecos reflectantes) in case of an accident or breakdown.
• Motorways have SOS emergency buttons approximately every 1.5km. You simply press the button and wait for assistance.
• If you break down on a motorway, pull over, put your hazard lights on and place your warning triangle 50m behind your car. If you are on a national road you must place two triangles, one behind and one in front both 50m from the car.

I've broken down	tengo una avería
	ten-go **oo**-na a-be-**ree**-a
what do I do?	¿qué hago?
	¿ke **a**-go?
I'm on my own (female)	estoy sola
	es-**toy so**-la
there are children in the car	hay niños en el coche
	aee **nee**-nyos en el **ko**-che
where's the nearest garage?	¿dónde está el taller más cercano?
	¿**don**-de es-**ta** el ta-**lyer** mas ther-**ka**-no?
is it serious?	¿es muy serio?
	¿es mwee **se**-ryo?
can you repair it?	¿puede arreglarlo?
	¿**pwe**-de a-rre-**glar**-lo?
when will it be ready?	¿para cuándo estará listo?
	¿**pa**-ra **kwan**-do es-ta-**ra lees**-to?
how much will it cost?	¿cuánto me costará?
	¿**kwan**-to me kos-ta-**ra**?

the car won't start	el coche no arranca
	el **ko**-che no a-**rran**-ka
I have a flat tyre	tengo una rueda pinchada
	ten-go **oo**-na **rwe**-da peen-**cha**-da
the engine is overheating	el motor se calienta
	el mo-**tor** se ka-**lyen**-ta
the battery is flat	la batería está descargada
	la ba-te-**ree**-a es-**ta** des-kar-**ga**-da
can you replace the windscreen?	¿me puede cambiar el parabrisas?
	¿me **pwe**-de kam-**byar** el pa-ra-**bree**-sas?

Car hire

- Cars can be hired at airports and main railway stations, and drivers must be over 21 and hold a valid EU driver's licence.
- Check what's covered in the price, particularly insurance.
- Most hire companies give information, often in English, on what to do in case of accident or breakdown.
- Bigger companies will be able to provide baby seats, etc.

I want to hire a car	quería alquilar un coche
	ke-**ree**-a al-kee-**lar** oon **ko**-che
for one day	para un día
	pa-ra oon **dee**-a
for ... days	para ... días
	pa-ra ... **dee**-as
I want...	quiero...
	kye-ro...
a large car	un coche grande
	oon **ko**-che **gran**-de
a small car	un coche pequeño
	oon **ko**-che pe-**ke**-nyo
an automatic	un coche automático
	oon **ko**-che ow-to-**ma**-tee-ko
how much is it?	¿cúanto es?
	¿**kwan**-to es?

is fully comprehensive insurance included in the price?	¿el seguro a todo riesgo va incluido en el precio?
	¿el se-**goo**-ro a **to**-do **ryes**-go ba een-kloo-**ee**-do en el **pre**-thyo?
what do we do if we break down?	¿qué hay que hacer si tenemos una avería?
	¿ke aee ke a-**ther** see te-**ne**-mos **oo**-na a-be-**ree**-a?
when must I return the car by?	¿a qué hora tengo que devolver el coche?
	¿a ke **o**-ra **ten**-go ke de-bol-**ber** el **ko**-che?
please show me the controls	¿me enseña cómo funcionan los mandos?
	¿me en-**se**-nya **ko**-mo foon-**thyo**-nan los **man**-dos?
where are the documents?	¿dónde están los papeles del coche?
	¿**don**-de es-**tan** los pa-**pe**-les del **ko**-che?
where is the nearest petrol station?	¿dónde está la gasolinera más cercana?
	¿**don**-de es-**ta** la ga-so-lee-**ne**-ra mas ther-**ka**-na?

Shopping

Shopping – holiday

- Opening hours vary considerably between region, city, town and type of shop, a rough guide is about 9.30am till 1.30pm then 5pm till 8pm. Food shops can open earlier. Large department stores, hypermarkets and many supermarkets stay open at lunchtime and until 10pm in the evening.
- The **estanco** sells a wide range of useful things: stamps, cigarettes, bus tickets and postcards.
- Postboxes are yellow, priority mail boxes are red.

do you sell...?	¿vende...?
	¿**ben**-de...?
batteries for this camera	**pilas para esta cámara**
	pee-las **pa**-ra **es**-ta **ka**-ma-ra
stamps	**sellos**
	se-lyos
where can I buy...?	¿**dónde puedo comprar...?**
	¿**don**-de **pwe**-do kom-**prar**...?
films	**carretes de fotos**
	ka-**rre**-tes de **fo**-tos
a memory card for the camera	**una tarjeta de memoria para la cámara**
	oo-na tar-**khe**-ta de me-**mo**-ree-a **pa**-ra la **ka**-ma-ra
10 stamps	**diez sellos**
	dyeth **se**-lyos
for postcards	**para postales**
	pa-ra pos-**ta**-les
to Britain	**para Gran Bretaña**
	pa-ra gran bre-**ta**-nya

45

a tape for this video camera	una cinta para esta videocámara
	oo-na **theen**-ta **pa**-ra **es**-ta **bee**-deo **ka**-ma-ra
I'm looking for a present...	estoy buscando un regalo...
	es-**toy** boos-**kan**-do oon re-**ga**-lo...
for my mother/son	para mi madre/hijo
	pa-ra mee **ma**-dre/**ee**-kho
have you anything cheaper?	¿tiene algo más barato?
	¿**tye**-ne **al**-go mas ba-**ra**-to?
it's a gift	es un regalo
	es oon re-**ga**-lo
please wrap it up	envuélvamelo por favor
	en-**bwel**-ba-me-lo por fa-**bor**
is there a market/ street market?	¿hay mercado/mercadillo?
	¿aee mer-**ka**-do/mer-ka-**dee**-lyo?
which day?	¿qué día?
	¿ke **dee**-a?

Shopping – clothes

• •

• Spain's largest department store is **El Corte Inglés**, which has branches in all major towns. It is generally open on the first Sunday of each month.
• If you want a refund you must produce your receipt, and you may only be offered a replacement or a credit note instead of your money back.

can I try this on?	¿puedo probarme esto?
	¿**pwe**-do pro-**bar**-me **es**-to?
where are the changing rooms?	¿dónde están los probadores?
	¿**don**-de es-**tan** los pro-ba-**do**-res?
it's too big	es demasiado grande
	es de-ma-**sya**-do **gran**-de
have you a smaller size?	¿tiene una talla menor?
	¿**tye**-ne **oo**-na **ta**-lya me-**nor**?
it's too small	es demasiado pequeño
	es de-ma-**sya**-do pe-**ke**-nyo

have you a larger size?	¿tiene una talla mayor?
	¿**tyen**-e **oo**-na **tal**-ya ma-**yor**?
it's too expensive	es demasiado caro
	es de-ma-**sya**-do **ka**-ro
I'm just looking	sólo estoy mirando
	so-lo es-**toy** mee-**ran**-do
I'll take this one	me llevo esto
	me **lye**-bo **es**-to
I take a size ... (shoe)	uso/tengo el ... (de zapatos)
	oo-so/**ten**-go el ... (de tha-pa-tos)
I take size ... clothes	uso/tengo la talla...
	oo-so/**ten**-go la **ta**-lya...
what shoe size are you?	¿qué número usa/tiene?
	¿ke **noo**-me-ro **oo**-sa/**tye**-ne?
does it fit?	¿le queda bien?
	¿le **ke**-da byen?

Shopping – food

. . . .

● Spanish shops are usually small family run affairs although many more hypermarkets and supermarkets have sprung up and are generally located on the outskirts of towns. In supermarkets you may have to leave your bags in a locker at the entrance, or with an attendant who will give you a token to get them back.
● The Spanish often don't believe in queuing so if it is your turn you need to speak up! You may be asked who is '**La Ultima**' (the last person in line).

where can I buy...?	¿dónde puedo comprar...?
	¿**don**-de **pwe**-do kom-**prar**...?
where is...?	¿dónde está...?
	¿**don**-de es-**ta**...?
the supermarket	el supermercado
	el soo-per-mer-**ka**-do
the baker's	la panadería
	la pa-na-de-**ree**-a

where is the market?	¿dónde está el mercado?
	¿**don**-de es-**ta** el mer-**ka**-do?
which day is the market?	¿qué día hay mercado?
	¿ke **dee**-a aee mer-**ka**-do?
it's me next	estoy yo ahora
	es-**toy** yo a-**o**-ra
that's enough	basta
	bas-ta
a litre of...	un litro de...
	oon **lee**-tro de...
a bottle of...	una botella de...
	oo-na bo-**te**-lya de...
a can of...	una lata de...
	oo-na **la**-ta de...
a carton of...	un cartón de...
	oon kar-**ton** de...

beer	cerveza	ther-**be**-tha
bread	pan	pan
coke	coca-cola	ko-ka-**ko**-la
fruit	fruta	**froo**-ta
milk	leche	**le**-che
oil	aceite	a-**they**-te
orange juice	zumo de naranja	**thoo**-mo de na-**ran**-kha
tonic water	tónica	**to**-nee-ka
water	agua	**a**-gwa
wine	vino	**bee**-no

- Many shops (including supermarkets) will gift-wrap presents.
- Big supermarkets have petrol stations and cash dispensers.
- You generally have to get fruit and vegetables weighed before going to the checkout.
- Bakers sell fresh bread, milk, fruit juice and sometimes sweets and cakes. Milk is almost always long-life.

| what would you like? | ¿qué desea? |
| | ¿ke de-**se**-a? |

anything else?	¿algo más?	
	¿**al**-go mas?	
a tin of tomatoes	una lata de tomates	
	oo-na **la**-ta de to-**ma**-tes	
a jar of jam	un tarro de mermelada	
	oon **ta**-rro de mer-me-**la**-da	
a loaf of bread	una barra de pan	
	oo-na **ba**-rra de pan	
three yogurts	tres yogures	
	tres yo-**goo**-res	
half a dozen eggs	media docena de huevos	
	me-dya do-**then**-a de **we**-bos	
a packet of...	un paquete de...	
	oon pa-**ke**-te de...	
100 grams of...	cien gramos de...	
	thyen **gra**-mos de...	
250 grams of...	un cuarto (de kilo) de...	
	oon **kwar**-to (de **kee**-lo) de...	
a kilo of...	un kilo de...	
	oon **kee**-lo de...	
8 slices of...	ocho lonchas de...	
	o-cho **lon**-chas de...	

apples	manzanas	man-**tha**-nas
biscuits	galletas	ga-**lyet**-tas
cheese	queso	**ke**-so
chorizo	chorizo	cho-**ree**-tho
cooked ham	jamón de York	kha-**mon** de york
cured ham	jamón serrano	kha-**mon** se-**rra**-no
mushrooms	champiñones	cham-pee-**nyo**-nes
potatoes	patatas	pa-**ta**-tas
sausages	salchichas	sal-**chee**-chas
sugar	azúcar	a-**thoo**-kar

Shopping – food

Daylife

Sightseeing

- Tourist offices provide town plans and info on accommodation, restaurants and attractions. Check out **www.spaintour.org** (or **www.spain.info**)
- Museum opening hours vary but are usually 10am-2pm and 5-8pm. They normally close on Mondays.
- In Madrid a 3-gallery ticket gives admission to the Reina Sofia Gallery, the Thyssen Gallery and the Prado.

where is the tourist office?	**¿dónde está la oficina de turismo?**
	¿**don**-de es-**ta** la o-fee-**thee**-na de too-**rees**-mo?
we'd like to visit...	**queríamos visitar...**
	ke-**ree**-a-mos bee-see-**tar**...
have you any leaflets?	**¿tiene algún folleto?**
	¿**tye**-ne al-**goon** fo-**lye**-to?
when can we visit...?	**¿cuándo se puede visitar...?**
	¿**kwan**-do se **pwe**-de bee-see-**tar**...?
do you have a town guide?	**¿tiene una guía de la cuidad?**
	¿**tye**-ne **oo**-na **gee**-a de la thyoo-**dad**?
what day does it close?	**¿qué día cierra?**
	¿ke **dee**-a **thye**-rra?
is it open to the public?	**¿está abierto al público?**
	¿es-**ta** a-**byer**-to al **poo**-blee-ko?
we'd like to go to...	**queríamos ir a...**
	ke-**ree**-a-mos eer a...
are there any excursions?	**¿hay alguna excursión organizada?**
	¿aee al-**goo**-na eks-koor-**syon** or-ga-nee-**tha**-da?

when does it leave?	**¿a qué hora sale?**
	¿a ke **o**-ra **sa**-le?
where does it leave from?	**¿de dónde sale?**
	¿de **don**-de **sa**-le?
how much is it to get in?	**¿cuánto cuesta entrar?**
	¿**kwan**-to **kwes**-ta en-**trar**?
is there a reduction for...?	**¿hay descuento para...?**
	¿aee des-**kwen**-to **pa**-ra...?
students	**estudiantes**
	es-too-**dyan**-tes
seniors	**jubilados**
	khoo-bee-**la**-dos

Beach

• Beaches which meet European standards of cleanliness are allowed to fly a blue flag.
• A green flag flying on a beach means it's safe to swim, a yellow flag means swimming isn't recommended, and a red flag means it's dangerous.
• You can hire a sunshade (**hamaca**) per day.

is there a quiet beach?	**¿hay alguna playa tranquila?**
	¿aee al-**goo**-na **pla**-ya tran-**kee**-la?
how do I get there?	**¿cómo se va hasta allí?**
	¿**ko**-mo se ba **as**-ta a-**yee**?
is there a swimming pool?	**¿hay piscina?**
	¿aee pees-**thee**-na?
can we swim in the river?	**¿podemos bañarnos en el río?**
	¿po-**de**-mos ba-**nyar**-nos en el **ree**-o?
is the water clean?	**¿está limpia el agua?**
	¿es-**ta leem**-pya el **a**-gwa?
is the water deep?	**¿es muy profundo?**
	¿es mwee pro-**foon**-do?
is the water cold?	**¿está fría el agua?**
	¿es-**ta free**-a el **a**-gwa?

is it dangerous?	¿es peligroso?
	¿es pe-lee-**gro**-so?
are there currents?	¿hay corrientes?
	¿aee ko-**rryen**-tes?
where can we...?	¿dónde se puede hacer...?
	¿**don**-de se **pwe**-de a-**ther**...?
windsurf	windsurfing
	ween-**soor**-feen
waterski	esquí acuático
	es-**kee** a-**kwa**-tee-ko
can I hire...?	¿puedo alquilar...?
	¿**pwe**-do al-kee-**lar**...?
a beach umbrella	una sombrilla
	oo-na som-**bree**-lya
a jetski	una moto acuática
	oo-na **mo**-to a-**kwa**-tee-ka
a pedal boat/pedalo	un hidropedal
	oon ee-dro-pe-**dal**

Sport

• Tourist offices will provide information on sports activities in their area.
• Swimming caps must be worn at all indoor pools.
• National parks generally have walking and cycling trails.
• If you want tickets to a local football match, go to the stadium ticket booth an hour before kick-off.

where can we...?	¿dónde se puede...?
	¿**don**-de se **pwe**-de...?
play tennis/golf	jugar al tenis/golf
	khoo-**gar** al **te**-nees/golf
go swimming	nadar
	na-**dar**
hire bikes	alquilar bicis
	al-kee-**lar bee**-thees

go fishing	**ir a pescar**
	eer a pes-**kar**
go riding	**montar a caballo**
	mon-**tar** a ka-**ba**-lyo
how much is it...?	**¿cuánto cuesta...?**
	¿**kwan**-to **kwes**-ta...?
per hour	**la hora**
	la **o**-ra
per day	**por día**
	por **dee**-a
how do I book a court?	**¿cómo se reserva una pista?**
	¿**ko**-mo se re-**ser**-ba **oo**-na **pee**-sta?
can I hire rackets?	**¿puedo alquilar raquetas?**
	¿**pwe**-do al-kee-**lar** ra-**ke**-tas?
is there a football match?	**¿hay algún partido de fútbol?**
	¿aee al-**goon** par-**tee**-do de foot-**bol**?
do I need walking boots?	**¿necesito botas de montaña?**
	¿ne-the-**see**-to **bo**-tas de mon-**ta**-nya?
where is there a sports shop?	**¿dónde hay una tienda de deportes?**
	¿**don**-de aee **oo**-na **tyen**-da de de-**por**-tes?

Skiing

• There are good skiing facilities in the Sierra Nevada and Catalonia. Check out skiing conditions on **www.snow-forecast.com** or **www.bbc.co.uk/weather/sports/snowsports**.
• Take passport-sized photos with you for passes.
• Cross-country skiing is **esquí de fondo**.

can I hire skis?	**¿puedo alquilar unos esquíes?**
	¿**pwe**-do al-kee-**lar oo**-nos es-**kee**-es?
how much is a pass?	**¿cuánto cuesta un forfait?**
	¿**kwan**-to **kwes**-ta oon for-**fa**-eet?
I'm a beginner	**soy principiante**
	soy preen-thee-**pyan**-te

which is an easy run?	**¿hay alguna pista fácil?**
	¿aee al-**goo**-na **pees**-ta **fa**-theel?
what is the snow like today?	**¿cómo está hoy la nieve?**
	¿**ko**-mo es-**ta** oy la **nye**-be?
is there a map of the ski runs?	**¿hay un mapa de pistas?**
	¿ee oon **ma**-pa de **pee**-stas?
my skis are...	**mis esquíes son...**
	mees es-**kee**-es son...
too long	**demasiado largos**
	de-ma-**sya**-do **lar**-gos
too short	**demasiado cortos**
	de-ma-**sya**-do **kor**-tos
my bindings are...	**tengo las fijaciones...**
	ten-go las fee-kha-**thyo**-nes...
too loose	**demasiado flojas**
	de-ma-**sya**-do **flo**-khas
very tight	**muy prietas**
	mwee **prye**-tas
where can we go cross-country skiing?	**¿dónde se puede hacer esquí de fondo?**
	¿**don**-de se **pwe**-de a-**ther** es-**kee** de **fon**-do?
what length skis do you want?	**¿de qué largo quiere los esquíes?**
	¿de ke **lar**-go **kye**-re los es-**kee**-es?
what is your shoe size?	**¿qué número de zapato tiene?**
	¿ke **noo**-me-ro de tha-**pa**-to **tye**-ne?

Nightlife

Nightlife – popular

• Spanish people tend to dine late and then go out afterwards. An evening out might not start until 10pm and typically involves visiting a series of bars, staying for only a short time in each one.
• The last film showing is usually midnight when tickets are cheaper.

what is there to do at night?	**¿qué se puede hacer por las noches?** ¿ke se **pwe**-de a-**ther** por las **no**-ches?
which is a good bar?	**¿qué bares buenos hay?** ¿ke **ba**-res **bwe**-nos aee?
which is a good disco?	**¿qué discotecas buenas hay?** ¿ke dees-ko-**te**-kas **bwe**-nas aee?
where can we hear live music?	**¿dónde hay música en vivo?** ¿**don**-de aee **moo**-see-ka en **bee**-bo?
is it expensive?	**¿es caro?** ¿es **ka**-ro?
where can we hear flamenco/salsa?	**¿dónde se puede escuchar flamenco/salsa?** ¿**don**-de se **pwe**-de es-koo-**char** fla-**men**-ko/**sal**-sa?
where do local people go at night?	**¿dónde va la gente de aquí por la noche?** ¿**don**-de ba la **khen**-te de a-**kee** por la **no**-che?
is it a safe area?	**¿es una zona segura?** ¿es **oo**-na **tho**-na se-**goo**-ra?
are there any concerts?	**¿hay algún concierto?** ¿aee al-**goon** kon-**thyer**-to?
do you want to dance?	**¿quieres bailar?** ¿**kye**-res baee-**lar**?
my name is...	**me llamo...** me **lya**-mo...

| what's your name? | ¿cómo te llamas? |
| | ¿**ko**-mo te **lya**-mas? |

Nightlife – cultural

• •

• Museums sometimes re-open between 5 and 8pm.
• There are many summer festivals featuring dance, music and drama, which generally begin around 10.30 or 11pm.
• In large cities you can often find **La Guia del Ocio**, a magazine listing events (**www.guiadelocio.com**). Newspapers usually carry a page called **Agenda Cultural** with local events.

is there a list of cultural events?	¿hay alguna guía del ocio?
	¿aee al-**goo**-na **gee**-a del **o**-thyo?
when is the local festival?	¿cuándo son las fiestas de aquí?
	¿**kwan**-do son las **fyes**-tas de a-**kee**?
we'd like to go...	queríamos ir...
	ke-**ree**-a-mos eer...
to the theatre/ to the opera	al teatro/a la ópera
	al te-**a**-tro/a la **o**-pe-ra
to the ballet/ to a concert	al ballet/a un concierto
	al ba-**le**/a oon kon-**thyer**-to
what's on?	¿qué ponen?
	¿ke **po**-nen?
do I need to get tickets in advance?	¿tengo que sacar antes las entradas?
	¿**ten**-go ke sa-**kar an**-tes las en-**tra**-das?
how much are the tickets?	¿cuánto cuestan las entradas?
	¿**kwan**-to **kwes**-tan las en-**tra**-das?
when does the performance end?	¿cuándo termina la representación?
	¿**kwan**-do ter-**mee**-na la re-pre-sen-ta-**thyon**?
2 tickets...	dos entradas...
	dos en-**tra**-das...
for tonight/ for tomorrow	para esta noche/para mañana
	pa-ra **es**-ta **no**-che/**pa**-ra ma-**nya**-na
for 5th August	para el cinco de agosto
	pa-ra el **theen**-ko de a-**gos**-to

Accommodation

Hotel

• Tourist offices have lists of hotels and other accommodation in their area. Hotels use a star grading system (from 1 to 5).
• **Hostales** and **pensiones** are generally family-owned guest-houses. The price doesn't usually include breakfast.
• **Paradores** are good-quality hotels, usually in monuments, castles, listed buildings etc. Check out **www.parador.es**.

have you a room for tonight?	**¿tiene una habitación para esta noche?** ¿**tye**-ne **oo**-na a-bee-ta-**thyon pa**-ra **es**-ta **no**-che?
a room	**una habitación** **oo**-na a-bee-ta-**thyon**
single/double/triple	**individual/doble/triple** een-dee-bee-**dwal**/**do**-ble/**tree**-ple
family	**familiar** fa-mee-**lyar**
with a shower	**con ducha** kon **doo**-cha
with a bath	**con baño** kon **ba**-nyo
how much is it per night?	**¿cuánto cuesta por noche?** ¿**kwan**-to **kwes**-ta por **no**-che?
is breakfast included?	**¿está incluido el desayuno?** ¿es-**ta** een-kloo-**ee**-do el de-sa-**yoo**-no?
I booked a room	**tengo reservada una habitación** **ten**-go re-ser-**ba**-da **oo**-na a-bee-ta-**thyon**
in the name of...	**a nombre de...** a **nom**-bre de...

I'd like to see the room	**quería ver la habitación**
	ke-**ree**-a ber la a-bee-ta-**thyon**
have you anything cheaper?	**¿tiene algo más barato?**
	¿**tye**-ne **al**-go mas ba-**ra**-to?
I want a room with three beds	**quiero una habitación con tres camas**
	kye-ro **oo**-na a-bee-ta-**thyon** kon tres **ka**-mas
can I leave this in the safe?	**¿puedo dejar esto en la caja fuerte?**
	¿**pwe**-do de-**khar es**-to en la **ka**-kha **fwer**-te?
can I have my key, please?	**¿puede darme la llave, por favor?**
	¿**pwe**-de **dar**-me la **lya**-be, por fa-**bor**?
are there any messages for me?	**¿hay algún mensaje para mí?**
	¿aee al-**goon** men-**sa**-khe **pa**-ra mee?
come in!	**¡pase!**
	¡**pa**-se!
please come back later	**por favor, vuelva más tarde**
	por fa-**bor**, **bwel**-ba mas **tar**-de
I'd like breakfast in my room	**quería desayunar en la habitación**
	ke-**ree**-a de-sa-yoo-**nar** en la a-bee-ta-**thyon**
please bring...	**por favor, ¿me trae...?**
	por fa-**bor**, ¿me **trae**...?
toilet paper	**papel higiénico**
	pa-**pel** ee-**khye**-nee-ko
soap	**jabón**
	kha-**bon**
clean towels	**toallas limpias**
	to-**a**-lyas **leem**-pyas
a glass	**un vaso**
	oon **ba**-so
could you clean...?	**¿puede limpiar...?**
	¿**pwe**-de leem-**pyar**?
my room	**la habitación**
	la a-bee-ta-**thyon**
the bath	**el baño**
	el **ba**-nyo
please call me...	**por favor, despiérteme...**
	por fa-**bor**, des-**pyer**-te-me...

at 8 o'clock	**a las ocho**
	a las **o**-cho
do you have a	**¿tienen servicio de lavandería?**
laundry service?	¿**tye**-nen ser-**beeth**-yo de la-ban-de-**ree**-a?
we're leaving	**nos vamos mañana**
tomorrow	nos **ba**-mos ma-**nya**-na
please prepare the	**¿me prepara la cuenta, por favor?**
bill	¿me pre-**pa**-ra la **kwen**-ta por fa-**bor**?

Self-catering

• More and more buildings now have what is called 'city gas' and don't need gas cylinders. Electric cookers are more common than gas.
• Electricity is mostly 220 volts with 2-pin round plugs. You can find adaptors for your appliances in most electricity shops or ironmonger's.
• You have to take care of your own rubbish which is collected daily from bins in the streets. Spanish people try to recycle as much as possible and there are special containers for organic waste, paper/cardboard (usually blue), plastic/metal containers and tetra-pak (usually yellow) and glass (usually green). Sometimes they are all green or grey with stickers for the type of waste you can throw in them.
• Youth hostels (**albergues**) can be booked in advance.

which is the key for	**¿cuál es la llave de esta puerta?**
this door?	¿kwal es la **lya**-be de **es**-ta **pwer**-ta?
please show us how	**enséñenos cómo funciona esto, por favor**
this works	en-**se**-nye-nos **ko**-mo foon-**thyo**-na **es**-to,
	por fa-**bor**
how does ... work?	**¿cómo funciona...?**
	¿**ko**-mo foon-**thyo**-na...?
the air conditioning	**el aire acondicionado**
	el **aee**-re a-kon-dee-thyo-**na**-do
the central heating	**la calefacción**
	la ka-le-fak-**thyon**

the waterheater	**el calentador del agua**
	el ka-len-ta-**dor** del **a**-gwa
is there always hot water?	**¿hay siempre agua caliente?**
	¿aee **syem**-pre **a**-gwa ka-**lyen**-te?
the washing machine	**la lavadora**
	la la-ba-**do**-ra
the cooker	**la cocina**
	la ko-**thee**-na
who do I contact if there are any problems?	**¿a quién aviso si hay algún problema?**
	¿a kyen a-**bee**-so see aee al-**goon** pro-**ble**-ma?
we need extra...	**nos hacen falta más...**
	nos **a**-then **fal**-ta mas...
cutlery	**cubiertos**
	koo-**byer**-tos
dishes	**platos**
	pla-tos
sheets	**sábanas**
	sa-ba-nas
blankets	**mantas**
	man-tas
bedspreads	**colchas**
	col-chas
the gas has run out	**se ha acabado el gas**
	se a a-ka-**ba**-do el gas
is there a heater/ventilator?	**¿hay una estufa/un ventilador?**
	¿aee **oo**-na es-**too**-fa/oon ben-tee-la-**dor**?
what do I do?	**¿qué hago?**
	¿ke **a**-go?
can we have an extra key?	**¿nos puede dar otro juego de llaves?**
	¿nos **pwe**-de dar **o**-tro **khwe**-go de **lya**-bes?
where are the fuses?	**¿dónde están los fusibles?**
	¿**don**-de es-**tan** los foo-**see**-bles?
where do I put the rubbish?	**¿dónde se deja la basura?**
	¿**don**-de se **de**-kha la ba-**soo**-ra?

Camping and caravanning

- When camping in Spain you must use approved sites. Campsites are graded (class 1 to 3). A useful website is **www.campinguia.com**.
- You usually pay per tent, per person and per car/caravan.
- If towing a caravan or trailer you must not exceed 50kph in built-up areas and 70 or 80 kph on other roads.

we're looking for a campsite	**estamos buscando un camping** es-**ta**-mos boos-**kan**-do oon **kam**-peen
have you a list of campsites?	**¿tiene una guía de campings?** ¿**tye**-ne **oo**-na **gee**-a de **kam**-peens?
where is the campsite?	**¿dónde está el camping?** ¿**don**-de es-**ta** el **kam**-peen?
have you any vacancies?	**¿tienen sitio?** ¿**tye**-nen **see**-tyo?
how much is it per night?	**¿cuánto cuesta por noche?** ¿**kwan**-to **kwes**-ta por **no**-che?
we'd like to stay for ... nights	**queríamos quedarnos ... noches** ke-**ree**-a-mos ke-**dar**-nos ... **no**-ches
is the campsite near the beach?	**¿está el camping cerca de la playa?** ¿es-**ta** el **kam**-peen **ther**-ka de la **pla**-ya?
do you have a more sheltered site?	**¿tienen algún sitio más resguardado?** ¿**tye**-nen al-**goon see**-tyo mas res-gwar-**da**-do?
it is very muddy here	**aquí hay mucho barro** a-**kee** aee **moo**-cho **ba**-rro
is there another site?	**¿hay otro sitio?** ¿aee **o**-tro **see**-tyo?
is there a shop on the site?	**¿hay alguna tienda en el camping?** ¿aee al-**goo**-na **tyen**-da en el **kam**-peen?
can we camp here?	**¿podemos acampar aquí?** ¿po-**de**-mos a-kam-**par** a-**kee**?
can we park our caravan here?	**¿podemos aparcar la caravana aquí?** ¿po-**de**-mos a-par-**kar** la ka-ra-**ba**-na a-**kee**?
for the night	**por esta noche** por **es**-ta **no**-che

Different travellers

Children

• •

• Children are accepted almost everywhere in Spain and will often be out with the family until late at night.
• Children under 4 go free on trains and buses; those between 4 and 13 pay 60% of the full fare on trains.
• Children under 12 cannot travel in the front seat and they must travel in the appropriate car seat according to their age.

a child's ticket	**un billete de niño**
(for transport)	oon bee-**lye**-te de **nee**-nyo
(for entertainment)	**una entrada de niño**
	oo-na en-**tra**-da de **nee**-nyo
is there a reduction for children?	**¿hay descuento para niños?**
	¿aee des-**kwen**-to **pa**-ra **nee**-nyos?
do you have a children's menu?	**¿tienen menú para niños?**
	¿**tye**-nen me-**noo pa**-ra **nee**-nyos?
do you have...?	**¿tiene...?**
	¿**tye**-ne...?
a high chair	**una trona**
	oo-na **tro**-na
a cot	**una cuna**
	oo-na **koo**-na
what's there for children to do?	**¿qué cosas hay para los niños?**
	¿ke **ko**-sas aee **pa**-ra los **nee**-nyos?
is there a playpark?	**¿hay algún parque infantil?**
	¿aee al-**goon par**-ke een-fan-**teel**?
is it safe for children?	**¿es seguro para los niños?**
	¿es se-**goo**-ro **pa**-ra los **nee**-nyos?

is it dangerous?	**¿es peligroso?**
	¿es pe-lee-**gro**-so?
I have two children	**tengo dos hijos**
	ten-go dos **ee**-khoss
he/she is 10 years old	**tiene diez años**
	tye-ne dyeth **a**-nyos
do you have children?	**¿tiene hijos?**
	¿**tye**-ne **ee**-khos?

Special needs

• •

• Tourist offices provide information on events and activities in their areas.
• Some youth hostels and a few hotels have facilities for disabled travellers.
• Check out disabled access carefully before your trip.
• Each town normally has a fleet of taxis designed to take wheelchairs. These have to be ordered specially.

is it possible to visit ... with a wheelchair?	**¿se puede entrar en ... con silla de ruedas?**
	¿se **pwe**-de en-**trar** en ... kon **see**-lya de **rwe**-das?
do you have toilets for the disabled?	**¿hay aseos para minusválidos?**
	¿aee a-**se**-os **pa**-ra mee-noos-**ba**-lee-dos?
I need a bedroom on the ground floor	**necesito una habitación en la planta baja**
	ne-the-**see**-to **oo**-na a-bee-ta-**thyon** en la **plan**-ta **ba**-kha
is there a lift?	**¿hay ascensor?**
	¿aee as-then-**sor**?
where is the lift?	**¿dónde está el ascensor?**
	¿**don**-de es-**ta** el as-then-**sor**?
I can't walk far	**no puedo andar mucho**
	no **pwe**-do an-**dar** moo-cho
are there many steps?	**¿hay muchos escalones?**
	¿aee **moo**-chos es-ka-**lo**-nes?

is there an entrance for wheelchairs?	¿hay acceso para sillas de ruedas?
	¿aee ak-**the**-so **pa**-ra **see**-lyas de **rwe**-das?
can I travel on this train with a wheelchair?	¿puedo viajar en este tren con silla de ruedas?
	¿**pwe**-do bya-**khar** en **es**-te tren kon **see**-lya de **rwe**-das?
is there a reduction for the disabled?	¿hay descuento para minusválidos?
	¿aee des-**kwen**-to **pa**-ra mee-noos-**ba**-lee-dos?

Exchange visitors

....

• These phrases are intended for families hosting Spanish-speaking visitors. We have used the more familiar **tú** form.
• Spanish people tend to eat dinner much later than in the UK, any time between 8.30 and 11pm. They may not be used to eating their main meal of the day as early as 6pm!

what would you like for breakfast?	¿qué quieres de desayuno?
	¿ke **kye**-res de de-sa-**yoo**-no?
do you eat...?	¿comes...?
	¿**ko**-mes...?
what would you like to eat?	¿qué quieres comer?/¿qué te apetece comer?
	¿ke **kye**-res ko-**mer**?/¿ke te a-pe-**te**-the ko-**mer**?
what would you like to drink?	¿qué quieres beber?/¿qué te apetece beber?
	¿ke **kye**-res be-**ber**?/¿ke te a-pe-**te**-the be-**ber**?
did you sleep well?	¿has dormido bien?
	¿as dor-**mee**-do byen?
would you like to take a shower?	¿quieres darte una ducha?
	¿**kye**-res **dar**-te **oo**-na **doo**-cha?
what would you like to do today?	¿qué quieres hacer hoy?/¿qué te apetece hacer hoy?
	¿ke **kye**-res a-**ther** oy?/¿ke te a-pe-**te**-the a-**ther** oy?

would you like to go shopping?	**¿quieres ir de compras?**
	¿**kye**-res eer de **kom**-pras?
I will pick you up at...	**te iré a recoger a...**
	te ee-**re** a re-ko-**kher** a...
take care	**ten cuidado**
	ten kwee-**da**-do
did you enjoy yourself?	**¿te lo has pasado bien?**
	¿te lo as pa-**sa**-do byen?
please be back by...	**vuelve antes de...**
	bwel-be **an**-tes de...
we'll be in bed when you get back	**estaremos acostados cuando vuelvas**
	es-ta-**re**-mos a-kos-**ta**-dos **kwan**-do **bwel**-bas

• These phrases are intended for those people staying with Spanish-speaking families.
• Take care to use the more formal **usted** form until you are invited to use **tú**, especially with older people.
• In spain the main meal is usually lunch and that's when families eat together. Dinner is usually a more informal meal unless there are guests.

I like...	**me gusta...**
	me **goos**-ta...
I don't like...	**no me gusta...**
	no me **goos**-ta...
that was delicious	**estaba buenísimo**
	es-**ta**-ba bwe-**nee**-see-mo
thank you very much	**muchas gracias**
	moo-chas **gra**-thyas
may I phone home?	**¿puedo llamar a casa?**
	¿**pwe**-do lya-**mar** a **ka**-sa?
may I make a reverse charge call?	**¿puedo hacer una llamada a cobro revertido?**
	¿**pwe**-do a-**ther oo**-na lya-**ma**-da a **ko**-bro re-ver-**tee**-do?
may I make a local call?	**¿puedo hacer una llamada local?**
	¿**pwe**-do a-**ther oo**-na lya-**ma**-da lo-**kal**?

can I have a key?	**¿me deja una llave?**
	¿me **de**-kha **oo**-na **lya**-be?
can you take me by car?	**¿puede llevarme en coche?**
	¿**pwe**-de lye-**bar**-me en **ko**-che?
can I borrow...?	**¿me deja/presta...?**
	¿me **de**-kha/**pres**-ta...?
an iron	**una plancha**
	oo-na **plan**-cha
a hairdryer	**un secador**
	oon se-ka-**dor**
what time do you get up?	**¿a qué hora se levanta?**
	¿a ke **o**-ra se le-**ban**-ta?
please could you call me at...?	**¿me puede llamar a las...?**
	¿me **pwe**-de lya-**mar** a las...?
I'm leaving in a week	**me voy dentro de una semana**
	me **boy den**-tro de **oo**-na se-**ma**-na
thanks for everything	**gracias por todo**
	gra-thyas por **to**-do
I've had a great time	**lo he pasado muy bien**
	lo e pa-**sa**-do mwee byen

Difficulties

Problems

....

- Always try to speak in Spanish – however bad! And then ask if there is someone who does speak some English.
- Try to stay calm. Not understanding each other can often aggravate the situation.
- Try to be as polite as possible, using **señor** or **señora** and the polite **usted** form.

can you help me, please?	**¿puede ayudarme, por favor?**
	¿**pwe**-de a-yoo-**dar**-me, por fa-**bor**?
I don't speak Spanish	**no hablo español**
	no **a**-blo es-pa-**nyol**
do you speak English?	**¿habla inglés?**
	¿**a**-bla een-**gles**?
does anyone speak English?	**¿hay alguien que hable inglés?**
	¿aee **al**-gyen ke **a**-ble een-**gles**?
I'm lost	**me he perdido**
	me e per-**dee**-do
how do I get to...?	**¿cómo se va a...?**
	¿**ko**-mo se ba a...?
I'm late	**llego tarde**
	lye-go **tar**-de
I need to get to...	**tengo que ir a...**
	ten-go ke eer a...
I've missed...	**he perdido...**
	e per-**dee**-do...
my plane/ my connection	**el vuelo/el enlace**
	el **bwe**-lo/el en-**la**-the

I've lost...	**he perdido...**
	e per-**dee**-do...
my wallet	**la cartera**
	la kar-**te**-ra
my passport	**el pasaporte**
	el pa-sa-**por**-te
my luggage has not arrived	**no ha llegado mi equipaje**
	no a **lye**-ga-do mee e-kee-**pa**-khe
I've left my bag in...	**me he dejado la bolsa en...**
	me e de-**kha**-do la **bol**-sa en...
leave me alone!	**¡déjeme en paz!**
	i**de**-khe-me en path!
go away!	**¡váyase!**
	i**ba**-ya-se!
I have no money	**no tengo dinero**
	no **ten**-go dee-**ne**-ro

Complaints

• •

• Spanish people tend not to complain much.
• Complaining does sometimes work, but don't expect miracles as it is not a major part of Spanish culture.
• There is sometimes a lack of flexibility to standard rules and regulations.
• Ask for the complaint form (**hoja** or **libro de reclamaciones**) in shops, hotels, restaurants, etc.

the light	**la luz**
	la looth
the air conditioning	**el aire acondicionado**
	el **aee**-re a-kon-dee-thyo-**na**-do
...doesn't work	**...no funciona**
	...no foon-**thyo**-na
the room is dirty	**la habitación está sucia**
	la a-bee-ta-**thyon** es-**ta soo**-thya

the bath is dirty	**el baño está sucio**
	el **ba**-nyo es-**ta soo**-thyo
there is no...	**no hay...**
	no aee...
hot water	**agua caliente**
	a-gwa ka-**lyen**-te
toilet paper	**papel higiénico**
	pa-**pel** ee-**khye**-nee-ko
it is too noisy	**hay demasiado ruido**
	aee de-ma-**sya**-do **rwee**-do
it is too small	**es demasiado pequeño**
	es de-ma-**sya**-do pe-**ke**-nyo
this isn't what I ordered	**esto no es lo que he pedido**
	es-to no es lo ke e pe-**dee**-do
I want to complain	**quiero hacer una reclamación**
	kye-ro a-**ther oo**-na re-kla-ma-**thyon**
I want my money back	**quiero que me devuelvan el dinero**
	kye-ro ke me de-**bwel**-ban el dee-**ne**-ro
we've been waiting for a very long time	**llevamos mucho tiempo esperando**
	lye-**ba**-mos **moo**-cho **tyem**-po es-pe-**ran**-do
there is a mistake	**hay un error**
	aee oon e-**rror**
this is broken	**esto está roto**
	es-to es-**ta ro**-to
can you repair it?	**¿puede arreglarlo?**
	¿**pwe**-de a-rre-**glar**-lo?

Emergencies

• Emergency numbers in Spain: Police (nationwide) – 091, (local) – 092; Fire Brigade (Madrid, Barcelona & Seville) – 080 or 112, (elsewhere) – check with the operator; Civil defense: 1006.
• For an ambulance, call the police and they will make arrangements, or call 061 or 112 for emergencies (the 061 number is for life-threatening emergencies). The ambulance service is private.

help!	**¿me puede ayudar?**
	¿me **pwe**-de a-yoo-**dar**?
can you help me?	**¿me puede ayudar?**
	¿me **pwe**-de a-yoo-**dar**?
there's been an accident	**ha habido un accidente**
	a a-**bee**-do oon ak-thee-**den**-te
someone is injured	**hay un herido**
	aee oon e-**ree**-do
call...	**llame a...**
	lya-me a...
the police	**la policía**
	la po-lee-**thee**-a
an ambulance	**una ambulancia**
	oo-na am-boo-**lan**-thya
he was driving too fast	**él iba demasiado rápido**
	el **ee**-ba de-ma-**sya**-do **ra**-pee-do
where's the police station?	**¿dónde está la comisaría?**
	¿**don**-de es-**ta** la ko-mee-sa-**ree**-a?
the insurance company requires me to report it	**la compañía de seguros me exige que lo notifique**
	la kom-pa-**nyee**-a de se-**goo**-ros me ek-**see**-khe ke lo no-tee-**fee**-ke
I've been robbed	**me han robado**
	me an ro-**ba**-do
I have no money	**no tengo dinero**
	no **ten**-go dee-**ne**-ro

English	Spanish	Pronunciation
I've been attacked	**me han agredido**	me an a-gre-**dee**-do
I've been raped	**me han violado**	me an byo-**la**-do
my car has been broken into	**me han entrado en el coche**	me an en-**tra**-do en el **ko**-che
my car has been stolen	**me han robado el coche**	me an ro-**ba**-do el **ko**-che
that man keeps following me	**ese hombre me está siguiendo**	**e**-se **om**-bre me es-**ta** see-**gyen**-do
how much is the fine?	**¿cuánto es la multa?**	¿**kwan**-to es la **mool**-ta?
I don't have enough	**no tengo suficiente**	no **ten**-go soo-fee-**thyen**-te
can I pay at the police station?	**¿puedo pagar en la comisaría?**	¿**pwe**-do pa-**gar** en la ko-mee-sa-**ree**-a?
I would like to phone my embassy	**quisiera llamar a mi embajada**	kee-**syer**-a lya-**mar** a mee em-ba-**kha**-da
where is the British/ American/ Australian Consulate?	**¿dónde está el consulado británico/ americano/australiano?**	¿**don**-de es-**ta** el kon-soo-**la**-do bree-**ta**-nee-ko/ a-me-ree-ka-no/awa-tra-lya-no?
I'm very sorry	**lo siento mucho**	lo **syen**-to **moo**-cho
we're on our way	**ahora vamos para allá**	a-**o**-ra **ba**-mos **pa**-ra a-**ya**

Health

Health

- EU citizens are entitled to free emergency treatment. You must have a European Health Insurance Card (from **www.dh.gov.uk/travellers**).
- If you need to see a doctor, go to the nearest clinic by 9am and you may get an appointment that day. Make sure you're being treated as a National Health patient and not privately.

have you something for...?	**¿tiene algo para...?**
	¿**tye**-ne **al**-go **pa**-ra...?
car sickness/ diarrhoea	**el mareo/la diarrea**
	el ma-**re**-o/la dee-a-**rre**-a
is it safe for children to take?	**¿lo pueden tomar los niños?**
	¿lo **pwe**-den to-**mar** los **neen**-yos?
I don't feel well	**no me encuentro bien**
	no me en-**kwen**-tro byen
I need a doctor	**necesito un médico**
	ne-the-**see**-to oon **me**-dee-ko
my son/daughter is ill	**mi hijo/hija está enfermo(a)**
	mee **ee**-kho/**ee**-kha es-**ta** en-**fer**-mo(a)
he/she has a temperature	**tiene fiebre**
	tye-ne **fye**-bre
I'm taking these drugs	**estoy tomando estos medicamentos**
	es-**toy** to-**man**-do **es**-tos me-dee-ka-**men**-tos
I have high blood pressure	**tengo la tensión alta**
	ten-go la ten-**syon al**-ta
I'm diabetic	**soy diabético(a)**
	soy dya-**be**-tee-ko(a)
I'm pregnant	**estoy embarazada**
	es-**toy** em-ba-ra-**tha**-da

I'm on the pill	**estoy tomando la píldora**
	es-**toy** to-**man**-do la **peel**-do-ra
I'm allergic to penicillin	**soy alérgico(a) a la penicilina**
	soy a-**ler**-khee-ko(a) a la pe-nee-thee-**lee**-na
my blood group is...	**mi grupo sanguíneo es...**
	mee **groo**-po san-**gee**-ne-o es...
I'm breastfeeding	**estoy dando el pecho/de mamar**
	es-**toy dan**-do el **pe**-cho/de ma-**mar**
is it safe to take?	**¿tiene contraindicaciones?**
	¿**tye**-ne con-tra-een-dee-ka-**thyo**-nes?
will he/she have to go to hospital?	**¿tendrá que ir al hospital?**
	¿ten-**dra** ke eer al os-pee-**tal**?
I need to go to casualty	**tengo que ir a urgencias**
	ten-go ke eer a oor-**khen**-thyas
where is the hospital?	**¿dónde está el hospital?**
	¿**don**-de es-**ta** el os-pee-**tal**?
when are visiting hours?	**¿cuáles son las horas de visita?**
	¿**kwa**-les son las **o**-ras de bee-**see**-ta?
which ward?	**¿qué planta?**
	¿ke **plan**-ta?
I need to see the dentist	**necesito ver al dentista**
	ne-the-**see**-to ber al den-**tees**-ta
I have toothache	**me duele una muela**
	me **dwe**-le **oo**-na **mwe**-la
the filling has come out	**se me ha caído el empaste**
	se me a ka-**ee**-do el em-**pas**-te
it hurts	**me duele**
	me **dwe**-le
my dentures are broken	**se me ha roto la dentadura postiza**
	se me a **ro**-to la den-ta-**doo**-ra pos-**tee**-tha
can you repair them?	**¿puede arreglarla?**
	¿**pwe**-de a-rre-**glar**-la?
I have an abscess	**tengo un absceso**
	ten-go oon ab-**the**-so
I need a receipt for my insurance	**necesito un recibo para el seguro**
	ne-the-**see**-to oon re-**thee**-bo **pa**-ra el se-**goo**-ro

Business

Business

- Office hours are generally 9am till 1pm, and 4 till 7pm.
- Government offices are open to the public from 9am till 2pm.
- Spanish company websites end .**es**.
- Often if a Spanish bank holiday falls on a Thursday people take Friday off to have a long weekend but there are regional differences.

I'm...	soy...
	soy...
where can I plug in my laptop?	¿dónde puedo enchufar el (ordenador) portátil?
	¿**don**-de **pwe**-do en-choo-**far** el (or-de-na-**dor**) por-**ta**-teel?
what is your website address?	¿cuál es su página web?
	¿kwal es su **pa**-khee-na web?
here's my card	aquí tiene mi tarjeta
	a-**kee tye**-ne mee tar-**khe**-ta
I'm from Jones Ltd	soy de la empresa Jones
	soy de la em-**pre**-sa Jones
I'd like to arrange a meeting with Mr/Ms...	quería tener una reunión con el señor/la señora...
	ke-**ree**-a te-**ner oo**-na re-oo-**nyon** kon el se-**nyor**/la se-**nyo**-ra...
can we meet at a restaurant?	¿podemos vernos en un restaurante?
	¿po-**de**-mos **ber**-nos en oon res-tow-**ran**-te?
I will send an e-mail to confirm	se lo confirmaré por email
	se lo kon-feer-ma-**re** por **ee**-meyl
I'm staying at Hotel...	estoy en el Hotel...
	es-**toy** en el o-**tel**...

how do I get to your office?	¿cómo se va a su oficina?
	¿**ko**-mo se ba a soo o-fee-**thee**-na?
here is some information about my company	aquí tiene información sobre mi empresa
	a-**kee tye**-ne een-for-ma-**thyon so**-bre mee em-**pre**-sa
I have an appointment with...	tengo una cita con...
	ten-go **oo**-na **thee**-ta kon...
at ... o'clock	a las...
	a las...
I'm delighted to meet you	encantado(a) de conocerle
	en-kan-**ta**-do(a) de ko-no-**ther**-le
my Spanish isn't very good	no hablo muy bien español
	no **a**-blo mwee byen es-pa-**nyol**
what's the managing director's name?	¿cómo se llama el director general?
	¿**ko**-mo se **lya**-ma el dee-rek-**tor** khe-ne-**ral**?
I would like some information about the company	quería información sobre la empresa
	ke-**ree**-a een-for-ma-**thyon so**-bre la em-**pre**-sa
do you have a press office?	¿tiene oficina de prensa?
	¿**tye**-ne o-fee-**thee**-na de **pren**-sa?
I need an interpreter	necesito un intérprete
	ne-the-**see**-to oon een-**ter**-pre-te
can you photocopy this for me?	¿me puede fotocopiar esto?
	¿me **pwe**-de fo-to-ko-**pyar es**-to?
is there a business centre?	¿hay algún centro de negocios?
	¿aee al-**goon then**-tro de ne-**go**-thyos?
do you have an appointment?	¿está usted citado(a)?
	¿es-**ta** oos-**ted** thee-**ta**-do(a)?

Phoning

- The international dialling code for the UK is oo 44. Spain is oo 34.
- You can buy phonecards (for 6 and 12 euros) from newspaper kiosks and tobacconists.
- For calls within Spain you must dial the area code and number (even for local calls).

a phonecard	una tarjeta telefónica
	oo-na tar-**khe**-ta te-le-**fo**-nee-ka
for ... euros	de ... euros
	de ... **eoo**-ros
I want to make a phone call	quiero hacer una llamada
	kye-ro a-**ther oo**-na lya-**ma**-da
I want to make a reverse charge call	quiero hacer una llamada a cobro revertido
	kye-ro a-**ther oo**-na lya-**ma**-da a **ko**-bro re-ber-**tee**-do
can I speak to...?	¿puedo hablar con...?
	¿**pwe**-do a-**blar** kon...?
this is...	soy...
	soy...
I'll call back later/tomorrow	le volveré a llamar más tarde/mañana
	le bol-be-**re** a lya-**mar** mas **tar**-de/ma-**nya**-na
can you give me an outside line, please	¿me da línea, por favor?
	¿me da **lee**-ne-a, por fa-**bor**?
hello/who is calling?	¿diga?/¿de parte de quién?
	¿**dee**-ga?/¿de **par**-te de kyen?
it's engaged	está comunicando
	es-**ta** ko-moo-nee-**kan**-do
I'll text you	te mando un mensaje
	te **man**-do oon men-**sa**-khe
can you text me?	¿me puedes mandar un mensaje?
	¿me **pwe**-des man-**dar** oon men-**sa**-khe?

E-mail/fax

. . . .

- There are a lot of internet cafés in Spain. Some deals look better than they actually are.
- www. is **tres uve dobles punto.** @ is **arroba.** Many English terms are used and understood. The Spanish word for 'password' is **contraseña** but 'password' is very common.
- The ending for Spanish websites is **.es**.

I want to send an e-mail	quiero mandar un email
	kye-ro man-**dar** oon **ee**-meyl
what's your e-mail address?	¿cuál es su email?
	¿kwal es soo **ee**-meyl?
my e-mail address is...	mi (dirección de) email es...
	mee (dee-rek-**thyon** de) **ee**-meyl es...
lydia.martin@villen.es	lydia punto martin arroba villen punto e s
	lee-dya **poon**-to mar-**teen** ar-**ro**-ba **uil**-yen **poon**-to e **e**-se (or es)
how do you spell it?	¿cómo se escribe?
	¿**ko**-mo se es-**kree**-be?
all one word	todo junto
	to-do **khoon**-to
all lower case (small letters)	todo en minuscula(s)
	to-do en mee-**noos**-koo-la(s)
did you get my e-mail?	¿le llegó mi email?
	¿le lye-**go** mee **ee**-meyl?
did you get the attachment?	¿recibió el documento adjunto?
	¿re-thee-**byo** el do-koo-**men**-to ad-**khoon**-to?
I want to send a fax	quiero mandar un fax
	kye-ro man-**dar** oon faks
what's your fax number?	¿cuál es su número de fax?
	¿kwal es soo **noo**-me-ro de faks?
did you get my fax?	¿le llegó mi fax?
	¿le lye-**go** mee faks?
can I send a fax from here?	¿puedo mandar un fax desde aquí?
	¿**pwe**-do man-**dar** oon faks **des**-de a-**kee**?

Internet/cybercafé

. . . .

• Some libraries in Spain have Internet access but it is not that common. You pay a fee for half an hour, an hour, two hours or you can buy a card for a number of sessions which will probably be cheaper. Cybercafés are common in Spain and also charge according to the time you are connected. In most cybercafés you can take photocopies and print out documents as well.

• There are some Spanish search engines but most people use google or yahoo. Internet terminology terms are generally borrowed from English, though sometimes 'adapted' to Spanish pronunciation.

I want to check my e-mail	quiero comprobar mi correo
	kye-ro kom-pro-**bar** mee ko-**rreo**
how much is it for 15 minutes?	¿cuánto cuestan 15 minutos?/¿cuánto cuesta conectarse 15 minutos?
	¿**kwan**-to **kwes**-tan **keen**-the mee-**noo**-tos?/¿**kwan**-to **kwes**-ta ko-nek-**tar**-se **keen**-the mee-**noo**-tos?
how much is it for an hour?	¿cuánto cuesta una hora?/¿cuánto cuesta conectarse una hora?
	¿**kwan**-to **kwes**-ta **oo**-na **o**-ra?/¿**kwan**-to **kwes**-ta ko-nek-**tar**-se **oo**-na **o**-ra?
how much is it to print something out?	¿cuánto cuesta imprimir algo?
	¿**kwan**-to **kwes**-ta eem-pree-**meer al**-go?
I'd like to put these photos onto CD	me gustaría grabar estas fotos en un CD
	me goos-ta-**ree**-a gra-**bar es**-tas **fo**-tos en oon the-**de**
can you print it out?	¿puede imprimir esto?
	¿**pwe**-de eem-pree-**meer es**-to?
where can I buy a memory stick?	¿dónde puedo comprar un lapis de memoria?
	¿**don**-de **pwe**-do kom-**prar** oon **la**-peeth de me-**mo**-rya?
can you help me, please?	¿me puede ayudar, por favor?
	¿me **pwe**-de a-yoo-**dar**, por fa-**bor**?
it doesn't work	no funciona
	no foon-**thyo**-na
this computer has crashed	este ordenador se ha bloqueado
	es-te or-de-na-**dor** se a blo-ke-**a**-do
the CD is stuck in the drive	el CD se ha quedado atascado en la unidad de disco
	el the-**de** se a ke-**da**-do a-tas-**ka**-do en la oo-nee-**dad** de **dees**-ko

Practical info

Numbers

0	cero	**the**-ro
1	uno	**oo**-no
2	dos	dos
3	tres	tres
4	cuatro	**kwa**-tro
5	cinco	**theen**-ko
6	seis	**se**-ees
7	siete	**sye**-te
8	ocho	**o**-cho
9	nueve	**nwe**-be
10	diez	dyeth
11	once	**on**-the
12	doce	**do**-the
13	trece	**tre**-the
14	catorce	ka-**tor**-the
15	quince	**keen**-the
16	dieciséis	dye-thee-**seys**
17	diecisiete	dye-thee-**sye**-te
18	dieciocho	dye-thee-**o**-cho
19	diencinueve	dye-thee-**nwe**-be
20	veinte	**beyn**-te
21	veintiuno	beyn-tee-**oo**-no
22	veintidós	beyn-tee-**dos**
30	treinta	**treyn**-ta
40	cuarenta	kwa-**ren**-ta
50	cincuenta	theen-**kwen**-ta
60	sesenta	se-**sen**-ta
70	setenta	se-**ten**-ta

80	ochenta	o-**chen**-ta
90	noventa	no-**ben**-ta
100	cien	thyen
110	ciento diez	**thyen**-to dyeth
200	doscientos	dos-**thyen**-tos
500	quinientos	kee-**nyen**-tos
1000	mil	meel
million	un millón	oon mee-**lyon**
1st	**1º/1ᵉʳ** primero/primer	pree-**me**-ro/pree-**mer**
2nd	**2º** segundo	se-**goon**-do
3rd	**3º/3ᵉʳ** tercero/tercer	ter-**the**-ro/ter-**ther**
4th	**4º** cuarto	**kwar**-to
5th	**5º** quinto	**keen**-to
6th	**6º** sexto	**seks**-to
7th	**7º** séptimo	**sep**-tee-mo
8th	**8º** octavo	ok-**ta**-bo
9th	**9º** noveno	no-**be**-no
10th	**10º** décimo	**de**-thee-mo

Days and months

. . . .

Monday	lunes	**loo**-nes
Tuesday	martes	**mar**-tes
Wednesday	miércoles	**myer**-ko-les
Thursday	jueves	**khwe**-bes
Friday	viernes	**byer**-nes
Saturday	sábado	**sa**-ba-do
Sunday	domingo	do-**meen**-go
January	enero	e-**ne**-ro
February	febrero	fe-**bre**-ro
March	marzo	**mar**-tho
April	abril	a-**breel**
May	mayo	**ma**-yo
June	junio	**khoo**-nyo

July	julio	**khoo**-lyo
August	agosto	a-**gos**-to
September	septiembre	sep-**tyem**-bre
October	octubre	ok-**too**-bre
November	noviembre	no-**byem**-bre
December	diciembre	dee-**thyem**-bre

what's the date?	¿qué fecha es hoy?
	¿ke **fe**-cha es oy?
which day?	¿qué día?
	¿ke **dee**-a?
day	día
	dee-a
week	semana
	se-**ma**-na
month	mes
	mes
year	año
	a-nyo
March 5th	el cinco de marzo
	el **theen**-ko de **mar**-tho
July 6th	el seis de julio
	el **se**-ees de **khoo**-lyo
on Saturday	el sábado
	el **sa**-ba-do
on Saturdays	los sábados
	los **sa**-ba-dos
every Saturday	todos los sábados
	to-dos los **sa**-ba-dos
this Saturday	este sábado
	es-te **sa**-ba-do
next Saturday	el próximo sábado/el sábado que viene
	el **prok**-see-mo **sa**-ba-do/el **sa**-ba-do ke **bye**-ne
last Saturday	el sábado pasado
	el **sa**-ba-do pa-**sa**-do
please can you confirm the date?	¿me puede confirmar la fecha?
	¿me **pwe**-de kon-feer-**mar** la **fe**-cha?

Time

am = **de la mañana** (de la ma-**nya**-na)   pm = **de la tarde** (de la **tar**-de)
- The 24-hour clock is used a lot more in Europe than in Britain.
- The words **cuarto** (quarter) and **media** (half) aren't used.

what time is it, please?	**¿qué hora es por favor?** ¿ke **o**-ra es por fa-**bor**?
am/pm	**de la mañana/de la tarde** de la ma-**nya**-na/de la **tar**-de
it's 1 o'clock	**es la una** es la **oo**-na
it's 2/3 o'clock	**son las dos/tres** son las dos/tres
it's half past 8	**son las ocho y media** son las **o**-cho ee **me**-dya
it is half past 10	**son las diez y media** son las dyeth ee **me**-dya
in an hour	**dentro de una hora** **den**-tro de **oo**-na **o**-ra
in half an hour	**dentro de media hora** **den**-tro de **me**-dya **o**-ra
until 8 o'clock	**hasta las ocho** **as**-ta las **o**-cho
until 4 o'clock	**hasta las cuatro** **as**-ta las **kwa**-tro
at 10am	**a las diez de la mañana** a las dyeth de la ma-**nya**-na
at 2200	**a las diez de la noche** a las dyeth de la **no**-che
at midday	**a las doce de la mañana** a las **do**-the de la ma-**nya**-na
at midnight	**a medianoche** a **me**-dya-**no**-che
soon/later	**pronto/más tarde** **pron**-to/mas **tar**-de

Eating out

One of the greatest pleasures of travelling in Spain is the discovery of regional cooking. Spain has many provinces, each with their own distinctive dishes using the best of local produce. Sampling the many tastes and textures of Spanish food couldn't be easier: just stop at a bar and order **tapas**. **Tapas** are a way of life in the whole of Spain and have become fashionable even outside the country. They have the advantage of allowing you to taste lots of dishes at once and are ideal as a quick snack or light meal. Some people have become addicted to visiting various bars, one after the other, to eat a few of their mini dishes instead of having a main meal. This can be great fun, especially in big cities, where there is an incredible variety of **tapas**.

The rich diversity of regional cooking, based on fresh local ingredients, reflects the diversity of Spain's landscape and climate. However, some elements are common to all areas, such as the use of **chorizo** (spicy pork sausage with paprika), peppers, olive oil and garlic. A number of regional dishes have become associated with Spain as a whole, such as **paella** (a rice dish), **tortilla** (potato omelette) and **fabada** (bean stew).

As far as eating out in Spain is concerned, the general rule is that you must expect meals to be served late. Lunches, starting at 2pm and going on until nearly 4pm are common. This makes for a very late dinner, lighter than lunch. Breakfast (**el desayuno**) is normally light, consisting of coffee/milk with bread and olive oil or butter. The main meal is eaten at lunchtime (2–3pm) and is very much a family event. Lunch (**el almuerzo**) is usually a 3-course meal, with the second course often being a piece of meat with no accompaniment. When people eat in the evening (**la cena**), either at home or out, their meal may not start until 10pm or later.

Ordering drinks

- Tea in Spain tends to be served weak and with lemon. If you want milk, ask for it to be served separately **aparte** (a-**par**-te), otherwise you may get a cup of hot milk with a teabag in it.
- If you want a strong black coffee, ask for **un café solo**.
- A white coffee is often served in a glass mug, **en caña**.

a black coffee	**un café solo**
	oon ka-**fe so**-lo
a white coffee	**un café con leche**
	oon ka-**fe** kon **le**-che
a tea with milk/ lemon	**un té con leche/limón**
	oon tekon **le**-che/lee-**mon**
a lager	**una cerveza**
	oo-na ther-**be**-tha
a dry sherry	**un fino**
	oon **fee**-no
a hot chocolate with churros, please	**un chocolate con churros, por favor**
	oon cho-ko-**la**-te kon **choo**-rros, por fa-**bor**
a bottle of mineral water	**una botella de agua mineral**
	oo-na bo-**te**-lya de **a**-gwa mee-ne-**ral**
sparkling/still	**con gas/sin gas**
	kon gas/sin gas
a glass of red wine/ white wine	**un vaso de tinto/vino blanco**
	oon **ba**-so de **teen**-to/**bee**-no **blan**-ko
a bottle of wine	**una botella de vino**
	oo-na bo-**te**-lya de **bee**-no
the wine list, please	**la carta de vinos, por favor**
	la **kar**-ta de **bee**-nos, por fa-**bor**
another bottle, please	**otra botella, por favor**
	o-tra bo-**te**-lya, por fa-**bor**
what will you have?	**¿qué quiere tomar?**
	¿ke **kye**-re to-**mar**?

Ordering food

• •

- Lunch is usually between 1 and 3pm, dinner between 8.30 and 11pm.
- Eating **tapas** in various bars is a good way of trying out various foods and lets you eat earlier.
- The equivalent to 'Bon appétit!' is **¡Qué aproveche!** The reply is **¡Gracias, igualmente!** (thanks, you too!)

can you recommend a good restaurant?	**¿puede recomendarme un buen restaurante?**
	¿**pwe**-de re-ko-men-**dar**-me oon bwen res-tow-**ran**-te?
I'd like to book a table for ... people	**quería reservar una mesa para ... personas**
	ke-**ree**-a re-ser-**bar oo**-na **me**-sa **pa**-ra ... per-**so**-nas
for tonight at 8pm	**para esta noche a las ocho**
	pa-ra **es**-ta **no**-che a las **o**-cho
the menu, please	**la carta, por favor**
	la **kar**-ta, por fa-**bor**
is there a dish of the day?	**¿hay plato del día?**
	¿aee **pla**-to del **dee**-a?
have you a set-price menu?	**¿tiene un menú del día?**
	¿**tye**-ne oon me-**noo** del **dee**-a?
I'll have this	**yo voy a tomar esto**
	yo boy a to-**mar es**-to
what do you recommend?	**¿qué recomienda?**
	¿ke re-ko-**myen**-da?
excuse me!	**¡oiga, por favor!**
	¡**oy**-ga, por fa-**bor**!
more bread/water	**más pan/agua**
	mas pan/**a**-gwa
the bill, please	**la cuenta, por favor**
	la **kwen**-ta, por fa-**bor**
is service included?	**¿está incluido el servicio?**
	¿es-**ta** een-kloo-**ee**-do el ser-**bee**-thyo?

Special requirements

- The words for 'gluten free' are **sin gluten**.
- **Biológico** or **bio** means organic.
- On labels, **hidratos de carbono** are 'carbohydrates'. **Grasos(as)** are fats.
- Health foods (**productos dietéticos**) are available in large supermarkets and specialist shops (**herbolarios**).

I'm vegetarian	**soy vegetariano/a**
	soy be-khe-ta-**rya**-no/a
do you have any vegetarian dishes?	**¿tiene algún plato vegetariano?**
	¿**tye**-ne al-**goon pla**-to be-khe-ta-**rya**-no?
what is in this?	**¿qué lleva esto?**
	¿ke **lye**-ba **es**-to?
I don't eat meat/ pork	**no como carne/cerdo**
	no **ko**-mo **kar**-ne/**ther**-do
I don't eat fish/ shellfish	**no como pescado/marisco(s)**
	no **ko**-mo pes-**ka**-do/ma-**rees**-ko(s)
I'm allergic to shellfish	**soy alérgico(a) al marisco**
	soy a-**ler**-khee-ko(a) al ma-**rees**-ko
I can't eat raw eggs	**no puedo comer huevos crudos**
	no **pwe**-do ko-**mer we**-bos **kroo**-dos
I can't eat liver	**no puedo comer higado**
	no **pwe**-do ko-**mer ee**-ga-do
I am on a diet	**estoy a dieta**
	es-**toy** a **dye**-ta
I am allergic to peanuts	**soy alérgico(a) a los cacahuetes**
	soy a-**ler**-khee-ko(a) a los ka-ka-**we**-tes
is it raw?	**¿está crudo?**
	¿es-**ta kroo**-do?
I don't drink alcohol	**no bebo alcohol**
	no **be**-bo al-**kol**
is it made with unpasteurised milk?	**¿está hecho con leche sin pasteurizar?**
	¿es-**ta e**-cho kon **le**-che seen pas-te-oo-ree-**thar**?

Eating photoguide

Eating places

Restaurant/Tavern Eating places must display menus and prices outside.

It is normal to pay for drinks as you leave the bar but in some outdoor cafés, the waiter will present the bill with the drink and you are expected to pay there and then.

Market Daily and weekly markets have cheese and local specialities as well as tomatoes and fruit for the perfect picnic.

fried fish	fish	RESTAURANTE EL ANCLA	shellfish	meat

PESCAITOS - PESCADOS - MARISCOS Y CARNES

At restaurants, be prepared to spend time at the table. You can order à la carte or from the set menu, in which case you will be served quicker. Note that large portions are generally served. Salads and vegetable dishes are considered as separate items and normally brought to the table before the main dish. Bread is always provided but not butter.

Eating places

Platos Combinados normally consists of meat or fish with rice, potatoes or chips and veg, i.e. a full dish. If what you order isn't a **platos combinados** and you order, for example, a piece of fish, you will only get fish. You need to ask for chips or veg.

Ración

Large Tapas

Heladeria = **Ice-cream Parlour**

PIZZERIA

Pizza and other Italian food are widely available in Spain.

A **cafetería** normally serves snacks (toasted sandwiches, **sándwiches**) as well as cakes, **pasteles**. Look out for local specialities. **Ensaimadas** are spiral-shaped cakes from Majorca which can be either sweet or savoury.

PEQUEÑA MEDIANA GRANDE	**BATIDOS** Milkshakes	**Pastelería** Cakes and Pastries
pequeña = small **mediana** = medium **grande** = large	**GRANIZADOS** Iced Drink	**Comedor** Dining Room

CONFITERIA **CAFETERIA**	Cake Shop and Café

Bars serve drinks, coffee and breakfasts Spanish-style. They may also offer **Tapas**, **pinchos** (snacks) and **bocadillos** (sandwiches).

Mesón This is a traditional-style tavern restaurant.

Bodega is a wine cellar. It is rather like a wine bar which serves some food.

Beach bars/restaurants are called **Chiringuitos**.

Bakers sell fresh bread and other basic items. You can also get breakfast and lunch.

Kiosks are good for soft drinks, crisps, sweets and ice creams.

Mesón is a traditional-style tavern/restaurant. **Cervecería** means beerhouse.

ALMENDRAS 100G 1€
AVELLANAS 100G 1€
PISTACHOS 250G 1€
CONGUITOS 100G 0,5€
PIPAS 1 BOLSA 1€
PATATAS FRITAS 1 BOLSA 1€

Snacks are often sold on the street in shopping areas and during fiestas. On offer here is almonds, hazelnuts, pistachios, chocolate peanuts, sunflower seeds, crisps (**bolsa** = bag).

Breakfast

Meals

Reading the menu

Menus will show the types of dishes available, divided into categories, i.e. soups, starters, fish dishes etc., in more or less detail, depending on the type of restaurant.

La Carta
Entremeses Starters (also **entrantes fríos** or **calientes** – starters, cold or hot)
Sopas Soups
Plato del día Dish of the day
Primer plato First course
Ensalada Salad
Verduras Vegetables
Huevos Egg dishes
Revueltos Scrambled eggs (usually cooked with something like mushrooms, asparagus or spinach)
Pastas Pasta dishes
Arroces Rice dishes. (Many rice dishes, such as paella, are normally only prepared for a minimum of two people)
Parrilladas Grilled food
Pescados Fish dishes
Carnes Meats
Postres Desserts
Quesos Cheeses

Menu Del Dia is a set-price menu. These usually include wine – **pan**, **postre**, **vino** (bread, dessert, wine).
1º (= **primero** 'first'),
2º (= **segundo** 'second').
Sólo arriba en el comedor means 'upstairs only in the dining room'. **El menú** is a set-price menu and **la carta** is the actual printed menu. Some dishes (usually snacks) will only be available at lunchtime, **sólo a medio día**. House speciality is **especialidad de la casa**.

 **TAPAS** Tapas bars usually have two price lists, depending on whether you sit at the bar or a table. At the bar, ordering **tapas** is simply a matter of pointing at what you want. Spaniards seldom drink without picking at some small **tapas** or snack. **Tapas** lets you taste lots of dishes at once, because they are often small portions of main dishes. Almost any dish can be served as **tapas**. Often each person orders two or three different **tapas**, so if you are eating with a group of friends you will have a dozen or so to share. **Tapas** are ideal as a quick snack or light meal.

Croquetas
Fish or meat
croquettes

Choirzo
Spicy salami-
type sausage

**Calamares
Fritos** Squid
in batter

**Jamón
Serrano**
Cured ham

Gambas
Prawns in
batter

Salmorejo
Cold vegetable
soup

Flamenquín
Rolled pork
and ham

Patatas Bravas
Fried potatoes
and spicy sauce

Chanquetes
Whitebait

Aceitunas
Olives

Queso
Cheese

Almejas
Clams

Drinks

Coffee comes in many varieties, the most common is **café con leche**; **café solo**, black coffee is like an espresso. If you want decaff, be careful to ask for **descafeinado de máquina** (from the espresso machine), or you are likely to get a cup of warm milk and a sachet of Nescafé. **Café con leche** is usually served in a glass (**en caña**). If you want it in a cup ask for it **en taza**.

gofres = waffles
helados = ice cream
granizados = iced drinks

Chocolate Con Churros is a popular breakfast and snack. **Merienda** is thick hot chocolate with **churros**, fried batter sticks for dipping.

servicio no incluido Service Not Included
If you wish to tip, 5 to 10% of the bill is the usual amount.

Ordering a tea **té** with milk will often get you a teabag put into hot milk, so you have to be quite specific and ask for a tea with cold milk separately, **un té con leche fría aparte**.

REFRESCOS
Soft Drinks

Beer in Spain means lager. Local brews are very good. You can order a bottle **un botellín** or a draught beer **una caña**, usually about half a pint.

CALIENTE Hot

FRÍO Cold

Reading The Wine Label Cosecha means vintage. The **DO (denominación de origen)** system is region based. In this case, **Penedès. DOC** (adding the word **calificada** indicates tighter growing and production controls) only applies to Rioja at present. For good wine, stick to **DO** and **DOC** – avoid lowlier **vino de la tierra** and **vino de mesa**.

Terms to look out for are **sin crianza** (new wine, so not aged), **crianza** (1 year old and often the best bet), **reserva** (3 year old) and **gran reserva** (5 year old). Rioja is aged in oak barrels, so if you don't like too much oak, go for **sin crianza** or **crianza**. 13% alcohol is high. 11.5% is average, 14% is pretty hefty.

Sherry is named after one of the main sherry towns, Jerez. The other two towns are El Puerto de Santa María and Sanlúcar. Avoid the cheapies. **Fino**: dry, lean, subtle and lemony from Jerez – drink chilled. **Amontillado**: an aged **Fino**, rich and nutty. **Manzanilla**: briny, dry and yeasty. **Oloroso**: rich, spicy and Christmassy. **Palo Cortado**: halfway between **Amontillado** and **Oloroso**.

Bodega is the word for wine cellar and is the term for a wine bar which usually serves food. Menus are displayed outside.

Menu reader

....

Tapas

There are many different varieties of **tapas** depending on the region. This is a list of some of the most common **tapas** that can be found in any part of Spain. A larger portion of **tapas** is called a **ración**. A **pincho** is a **tapa** on a cocktail stick.

asadillo/asadura de pimientos roasted red peppers marinated in olive oil and garlic

berenjenas fritas fried aubergines

boquerones en vinagre fresh anchovies marinated in garlic (sometimes also in onions), parsley and olive oil

croquetas de carne/pescado meat/fish croquettes with bechamel

ensaladilla rusa potato salad with vegetables, tuna, hard-boiled eggs and mayonnaise

frituría de pescado assorted deep-fried fish

gambas al ajillo grilled shrimps sautéed in olive oil, garlic, parsley and dry white wine

gambas plancha grilled shrimps

japuta/Cazón en adobo marinated pomfret/dogfish

montadito de lomo grilled pork fillet marinated in paprika and garlic, served on toasted bread

patatas alioli potato in garlic and olive oil vinaigrette

patatas bravas fried potato cubes with a spicy tomato sauce

pinchitos morunos grilled skewers of pork tenderloin marinated in spices, garlic and olive oil

pincho de tortilla small portion of Spanish omelette

pulpo a la vinagreta octopus marinated in garlic, onions, peppers, olive oil and lemon juice

rabo de toro en salsa oxtail stew

salmorejo thick cold tomato soup made with tomatoes, bread, garlic and olive oil

...**a la/al** in the style of
...**a la Navarra** stuffed with ham
...**a la parilla/plancha** grilled
...**a la romana** fried in batter
...**al horno** baked/roast
aceite oil
aceite de oliva olive oil
aceitunas olives
aceitunas rellenas stuffed olives
acelgas Swiss chard
adobo, ...en marinated
agua water
agua mineral mineral water
agua con gas sparkling water
agua sin gas still water
aguardiente a kind of clear brandy
ahumado smoked
ajetes garlic shoots
ajillo, ...al with garlic
ajo garlic
ajo blanco kind of garlic, bread and almond soup served cold. Usually served with diced apple and raisins
ajo de las manos sliced, boiled potatoes mixed with a garlic, oil and vinegar dressing, and flavoured with red chillies
albahaca basil
albaricoque apricot
albóndigas meatballs in sauce
alcachofas artichokes
alcachofas a la vinagreta artichokes served with a strong vinaigrette
alcachofas con jamón sautéed artichoke hearts with cured ham
alcachofas rellenas stuffed artichokes
alcaparras capers
aliño dressing
alioli/allioli olive oil and garlic mashed together into a creamy paste similar to mayonnaise. Served with meat, potatoes or fish
almejas clams
almejas a la marinera steamed clams cooked with parsley, wine and garlic
almendras almonds
alubias large white beans found in many stews
amontillado medium-dry to dry sherry
ancas de rana frogs' legs
anchoa anchovy
anguila eel
angulas baby eels, highly prized
angulas al ajillo baby eels cooked with garlic
angulas en cazuelita garlic-flavoured, fried baby eels seasoned with hot pepper
anís (seco or dulce) aniseed liqueur, dry or sweet, normally drunk as a long drink with water and ice
apio celery
arenque herring
arroz rice
arroz a banda a dish of rice and fish. The dish is served in two courses: first the rice cooked with

saffron is served and then the fish
that has been cooked in it

arroz a la cubana rice with fried
egg and tomato sauce

arroz a la levantina rice with
shellfish, onions, artichokes, peas,
tomatoes and saffron

arroz a la marinera rice with
seafood

arroz a la valenciana Valencian
version of paella, sometimes
cooked with eel

arroz a la zamorana rice with
pork, peppers and garlic

arroz blanco boiled rice

arroz con costra rice with
chicken, rabbit, sausages,
chickpeas and pork meatballs
baked in oven with egg topping

arroz con leche rice pudding
flavoured with cinnamon

arroz con pollo rice with chicken,
garnished with peas and peppers

arroz negro black rice (with squid
in its own ink)

arroz santanderino rice cooked
with salmon and milk

asado roasted

asadillo roasted sliced red peppers
in olive oil and garlic

asadillo/asadura de pimientos
roasted peppers

atún tuna (usually fresh)

atún con salsa de tomate tuna
fish in tomato sauce

avellana hazelnut

azafrán saffron

azúcar sugar

bacalao salt cod, cod

bacalao a la vizcaína salt cod
cooked with dried peppers, onions
and parsley

bacalao al ajo arriero salt cod
fried with garlic to which is added
vinegar, paprika and parsley

bacalao al pil-pil a Basque
speciality – salt cod cooked in a
creamy garlic and olive oil sauce

bacalao con patatas salt cod
slowly baked with potatoes,
peppers, tomatoes, onions, olives
and bay leaves

bacalao de convento salt cod
cooked with spinach and potato

bajoques farcides peppers
stuffed with rice, pork, tomatoes
and spices

bandeja de quesos cheese
platter

barbacoa, ...a la barbecued

berenjena aubergine (eggplant)

berenjenas a la catalana
aubergines with tomato sauce,
Catalan style

berenjenas rellenas stuffed
aubergines (usually with mince)

berenjenas salteadas
aubergines sautéed with tomatoes
and onions

besugo red bream

bistec steak

bizcocho sponge

bizcocho borracho sponge
soaked in wine and syrup

blanco y negro a milky coffee with ice

bocadillo sandwich (French bread)

bocadillo (de...) sandwich

bogavante lobster

bonito tunny fish, lighter than tuna, good grilled

boquerones fresh anchovies

boquerones fritos fried anchovies

brandy Spanish brandy; if you want what we would call brandy ask for **coñac**

brasa, ...a la barbecued

buñuelos type of fritter. Savoury ones are filled with cheese, ham, mussels or prawns. Sweet ones can be filled with fruit

buñuelos de bacalao salt cod fritters

butifarra special sausage from Catalonia

butifarra blanca white sausage containing pork and tripe

butifarra negra black sausage containing pork blood, belly and spices

caballa mackerel

cabello de ángel sweet pumpkin filling

cabrito kid (goat)

cabrito al horno roast kid

cacahuete peanut

cachelada chopped boiled potatoes and cabbage with garlic, red pepper and fried bacon. Often served with **chorizo**

café coffee

café con leche white coffee

café cortado coffee with only a little milk

café descafeinado decaffeinated coffee

café helado iced coffee

café solo black coffee

calabacines courgettes

calabacines rellenos stuffed courgettes

calabaza guisada stewed pumpkin

calamares squid

calamares a la romana fried squid rings in batter

calamares en su tinta squid cooked in its own ink

calamares fritos fried squid

calamares rellenos stuffed squid

calçotada roasted spring onion with olive oil and almonds, typical of Tarragona

caldeirada fish soup from Galicia

caldereta stew/casserole

caldereta de cordero lamb casserole

caldereta de langosta lobster stew

caldereta de pescado fish stew

caldo clear soup

caldo de pescado fish soup

caldo gallego clear soup with green vegetables, beans, pork and **chorizo**

caliente hot

callos tripe

callos a la madrileña fried tripe casseroled in a spicy paprika sauce with tomatoes and **chorizo**

camarones shrimps

canela cinnamon

cangrejo crab

caracoles snails

caracoles de mar winkles

caracolillos winkles

carajillo black coffee with brandy which may be set alight depending on regional customs

cardo cardoon, plant related to the artichoke

carne meat

carne de buey beef

carne picada minced meat

carnero mutton

cassolada pork and vegetable stew from Catalonia

castaña chestnut

cava champagne-style sparkling wine

cazuela de fideos legumes, meat and noodle stew

cebolla onion

cebollas rellenas stuffed onions

cebollas rojas red onions

centollo spider crab

cerdo pork

cerdo asado roast pork

cerezas cherries

cerveza beer

champán champagne

champiñones mushrooms

chanfaina a stew made from pig's liver and other parts

chanquetes whitebait

chilindrón, ...al sauce made with pepper, tomato, fried onions and meat (pork or lamb)

chistorra spicy sausage from Navarra

chocolate either chocolate (for eating) or a hot thick drinking chocolate **un chocolate**

chorizo spicy red sausage. The larger type is eaten like salami, the thinner type is cooked in various dishes

choto kid or calf

choto albaicinero kid fried with garlic, from Granada

chuleta chop

chuleta de cerdo pork chop

chuleta de ternera veal/beef chop

chuletas de cordero grilled lamb chops

chuletón large steak

churrasco barbecued steak

churros fried batter sticks sprinkled with sugar, usually eaten with thick hot chocolate

ciervo deer (venison)

cigalas king prawns

cilantro coriander

ciruelas plums

coca (coques) type of pizza with meat, fish or vegetables served in the Balearic Islands. They can also be sweet

cochinillo roast suckling pig

cocido stew made with various

meats, vegetables and chickpeas. There are regional variations of this dish and it is worth trying the local version

cocido de lentejas thick stew of lentils and **chorizo**

cocido de pelotas a rich spicy stew with mince wrapped in cabbage leaves containing pork and chickpeas

coco coconut

cóctel de gambas prawn cocktail

codillo de cerdo pig's trotter

codornices asadas roast quail

codorniz quail

col cabbage

coles de Bruselas Brussels sprouts

coliflor cauliflower

comino cumin

coñac brandy

conchas finas large scallops

conejo rabbit

consomé consommé

consomé al jerez consommé with sherry

consomé de gallina chicken consommé

copa goblet

copa de helado ice cream sundae

coques see **coca**

coques de torró wafers filled with almonds, sold at Christmas in Majorca

cordero lamb

cordero al chilindrón lamb in a spicy pepper sauce

cordero asado roast lamb

cordero asado a la manchega spit-roasted young lamb

cordero relleno trufado lamb stuffed with truffles

costillas ribs

costillas de cerdo pork ribs

crema cream soup/cream

crema catalana similar to crème brûlée

crema de espárragos cream of asparagus

crema de tomate cream of tomato soup

crema generic name given to smooth liqueurs, e.g. **crema de naranja** (orange cream)

cremat coffee with brandy and rum, served in Catalonia

croquetas croquettes (made with thick bechamel sauce)

croquetas de camarones shrimp croquettes

crudo raw

cuajada cream-based dessert like junket, served with honey or sugar

cubalibre coca-cola mixed with rum or gin

cucurucho de helado ice cream cone

culantro coriander

dátiles dates

descafeinado decaffeinated

dorada sea bream

dorada a la sal sea bream cooked in the oven, covered only with salt, forming a crust

dorada al horno baked sea bream
dulce sweet
dulces cakes and pastries
embutido sausage, cold meat
empanada pastry/pie filled with meat or fish and vegetables
empanadilla pasty/small pie filled with meat or fish
empanado breadcrumbed and fried
ensaimada sweet spiral-shaped yeast bun from Majorca
ensalada (mixta/verde) (mixed/green) salad
ensalada de la casa lettuce, tomato and onion salad (may include tuna)
ensalada de huevos salad with hard boiled eggs
ensaladilla rusa diced cooked vegetables and potatoes in mayonnaise
entrecot entrecôte steak
entremeses starters
entremeses de fiambre cold meat hors d'œuvres
entremeses de pescado fish hors d'œuvres
escabeche, ...en pickled
escabeche de pescado fish marinated in oil and served cold
escalfado poached
escalivada salad of chargrilled or baked vegetables such as peppers and aubergines soaked in olive oil
escalope de ternera veal/beef escalope

escarola endive
escudella meat, vegetable and chickpea stew. Traditionally served as two courses: a soup and then the cooked meat and vegetables
escudilla de pages white bean, sausage, ham and pork soup
espárragos asparagus
espárragos con mahonesa asparagus with mayonnaise
espinacas gratinadas spinach au gratin
esqueixada salad made with salt cod
estofado braised/stewed
estofado de cordero lamb stew
estofado de ternera veal/beef stew
estragón tarragon
fabada asturiana pork, cured ham, black pudding, large butter beans or sausage stew with **chorizo** and **morcilla**
fabes large white haricot beans
faisán pheasant
farinatos fried sausages served with eggs
fiambre cold meat
fiambre de tenera veal pâté
fiambres surtidos assorted cold meats
fideos noodles/thin ribbons of pasta (vermicelli)
fideos a la cazuela noodles cooked with pork, sausages, ham and **sofrito** (fried onions, garlic and tomato)

fideuà amb marisc seafood dish with fine pasta (vermicelli)

filete fillet steak

filete de ternera veal/beef steak

filete a la plancha grilled fillet steak

filetes de lenguado sole fillets

fino pale, very dry sherry

flamenquín fried breaded meat roll, containing cured or smoked ham and sometimes cheese; typical of southern Spain

flan crème caramel

frambuesas raspberries

fresas strawberries

fresas con nata strawberries and cream

frijoles beans (name used in the Canary Islands)

frío cold

frite pieces of lamb fried in olive oil and paprika

frito fried

fritura de pescado fried assortment of fish

fruta fruit

fruta del tiempo fruit in season

frutos secos nuts

galleta biscuit

gallina hen

gambas prawns

gambas a la plancha grilled prawns

gambas al ajillo grilled prawns with garlic

gambas al pil-pil sizzling prawns cooked with chillies

ganso goose

garbanzos chickpeas

garbanzos con espinacas chickpeas with spinach

garrotxa goat's cheese

gazpacho traditional cold tomato soup of southern Spain. There are many different recipes. Basic ingredients are water, tomatoes, garlic, fresh bread-crumbs, salt, vinegar and olive oil. Sometimes served with diced cucumbers, hard-boiled eggs and cured ham

gazpacho extremeño a version of gazpacho made with finely chopped green peppers and onions

ginebra gin

gofio toasted corn meal often rolled into balls and eaten as a bread substitute in the Canary Islands

gran reserva classification given to aged wines of exceptional quality

granada pomegranate

granizado fruit drink with crushed ice

gratinado au gratin

grelos young turnip tops

guindilla chilli

guisado stew or casserole

guisantes peas

guisantes a la española boiled peas with cured ham, lettuce, carrots and onions

gulas the cheap alternative to **angulas**, made of fish (mainly haddock) and squid ink

habas broad beans

habas a la catalana broad beans cooked in pork fat often served with **chorizo**

habas con jamón broad beans with cured ham

hamburguesa hamburger

helado ice cream

hervido boiled

hígado liver

hígado con cebolla fried calf's liver with onions

higos figs

higos secos dried figs

horchata de chufas cool drink made with tiger nuts

horno, ...al baked (in oven)

huevos eggs

huevos a la española stuffed eggs with a cheese sauce

huevos a la flamenca baked eggs with tomatoes, peas, peppers, asparagus and **chorizo**

huevos al plato eggs baked in butter

huevos con jamón fried eggs and cured ham

ibéricos traditional Spanish gourmet products; a **surtido de ibéricos** means assorted products such as cured ham, cheese, **chorizo** and **salchichón**

infusión herbal tea

intxaursalsa whipped cream and walnut pudding

jamón ham

jamón de Jabugo Andalusian prime-quality cured ham from Jabujo, a small town in Huelva

jamón de pata negra prime cured ham (the best quality)

jamón serrano dark red cured ham

jamón de York cooked ham

jengibre ginger

jerez sherry

jibia cuttlefish

judías beans

judías blancas haricot beans

judías verdes green beans

judías verdes a la castellana/ española boiled green beans mixed with fried parsley, garlic and peppers

jurel horse mackerel

kokotxas hake's cheek usually fried

lacón con grelos salted pork with young turnip tops and white cabbage

langosta lobster

langosta a la catalana potatoes with a lobster filling served with mayonnaise

langostinos king prawns

langostinos a la plancha grilled king prawns

langostinos a la vinagreta casseroled crayfish with hardboiled eggs served in a vinaigrette sauce

laurel bay leaf

lechazo young lamb (roasted)

leche milk

leche caliente hot milk

leche condensada condensed milk

leche evaporada evaporated milk

leche fría cold milk

leche frita very thick custard dipped into an egg and breadcrumb mixture, fried and served hot in squares

leche merengada type of ice cream made with egg whites, sugar and cinnamon (can be drunk as a milkshake)

leche preparada boiled milk with sugar, cinnamon and lemon peel, usually drunk in summer as a milkshake

lechuga lettuce

legumbres fresh or dried pulses

lengua tongue

lenguado sole

lenguado a la romana sole fried in batter

lenguados fritos fried fillets of sole often served on a bed of mixed sautéed vegetables

lenguados rellenos fillets of sole stuffed with shrimps or prawns

lentejas lentils (very popular in Spain)

licor liqueur

liebre hare

liebre estofada stewed hare

limón lemon

limonada lemonade (normally canned and fizzy)

lomo loin of pork

longaniza spicy pork sausage

longaniza con judías blancas spicy pork sausage with white beans

lubina sea bass

lubina a la asturiana Asturian-style sea bass, with cider

lubina al horno baked sea bass with potatoes, onion, tomato and garlic

macarrones macaroni

macedonia de fruta fruit salad

magras con tomate slices of fried ham dipped into tomato sauce

mahonesa mayonnaise

maíz sweetcorn

majorero goat's cheese from Canary Islands

manitas de cerdo pig's trotters

mantequilla butter

manzana apple

manzanas rellenas stuffed baked apples

manzanilla camomile tea, or a very dry sherry from Sanlúcar de Barrameda

margarina margerine

marinado marinated

mariscada mixed shellfish

marisco shellfish ; seafood

marmitako tuna fish and potato stew

mayonesa mayonnaise

mazapán marzipan

medallón thick steak (medallion)

mejillones mussels

mejillones a la marinera mussels steamed in wine

mejillones al vapor mussels (steamed)

melocotón peach

melocotón en almíbar peaches in syrup

melón melon

melón con jamón melon and cured ham

membrillo quince jelly

menestra de verduras fresh vegetable stew often cooked with cured ham

merluza hake, one of the most popular fish in Spain

merluza a la asturiana boiled hake served with mayonnaise and garnished with hard boiled eggs

merluza a la sidra hake baked with clams, onions and cider

merluza en salsa verde hake with green sauce (with parsley)

mermelada jam

mero grouper

miel honey

migas breadcrumbs or croûtons usually fried in garlic and olive oil, sometimes with streaky bacon and **chorizo**

migas con jamón ham with breadcrumbs

migas extremeñas breadcrumbs fried with egg and spicy sausage

mollejas sweetbreads

mojama cured tuna fish, a delicacy

mojo a sauce made from olive oil, vinegar, garlic and different spices. Paprika is added for the red mojo. Predominantly found in the Canaries

mojo picón spicy **mojo** made with chilli peppers

mojo verde made with fresh coriander

mollejas sweetbreads

mollejas de ternera calves' sweetbreads

morcilla black pudding

moros y cristianos rice, black beans and onions with garlic sausage

moscatel sweet dessert wine from the muscat grape wine

mostaza mustard

nabo turnip

naranja orange

naranjada orangeade

nata cream

natillas sort of custard

navajas razor clams

nécora sea crab

nectarinas nectarines

níspero medlar

nuez moscada nutmeg

olla stew made traditionally with white beans, beef and bacon

olla gitana thick stew/soup made with chickpeas, pork and vegetables and flavoured with almonds and saffron

olla podrida thick cured ham, vegetable and chickpea stew/soup

oloroso sweet, dark, full-bodied sherry

orejas de cerdo a la plancha grilled pigs' ears

ostras oysters

paella one of the most famous of Spanish dishes. Paella varies from region to region but usually consists of rice, chicken, shellfish, vegetables, garlic and saffron. The dish's name derives from the large shallow pan in which it is cooked. The traditional paella Valenciana contains rabbit, chicken and sometimes eel

paella de mariscos rice and shellfish paella

pan bread

pan de higos dried figs pressed together in the shape of a small cake

panades lamb pasties eaten at Easter in the Balearics

panchineta almond and custard tart

panecillo bread roll

panelleta small cakes with pine nuts and almonds

papas arrugadas potatoes cooked in skins in salty water

parrilla, ...a la grilled

parrillada mixed grill (can be meat or fish)

parrillada de mariscos mixed grilled shellfish

pasas raisins

pasta pasta

pastel cake/pastry

pastel de carne meat pie

pastel de ternera veal/beef pie

patatas potatoes

patatas arrugadas potatoes cooked in their skins

patatas bravas fried diced potatoes mixed with a garlic, oil and vinegar dressing and flavoured with tomatoes and red chilli peppers

patatas con chorizo potatoes cooked with **chorizo**

patatas fritas chips/crisps

patatas nuevas new potatoes

pato duck

pato a la sevillana joints of wild duck cooked with sherry, onion, tomatoes, herbs and garlic, served in an orange and olive sauce

pavo turkey

pavo relleno stuffed turkey

pechuga de pollo chicken breast

pechugas en bechamel chicken breasts in bechamel sauce

Pedro Ximénez sweet, rich sherry-type dessert wine

pepino cucumber

pepitoria de pavo/pollo turkey/chicken fricassée

pera pear

percebes goose-neck barnacle, a Galician shellfish

perdices con chocolate partridges with a chocolate sauce

perdiz partridge

perejil parsley

pescado fish

pescaíto frito mixed fried fish

pez espada swordfish

picada sauce made of chopped parsley, almonds, pine nuts and garlic

pichones young pigeon

pimentón (sweet) paprika; (spicy) cayenne pepper

pimienta pepper (spice)

pimientos red and green peppers, one of the typical Spanish flavours

pimientos de piquillo pickled red peppers

pimientos morrones sweet red peppers

pimientos rellenos peppers stuffed with meat or fish

piña pineapple

pinchos small tapas

pinchos morunos pork grilled on a skewer. If you ask for a **pinchito** you can omit the word **moruno**, but if you say **pincho** you have to specify it and say **moruno**

piperrada type of scrambled eggs with red and green peppers, tomato, onion, garlic and paprika. A typical dish from the Basque country.

pipirrana a salad of fish, roast red peppers, tomatoes, hard-boiled eggs and onions, from Andalusia

pisto manchego a mixture of sautéed peppers, onions, aubergines, tomatoes, garlic

and parsley. Similiar to French ratatouille. Served hot or cold

plancha, ...a la grilled

plátano banana

platija plaice (flounder)

plato dish

plato del día dish of the day

plato combinado assorted food served together on one plate rather than as separate dishes as is more usual in Spain

pollo chicken

pollo al chilindrón chicken cooked with onion, ham, garlic, red pepper and tomatoes

pollo asado roast chicken

pollo con patatas chicken and chips

pollo en pepitoria breaded chicken pieces fried, then casseroled with herbs, almonds, garlic and sherry

pollo estofado chicken stewed with potatoes, mushrooms, shallots, bay leaves and mushrooms

pollo relleno stuffed chicken

polvorones very crumbly cakes made with almonds and often eaten with a glass of **anís**

pomelo grapefruit

porras fried sticks of batter; in some parts of Spain they are called **churros**

postres desserts

potaje thick soup/stew often with pork and pulses

potaje murciano red bean, French bean and rice soup

pote thick soup with beans and sausage which has many regional variations

pote gallego thick soup made with cabbage, white kidney beans, potatoes, pork and sausage

primer plato starter, first course

puchero hotpot made from meat or fish

puchero canario salted fish and potatoes served with **mojo** sauce

puerros leeks

pulpo octopus

puré de garbanzos thick chickpea soup

puré de patatas mashed potatoes

queimada warm drink made with **aguardiente** (clear brandy) sweetened with sugar and flambéed, a speciality of Galicia

quesada dessert similar to cheesecake

queso cheese

queso curado/semicurado cured/semi-cured cheese. Cured cheese has a strong flavour

queso de Burgos curd cheese from Burgos

queso de cabrales strong blue cheese from Asturias

queso de Idiazábal smoked sheep's milk cheese from the Basque country

queso de Mahón strong hard cheese from Menorca

queso de oveja mild sheep's cheese from León

queso de Roncal hard, smoked sheep's cheese

queso de tetilla soft, white cheese made in the form of a woman's breast

queso fresco green cheese

queso manchego hard sheep's curd cheese from La Mancha

queso rallado grated cheese

rábanos radishes

rabo de toro bull's tail, usually cooked in a stew

rancio dessert wine

ración small taster portion/a kind of **tapa**. You can also ask for **media ración** (also written ½ **ración**) in many bars and restaurants (a ración is bigger than a tapa. The size of a dessert plate)

rape monkfish

rape a la marinera monkfish cooked with wine

raya skate

rebozado in batter

refresco de fruta fruit drink with ice

rehogado lightly fried

relleno stuffed

remolacha beetroot

repollo cabbage

requesón cottage cheese

reserva wines of good quality that have been aged, but not as long as **gran reserva**

revuelto scrambled eggs often cooked with another ingredient

revuelto de champiñones scrambled eggs with mushrooms

revuelto de espárragos scrambled eggs with asparagus

revuelto de espinacas scrambled eggs with spinach

revuelto de gambas scrambled eggs with prawns

revuelto de morcilla scrambled eggs with black pudding

riñones al jerez kidneys in sherry sauce

rodaballo turbot

romana, ...a la fried in batter (generally squid – **calamares**)

romero rosemary

romesco sauce made traditionally with olive oil, red pepper and bread. Other ingredients are often added, such as almonds and garlic

romesco de pescado fish in a sauce of peppers, olive oil and bread with almonds

ron rum

rosco type of doughnut

roscón de reyes a large bun-like cake in the shape of a ring (usually filled with cream, mustard, chocolate or meringue), similar to Italian panettone and eaten at Epiphany

sal salt

salchicha sausage

salchichón salami-type sausage

salmón salmon

salmón a la parilla grilled salmon

salmón a la ribereña salmon fried with ham cooked with cider

salmón ahumado smoked salmon

salmonete red mullet

salmonete frito fried red mullet

salpicón (de marisco) chopped seafood or meat with tomato, onion, garlic and peppers

salsa sauce

salsa de tomate tomato sauce

salsa romesco sauce made of almonds and hazelnuts with mild chilli. Often served with fish and chicken

salsa verde garlic, olive oil and parsley sauce often served with fish

salteado sautéed

samfaina a dish of peppers, aubergines and tomatoes to which meat is often added

sandía watermelon

sándwich sandwich (usually toasted)

sangría red wine mixed with fruit, lemonade, sugar and ice often with cinnamon added. **Sangría** is always made of red wine but you can also find **sangría de champán** 'champagne sangría'

sardinas sardines

sardinas a la santanderina sardines cooked with tomato, Santander style

sardinas asadas barbecued sardines

sardinas frescas/fritas fresh/fried sardines

sardinas rebozadas sardines cooked in batter

sargo type of bream

seco dry

sepia cuttlefish

sesos brains

sesos a la romana brains fried in batter

sesos fritos fried brains

setas wild mushrooms

sidra cider

sifón soda water

sobrasada a paprika-flavoured pork sausage from Mallorca

sofrito basic sauce made with slowly fried onions, garlic and tomato

solomillo sirloin

solomillo de ternera veal/beef sirloin

sopa soup

sopa castellana or **sopa de ajo** garlic soup with bread. May contain poached egg or cured ham

sopa de arroz rice soup

sopa de cebolla onion soup

sopa de cocido meat soup

sopa de fideos noodle soup

sopa de gallina chicken soup

sopa de mariscos shellfish soup

sopa de pescado fish soup

sopa de pollo chicken soup

sopa de rabo oxtail/bull's tail soup

sopa de verduras vegetable soup

sopa mallorquina tomato, onion and pepper soup thickened with breadcrumbs

sorbete sorbet

sorbetes de frutas fruit sorbets

suquet fish, potato and tomato stew

suspiros meringues

suspiros de monja meringues served with thick custard

tapas appetizers; snacks

tarta cake or tart

tarta de manzana apple tart

tarta de Santiago flat almond cake

tarta helada ice-cream cake

té tea

té con leche tea with milk

té con limón tea with lemon

té helado iced tea (Nestea®, Lipton®)

ternasco young lamb

ternera veal/beef

ternera con naranja veal/beef cooked with orange

ternera rellena stuffed veal/beef

tisana herbal tea

tocinillo (de cielo) sweet made with egg yolk and sugar

tocino bacon

tomates tomatoes

tomates rellenos stuffed tomatoes

tomillo thyme

toronja grapefruit

torrija bread dipped in milk and then fried and sprinkled with sugar and cinnamon

tortilla (española) traditional potato and onion omelette, often served as a tapa

tortilla de champiñones mushroom omelette

tortilla de chorizo chorizo omelette

tortilla de espárragos asparagus omelette

tortilla de jamón cured ham omelette

tortilla murciana tomato and pepper omelette

trucha trout

trucha a la navarra trout stuffed with cured ham

trucha con almendras fried trout with almonds

tumbet layers of peppers, aubergine and tomato cooked with potato in an earthenware dish. Originally from Majorca

turrón nougat

turrón de Alicante, turrón duro hard nougat

turrón de Jijona, turrón blando soft nougat

txangurro spider crab

uvas grapes

vapor, ...al steamed

verduras vegetables

verduras con patatas boiled potatoes with greens

vermú vermouth

vieiras scallops

vieiras de Santiago scallops served in their shell, cooked in brandy, topped with breadcrumbs and grilled

vinagre vinegar

vinagreta vinaigrette

vino wine

vino blanco white wine

vino clarete rosé

vino de jerez sherry

vino de mesa table wine

vino rosado rosé wine

vino tinto red wine

yemas small cakes that look like egg yolks

yogur yoghurt

zanahorias carrots

zarzuela de mariscos mixed seafood with wine and saffron

zarzuela de pescado fish stew

zumo juice

zumo de albaricoque apricot juice

zumo de fruta fruit juice

zumo de lima lime juice

zumo de melocotón peach juice

zumo de naranja orange juice

zumo de naranja natural fresh orange juice

zumo de piña pineapple juice

zumo de tomate tomato juice

zurrukutuna salt cod cooked with green peppers

Grammar

Nouns

A noun is a word such as 'car', 'horse' or 'Mary' which is used to refer to a person or thing.

Unlike English, Spanish nouns have a gender: they are either masculine (el) or feminine (la). Therefore words for 'the' and 'a(n)' must agree with the noun they accompany – whether masculine, feminine or plural:

	masc.	*fem.*	*plural*
the	el gato	la plaza	los gatos, las plazas
a, an	un gato	una plaza	unos gatos, unas plazas

The ending of the noun will usually indicate whether it is masculine or feminine:

> o or -or are generally masculine
> a, -dad, -ión, -tud, -umbre are generally feminine

Note: Feminine nouns beginning with a stressed a- or ha- take the masculine article el, though the noun is still feminine.

Formation of plurals
The articles el and la become los and las in the plural. Nouns ending with a vowel become plural by adding -s.

> el gato → los gatos
> la plaza → las plazas
> la calle → las calles

Where the noun ends in a consonant, -es is added.

> el color → los colores
> la ciudad → las ciudades

Nouns ending in -z change their ending to -ces in the plural.

> el lápiz → los lápices
> la voz → las voces

Adjectives

An adjective is a word such as 'small', 'pretty' or 'practical' that describes a person or thing, or gives extra information about them. Adjectives normally follow the nouns they describe in Spanish, e.g. la manzana roja (the red apple). Some exceptions which go before the noun are:

buen good	gran great
ningún no, not any	mucho much, many
poco little, few	primer/primero first
tanto so much, so many	último last

e.g. el último tren (the last train)

Spanish adjectives also reflect the gender of the noun they describe. To make an adjective feminine, the masculine -o ending is changed to -a; and the endings -án, -ón, -or, -és change to -ana, -ona, -ora, -esa.

masc.	el libro rojo	*fem.*	la manzana roja
	(the red book)		(the red apple)
masc.	el hombre hablador	*fem.*	la mujer habladora
	(the talkative man)		(the talkative woman)

To make an adjective plural an -s is added to the singular form if it ends in a vowel. If the adjective ends in a consonant, -es is added.

| *masc.* | los libros rojos (the red books) | *fem.* | las manzanas rojas (the red apples) |
| *masc.* | los hombres habladores (the talkative men) | *fem.* | las mujeres habladoras (the talkative women) |

My, your, his, her...
These words also depend on the gender and number of the noun
they accompany and not on the sex of the 'owner'.

	with masc. *sing. noun*	*with fem.* *sing. noun*	*with plural* *nouns*
my	mi	mi	mis
your *(familiar sing.)*	tu	tu	tus
your *(polite sing.)*	su	su	sus
his/her/its	su	su	sus
our	nuestro	nuestra	nuestros/nuestras
your *(familiar pl.)*	vuestro	vuestra	vuestros/vuestras
their	su	su	sus
your *(polite pl.)*	su	su	sus

There is no distinction between 'his' and 'her' in Spanish: su billete
can mean either 'his' or 'her ticket'.

Pronouns

. . . .

A pronoun is a word that you use to refer to someone or something
when you do not need to use a noun, often because the person
or thing has been mentioned earlier. Examples are 'it', 'she',
'something' and 'myself'.

subject		*object*	
I	yo	me	me
you *(familiar sing.)*	tú	you	te
you *(polite sing.)*	usted (Ud.)	you	le
he/it	él	him/it	le, lo
she/it	ella	her/it	le, la

we	nosotros	us	nos
you (familiar pl.)	vosotros	you	os
you (polite pl.)	ustedes (Uds.)	you	les
they (masc.)	ellos	them	les, los
they (fem.)	ellas	them	les, las

Subject pronouns ('I', 'you', 'he', etc.) are generally omitted in Spanish, since the verb ending distinguishes the subject.

> hablo   I speak
> hablamos   <u>we</u> speak

However, they are used for emphasis or to avoid confusion.

> yo voy a Mallorca y él va a Alicante
> <u>I</u> am going to Mallorca and <u>he</u> is going to Alicante

Object pronouns are placed before the verb in Spanish.

> la veo   I see <u>her</u>
> los conocemos   we know <u>them</u>

However, in commands or requests they follow the verb.

> ¡ayúdame!   help <u>me</u>!
> ¡escúchale!   listen to <u>him</u>!

Except when they are expressed in the negative.

> ¡no me ayudes!   don't help <u>me</u>
> ¡no le escuches!   don't listen to <u>him</u>

The object pronouns shown above can be used to mean 'to me', 'to us', etc., but 'to him/to her' is **le** and 'to them' is **les**. If **le** and **les** occur in combinations with **lo/la/las/los** then **le/les** change to **se**, e.g. **se lo doy** (I give it to him).

Verbs

A verb is a word such as 'sing', 'walk' or 'cry' which is used with a subject to say what someone or something does or what happens to them. Regular verbs follow the same pattern of endings. Irregular verbs do not follow a regular pattern so you need to learn the different endings.

There are three main patterns of endings for Spanish verbs – those ending -ar, -er and -ir in the dictionary.

	cantar	**to sing**
	canto	I sing
	cantas	you sing
(usted)	canta	(s)he sings/you sing
	cantamos	we sing
	cantáis	you sing
(ustedes)	cantan	they sing/you sing
	vivir	**to live**
	vivo	I live
	vives	you live
(usted)	vive	(s)he lives/you live
	vivimos	we live
	vivís	you live
(ustedes)	viven	they live/you live
	comer	**to eat**
	como	I eat
	comes	you eat
(usted)	come	(s)he eats/you eat
	comemos	we eat
	coméis	you eat
(ustedes)	comen	they eat/you eat

Grammar

115

Like French, in Spanish there are two ways of addressing people: the polite form (for people you don't know well or who are older) and the familiar form (for friends, family and children). The polite 'you' is usted in the singular, and ustedes in the plural. You can see from below that usted uses the same verb ending as for he and she; ustedes the same ending as for they. Often the words usted and ustedes are omitted, but the verb ending itself indicates that you are using the polite form. The informal words for 'you' are tú (singular) and vosotros (plural).

The verb 'to be'
There are two different Spanish verbs for 'to be' – ser and estar. Ser is used to describe a permanent state.

| soy inglés | I am English |
| es una playa | it is a beach |

Estar is used to describe a temporary state or where something is located.

| ¿cómo está? | how are you? |
| ¿dónde está la playa? | where is the beach? |

	ser	**to be**
	soy	I am
	eres	you are
(usted)	es	(s)he is/you are
	somos	we are
	sois	you are
(ustedes)	son	they are/you are

	estar	**to be**
	estoy	I am
	estás	you are
(usted)	está	(s)he is/you are
	estamos	we are
	estáis	you are
(ustedes)	están	they are/you are

Other common irregular verbs include:

	tener	**to have**
	tengo	I have
	tienes	you have
(usted)	tiene	(s)he has/you have
	tenemos	we have
	tenéis	you have
(ustedes)	tienen	they have/you have
	ir	**to go**
	voy	I go
	vas	you go
(usted)	va	(s)he goes/you go
	vamos	we go
	vais	you go
(ustedes)	van	they go/you go
	poder	**to be able**
	puedo	I can
	puedes	you can
(usted)	puede	(s)he can/you can
	podemos	we can
	podéis	you can
(ustedes)	pueden	they can/you can
	querer	**to want**
	quiero	I want
	quieres	you want
(usted)	quiere	(s)he wants/you want
	queremos	we want
	queréis	you want
(ustedes)	quieren	they want/you want
	hacer	**to do**
	hago	I do
	haces	you do

(usted)	hace	(s)he does/you do
	hacemos	we do
	hacéis	you do
(ustedes)	hacen	they do/you do
	venir	**to come**
	vengo	I come
	vienes	you come
(usted)	viene	(s)he comes/you come
	venimos	we come
	venís	you come
(ustedes)	vienen	they come/you come

Past tense

To form the past tense, for example: 'I gave/I have given', 'I finished/ I have finished', combine the present tense of the verb haber – 'to have' with the past participle of the verb (cantado, comido, vivido):

	haber	**to have**
	he	I have
	has	you have
(usted)	ha	(s)he has/you have
	hemos	we have
	habéis	you have
(ustedes)	han	they have/you have
e.g.	he cantado	I sang/I have sung
	ha comido	he ate/he has eaten
	hemos vivido	we lived/we have lived

To form a negative no is placed before all of the verb:

e.g.	no he cantado	I haven't sung
	no ha comido	he hasn't eaten
	no hemos vivido	we haven't lived

Dictionary

A

a(n) un(a)
abbey la abadía
able: *to be able* poder
abortion el aborto
about (concerning) sobre
about 2 o'clock alrededor de las dos
above arriba; por encima
abroad en el extranjero
abscess el absceso
accelerator el acelerador
accent (pronunciation) el acento
to accept aceptar
do you accept this card? ¿acepta esta tarjeta?
access el acceso
wheelchair access el acceso para sillas de ruedas
accident el accidente
accident & emergency department las urgencias
accommodation el alojamiento
to accompany acompañar
account (bank, etc) la cuenta
account number el número de cuenta
to ache doler
it aches duele
my head aches me duele la cabeza
acid el ácido
actor/actress el actor/la actriz
adaptor el adaptador
address la dirección
what's the address? ¿cuál es la dirección?
address book la agenda
admission charge/fee el precio de entrada
to admit (to hospital) ingresar
adult el/la adulto(a)
for adults para adultos
advance: *in advance* por adelantado
advertisement el anuncio
to advise aconsejar

A&E las urgencias
aerial la antena
aeroplane el avión
aerosol el aerosol
afraid: *to be afraid of* tener miedo de
after después
afternoon la tarde
in the afternoon por la tarde
this afternoon esta tarde
tomorrow afternoon mañana por la tarde
aftershave el aftershave
again otra vez
against contra
age la edad
agency la agencia
ago: *a week ago* hace una semana
to agree estar de acuerdo
agreement el acuerdo
AIDS el sida
air el aire
by air en avión
air ambulance avión sanitario; ambulancia aérea
airbag (in car) el airbag
air bed el colchón inflable
air conditioning el aire acondicionado
air-conditioning unit el aparato de aire acondicionado
air freshener el ambientador
airline la linea aérea
air mail: *by airmail* por avión
airplane el avión
airport el aeropuerto
airport bus el autobús del aeropuerto
air ticket el billete de avión
aisle el pasillo
alarm la alarma
alarm clock el despertador
alcohol el alcohol
alcohol-free sin alcohol
alcoholic alcohólico(a)
is it alcoholic? ¿tiene alcohol?
all todo(a)/todos(as)

allergic to alérgico(a) a
I'm allergic to... soy alérgico(a) a...
allergy la alergia
to allow permitir
it's not allowed no está permitido
all right (agreed) de acuerdo
(OK) vale
are you all right? ¿está bien?
almost casi
alone solo(a)
alphabet el alfabeto
already ya
also también
altar el altar
always siempre
a.m. de la mañana
amber (traffic light) amarillo
(substance) ámbar
ambulance la ambulancia
America Norteamérica
American norteamericano(a)
amount el total
anaesthetic la anestesia
general anaesthetic la anestesia
  general
local anaesthetic la anestesia local
anchor el ancla
ancient antiguo(a)
and y
angina la angina (de pecho)
angry enfadado(a)
animal el animal
aniseed el anís
ankle el tobillo
anniversary el aniversario
to announce anunciar
announcement el anuncio
annual anual
another otro(a)
another beer, please otra cerveza,
  por favor
answer la respuesta
to answer responder
answerphone el contestador
  (automático)
antacid el antiácido
antenna la antena
antibiotic el antibiótico

antifreeze el anticongelante
antihistamine el antihistamínico
anti-inflammatory
  antiinflamatorio(a)
antiques las antigüedades
antique shop el anticuario
antiseptic el antiséptico
any alguno(a)
have you any pears? ¿tiene peras?
anyone alguien
anything algo
anywhere en cualquier parte
apartment el apartamento
appendicitis la apendicitis
apple la manzana
application form el impreso
  de solicitud
appointment (meeting) la cita
(dentist, hairdresser) la hora
approximately aproximadamente
apricot el albaricoque
April abril
apron el delantal
architect el/la arquitecto(a)
architecture la arquitectura
arm el brazo
armbands (to swim) los manguitos
  de nadar
armchair el sillón
to arrange organizar
to arrest detener
arrival la llegada
to arrive llegar
art el arte
art gallery la galería de arte
arthritis la artritis
artificial artificial
artist el/la artista
ashtray el cenicero
to ask (question) preguntar
(ask for something) pedir
asparagus el espárrago
aspirin la aspirina
asthma el asma
I have asthma tengo asma
at a; en
at home en casa
at night por la noche

at once ahora mismo
at 8 o'clock a las ocho
Atlantic Ocean el Océano Atlántico
attack (terrorist) el atentado
(medical) el ataque
to attack atacar
attractive atractivo(a)
aubergine la berenjena
auction la subasta
audience el público
August agosto
aunt la tía
au pair el/la au pair
Australia Australia
Australian australiano(a)
author el/la autor(a)
automatic automático(a)
automatic car el coche automático
auto-teller el cajero automático
autumn el otoño
available disponible
avalanche la avalancha
avenue la avenida
average medio(a)
to avoid (issue) evitar
(obstacle) esquivar
awake: *to be awake* estar
despierto(a)
away: *far away* lejos
awful espantoso(a)
awning (for caravan, etc) el toldo
axle (in car) el eje

B

baby el bebé
baby food los potitos
baby milk la leche infantil
baby's bottle el biberón
babyseat (in car) el asiento del bebé
babysitter el/la canguro
baby wipes las toallitas infantiles
back (of body) la espalda
backpack la mochila
bacon el beicon/bacon
bad (weather, news) mal/malo(a)
(fruit and vegetables) podrido(a)
badminton el bádminton
bag la bolsa

baggage el equipaje
baggage allowance el equipaje
permitido
baggage reclaim la recogida de
equipajes
bail bond la fianza
bait (for fishing) el cebo
baked al horno
baker's la panadería
balcony el balcón
bald (person) calvo(a)
(tyre) gastado(a)
ball (large: football, etc) el balón
(small: golf, tennis, etc) la pelota
ballet el ballet
balloon el globo
banana el plátano
band (rock) el grupo
bandage la venda
bank el banco
(river) la ribera
bank account la cuenta bancaria
banknote el billete
bar el bar
bar of chocolate la tableta
de chocolate
barbecue la barbacoa
to have a barbecue hacer una
barbacoa
barber's la barbería
to bark ladrar
barn el granero
barrel (wine/beer) el barril
basement el sótano
basil la albahaca
basket la cesta
basketball el baloncesto
bat (baseball, cricket) el bate
(creature) el murciélago
bath el baño
to have a bath bañarse
bathing cap el gorro de baño
bathroom el cuarto de baño
with bathroom con baño
battery (radio, camera, etc) la pila
(in car) la batería
bay (along coast) la bahía
Bay of Biscay el golfo de Vizcaya

to be estar; ser
beach la playa
nudist beach la playa nudista
private beach la playa privada
sandy beach la playa de arena
beach hut la caseta de playa
bean la alubia
beard la barba
beautiful hermoso(a)
beauty salon el salón de belleza
because porque
to become hacerse; convertirse en;
 llegar a ser
bed la cama
double bed la cama de matrimonio
single bed la cama individual
sofa bed el sofá-cama
twin beds las camas individuales
bed and breakfast alojamiento
 y desayuno
bed clothes la ropa de cama
bedroom el dormitorio
bee la abeja
beef la ternera
beer la cerveza
before antes de
before breakfast antes de desayunar/
 del desayuno
to begin empezar
behind detrás de
behind the house detrás de la casa
beige beige; beis
to believe creer
bell (church) la campana
(door bell) el timbre
to belong to pertenecer a
(club) ser miembro de
below debajo; por debajo
belt el cinturón
bend (in road) la curva
berth la litera
beside (next to) al lado de
beside the bank al lado del banco
best el/la mejor
bet la apuesta
to bet on apostar por
better mèjor
better than mejor que

between entre
bib el babero
bicycle la bicicleta
by bicycle en bicicleta
bicycle pump bomba de bicicleta
bicycle repair kit la caja de
 herramientas
bidet el bidé
big grande
bigger than mayor que
bike (pushbike) la bicicleta
(motorbike) la moto
bike lock el candado de la bicicleta
bikini el bikini
bill la factura
(in restaurant) la cuenta
bin el cubo; la papelera
bin liner la bolsa de (la) basura
binoculars los prismáticos
bird el pájaro
biro el boli
birth el nacimiento
birth certificate la partida de
 nacimiento
birthday el cumpleaños
happy birthday! ¡feliz cumpleaños!
my birthday is on... mi cumpleaños
 es el...
birthday card la tarjeta de
 cumpleaños
birthday present el regalo
 de cumpleaños
biscuits las galletas
bit: *a bit of* un poco de
bite (insect) la picadura
(animal) la mordedura
to bite morder
(insect) picar
bitten (by animal) mordido(a)
(by insect) picado(a)
bitter (taste) amargo(a)
black negro(a)
black ice la capa invisible de hielo
 en la carretera
blank (disk, tape) virgen
blanket la manta
bleach (household) la lejía
to bleed sangrar

blender (for food) la licuadora
blind (person) ciego(a)
(for window) la persiana
(roman) el estor
blister la ampolla
blocked (road) cortado(a)
(pipe) obstruido(a)
blond (person) rubio(a)
blood la sangre
blood group el grupo sanguíneo
blood pressure la presión sanguínea
blood test el análisis de sangre
blouse la blusa
blow-dry el secado a mano
blowout *n* (of tyre) el reventón
blue azul
dark blue azul marino
light blue azul claro
blunt (knife, blade) desafilado(a)
BMX la BMX; la bicicleta de cross
boar el jabalí
to board (train, etc) subir
boarding card/pass la tarjeta de embarque
boarding house la pensión
boat (large) el barco
(small) la barca
boat trip la excursión en barco
body el cuerpo
to boil hervir
boiled hervido(a)
boiler la caldera
bomb la bomba
bone el hueso
(fish bone) la espina
bonfire la hoguera
bonnet (car) el capó
book el libro
to book reservar
booking la reserva
booking office (train) la ventanilla de billetes
bookshop la librería
booster seat el asiento elevador
boot (car) el maletero
boots las botas
border (of country) la frontera
boring aburrido(a)

born: *I was born in...* nací en...
to borrow pedir prestado
boss el/la jefe(a)
both ambos(as)
bottle la botella
a bottle of wine una botella de vino
a half-bottle of... media botella de...
bottle opener el abrebotellas
bottom (of pool, garden) el fondo
bowl (for soup, etc) el bol
bow tie la pajarita
box la caja
box office la taquilla
boxer shorts los calzoncillos
boy el chico
boyfriend el novio
bra el sujetador
bracelet la pulsera
brain el cerebro
brake el freno
to brake frenar
brake cable cable de freno
brake fluid el líquido de frenos
brake light la luz de freno
brake pads las pastillas de freno
branch (of tree) la rama
(of bank, etc) la sucursal
brand (make) la marca
brass el latón
brave valiente
bread el pan
French bread la barra de pan
sliced bread el pan de molde
wholemeal bread el pan integral
bread roll el panecillo
to break romper
breakable frágil
breakdown (car) la avería
(nervous) la crisis nerviosa
breakdown van la grúa
breakfast el desayuno
breast el pecho
to breast-feed amamantar; dar el pecho
to breathe respirar
brick el ladrillo
bride la novia
bridegroom el novio

bridge el puente
briefcase la cartera
bright (colour) vivo(a)
Brillo pad® el nanas®
to bring traer
Britain Gran Bretaña
British británico(a)
broadband *n* la banda ancha
broccoli el brócoli
brochure el folleto
broken roto(a)
my leg is broken me he roto la pierna
broken down (car, etc) averiado(a)
bronchitis la bronquitis
bronze el bronce
brooch el broche
broom (brush) la escoba
brother el hermano
brother-in-law el cuñado
brown marrón
bruise el moratón; el cardenal
brush el cepillo
to brush cepillar
bubble bath el baño de espuma
bucket el cubo
buckle la hebilla
buffet car el coche comedor
to build construir
building el edificio
bulb (electric) la bombilla
bull el toro
bullfight la corrida de toros
bullfighter el torero
bullring la plaza de toros
bumbag la riñonera
bumper (car) el parachoques
bunch (of flowers) el ramo
(grapes) el racimo
bungee jumping el banyi
buoy la boya
bureau de change la oficina
de cambio
burger la hamburguesa
burglar el/la ladrón/ladrona
burglar alarm la alarma antirrobo
to burn quemar
burnt (food) quemado(a)
to burst reventar

bus el autobús
bus pass el bonobús
bus station la estación de autobuses
bus stop la parada de autobús
bus ticket el billete de autobús
business el negocio
on business de negocios
business card la tarjeta de visita
business centre centro de negocios
business class la clase preferente
businessman/woman el hombre/
la mujer de negocios
business trip el viaje de negocios
busy ocupado(a)
but pero
butcher's la carnicería
butter la mantequilla
butterfly la mariposa
button el botón
to buy comprar
by (via) por
(beside) al lado de
by air en avión
by bus en autobús
by car en coche
by ship en barco
by train en tren
bypass (road) la carretera
de circunvalación

C

cab (taxi) el taxi
cabaret el cabaré
cabin (on boat) el camarote
cabin crew la tripulación de cabina
cablecar el teleférico
café el café
internet café el cibercafé
cafetiere la cafetera
cake (big) la tarta
(little) el pastel
cake shop la pastelería
calculator la calculadora
calendar el calendario
call (telephone) la llamada
a long distance call una conferencia
to call (phone) llamar por teléfono
calm tranquilo(a)

124

camcorder la videocámara
(digital) la cámara digital
camera la cámara
camera case la funda de la cámara
camera shop la tienda de fotografía
camera phone el teléfono con cámara
to camp acampar
camping gas el camping gas
camping stove el hornillo de gas
campsite el camping
to can (to be able) poder
I can puedo
we can podemos
I cannot no puedo
we cannot no podemos
can la lata
can opener el abrelatas
Canada (el) Canadá
Canadian canadiense
canal el canal
to cancel anular; cancelar
cancellation la cancelación
cancer el cáncer
candle la vela
canoe la canoa
canoeing: to go canoeing hacer
  piragüismo
cap (hat) la gorra
(diaphragm) el diafragma
capital (city) la capital
cappuccino el capuchino
car el coche
car alarm la alarma de coche
car ferry el transbordador; el ferry
car hire el alquiler de coches
car insurance el seguro del coche
car keys las llaves del coche
car park el aparcamiento
car parts los accesorios para el coche
car port el puerto del coche
car radio la radio del coche
car seat (child) el asiento para niños
car wash el lavado (automático)
  de coches
carafe la jarra
caravan la caravana
carburettor el carburador
card (greetings, business) la tarjeta

playing cards las cartas
cardboard el cartón
cardigan la chaqueta de punto
careful cuidadoso(a)
be careful! ¡cuidado!
carpet (rug) la alfombra
(fitted) la moqueta
carriage (railway) el vagón
carrot la zanahoria
to carry llevar
carton la caja
(of cigarettes) el cartón
case (suitcase) la maleta
cash el dinero en efectivo
to cash (cheque) cobrar
cash desk la caja
cash dispenser el cajero automático
cashier el/la cajero(a)
cashpoint el cajero automático
casino el casino
casserole la cazuela
cassette el casete
cassette player el radiocasete
castanets las castañuelas
castle el castillo
casualty department las urgencias;
  el servicio de urgencias
cat el gato
cat food la comida para gatos
catalogue el catálogo
catalytic converter el catalizador
to catch (bus, train, etc) coger
cathedral la catedral
Catholic católico(a)
cauliflower la coliflor
cave la cueva
cavity (in tooth) la caries
CD el CD
CD player el lector de CD
CD ROM el CD-ROM
CD-RW (el) CD regrabable
CD writer (el) CD de escritura
ceiling el techo
cellar la bodega
cemetery el cementerio
cent el céntimo
centimetre el centímetro
central central

central heating la calefacción central
central locking (car) el cierre centralizado
centre el centro
century el siglo
ceramic la cerámica
cereal los cereales
certain (sure) seguro(a)
certificate el certificado
chain la cadena
chair la silla
chairlift el telesilla
chalet el chalet
chambermaid la camarera
champagne el champán
change el cambio
(small coins) el *or* lo suelto
(money returned) la vuelta
to change cambiar
(clothes) cambiarse
(train) hacer transbordo
to change money cambiar dinero
changing room el probador
chapel la capilla
charcoal el carbón vegetal
charge (fee) el precio
(electrical) la carga
I've run out of charge no tengo batería
to charge (money) cobrar
(battery) cargar
please charge it to my account cárguelo a mi cuenta, por favor
I need to charge my phone necesito cargar el teléfono
charger (for battery) el cargador
charter flight el vuelo chárter
chatroom la sala de chat
cheap barato(a)
cheaper más barato(a)
cheap rate la tarifa baja
to check revisar; comprobar
to check in (at airport) facturar el equipaje
(at hotel) registrarse
check-in la facturación
cheek la mejilla
cheers! ¡salud!

cheese el queso
chef el chef
chemist's la farmacia
cheque el cheque
cheque book el talonario
cheque card la tarjeta bancaria
cherry la cereza
chest (of body) el pecho
chewing gum el chicle
chicken el pollo
chickenpox la varicela
child (boy) el niño
(girl) la niña
children (infants) los niños
for children para niños
child seat (car) el asiento de niños
chilli la guindilla; el chile
chimney la chimenea
chin la barbilla
china la porcelana
chips las patatas fritas
chiropodist el/la podólogo(a)
chocolate el chocolate
chocolates los bombones
to choose escoger
chop (meat) la chuleta
chopping board la tabla de cortar
christening el bautizo
Christian name el nombre de pila
Christmas la Navidad
Merry Christmas! ¡Feliz Navidad!
Christmas card la tarjeta de Navidad
Christmas Eve la Nochebuena
church la iglesia
cigar el puro
cigarette el cigarrillo
cigarette lighter el mechero
cigarette paper el papel de fumar
cinema el cine
circle (theatre) el anfiteatro
circuit breaker el cortacircuitos
circus el circo
cistern la cisterna
city la ciudad
city centre el centro de la ciudad
class: *first class* primera clase
second class segunda clase
clean limpio(a)

to clean limpiar
cleaner (person) el/la encargado(a) de la limpieza
cleanser (for face) la crema limpiadora
clear claro(a)
client el/la cliente
cliff (along coast) el acantilado (in mountains) el precipicio
to climb (mountains) escalar
climbing boots las botas de escalar
Clingfilm® el papel de plástico transparente
clinic la clínica
cloakroom el guardarropa
clock el reloj
close by muy cerca
to close cerrar
closed (shop, etc) cerrado(a)
cloth (rag) el trapo (fabric) la tela
clothes la ropa
clothes line el tendedero
clothes peg la pinza
clothes shop la tienda de ropa
cloudy nublado(a)
club el club
clutch (in car) el embrague
clutch fluid el líquido del embrague
coach (bus) el autocar
coach station la estación de autobuses
coach trip la excursión en autocar
coal el carbón
coast la costa
coastguard el/la guardacostas
coat el abrigo
coat hanger la percha
cockroach la cucaracha
cocktail el cóctel
cocktail bar el bar de cóctel
cocoa el cacao
code el código
coffee el café
black coffee el café solo
cappuccino el capuchino
decaffeinated coffee el (café) descafeinado
white coffee el café con leche

coffee-shop el café
coil (IUD) el DIU
coin la moneda
Coke® la Coca Cola®
colander el colador
cold frío(a)
cold water el agua fría
I'm cold tengo frío
it's cold hace frío
cold (illness) el resfriado
I have a cold estoy resfriado(a)
cold sore la calentura
collar el cuello
collar bone la clavícula
colleague el/la compañero(a) de trabajo
to collect recoger
collection la recogida
colour el color
colour-blind daltónico(a)
colour film (for camera) el carrete en color
comb el peine
to come venir (to arrive) llegar
to come back volver
to come in entrar
come in! ¡pase!
comedy la comedia
comfortable cómodo(a)
company (firm) la empresa
compartment el compartimento
compass la brújula
to complain reclamar
complaint la reclamación; la queja
complete completo(a)
to complete terminar
compulsory obligatorio(a)
computer el ordenador
computer disk (floppy) el disquete
computer game el juego de ordenador
computer program el programa de ordenador
concert el concierto
concert hall la sala de conciertos
concession el descuento
concussion la conmoción cerebral

conditioner el suavizante
condom el condón
conductor (on bus) el/la cobrador(a)
(on train) el/la revisor(a)
conference el congreso
to confirm confirmar
please confirm por favor, confirme
confirmation (flight, booking) la
confirmación
congratulations! ¡enhorabuena!
connection (train, etc) el enlace
constipated estreñido(a)
consulate el consulado
to consult consultar
to contact ponerse en contacto con
contact details la información de
contacto
contact lens la lentilla
contact lens cleaner la solución
limpiadora para lentillas
to continue continuar
contraceptive el anticonceptivo
contract el contrato
convenient: is it convenient?
¿le viene bien?
convulsions las convulsiones
to cook cocinar
cooked preparado(a)
cooker la cocina
cookies las galletas
cool fresco(a)
cool-box la nevera portátil
copper el cobre
copy (duplicate) la copia
(of book) el ejemplar
to copy copiar
coral el coral
cordless phone el teléfono
inalámbrico
cork el corcho
corkscrew el sacacorchos
corner la esquina
cornflakes los copos de maíz;
los cornflakes
corridor el pasillo
cortisone la cortisona
cosmetics los cosméticos
cost (price) el precio

to cost costar
how much does it cost? ¿cuánto
cuesta?
costume (swimming) el bañador
cot la cuna
cottage la casita de campo
cotton el algodón
cotton buds los bastoncillos
cotton wool el algodón hidrófilo
couchette la litera
to cough toser
cough la tos
cough mixture el jarabe para la tos
cough sweets los caramelos para
la tos
counter (in shop) el mostrador
(in bar) la barra
country (not town) el campo
(nation) el país
countryside el campo
couple (2 people) la pareja
a couple of... un par de...
courgette el calabacín
courier service el servicio
de mensajero
course (of study) el curso
(of meal) el plato
cousin el/la primo(a)
cover charge (in restaurant)
el cubierto
cow la vaca
crafts la artesanía
craft fair la feria de artesanía(s)
craftsperson el/la artesano(a)
cramps los calambres
cranberry juice el zumo de arándanos
crash (car) el accidente
to crash (car) chocar
crash helmet el casco protector
cream (lotion) la crema
(on milk) la nata
soured cream la nata cortada
whipped cream la nata montada
creche la guardería
credit *n* (on mobile phone) el saldo
credit card la tarjeta de crédito
crime el delito
crisps las patatas fritas

128

cross (crucifix) la cruz
to cross (road) cruzar
cross country skiing el esquí de fondo
crossing (sea) la travesía
crossroads el cruce
crossword puzzle el crucigrama
crowd la multitud
crowded concurrido(a)
crown la corona
cruise el crucero
crutches las muletas
to cry (weep) llorar
crystal el cristal
cucumber el pepino
cufflinks los gemelos
cul-de-sac el callejón sin salida
cup la taza
cupboard el armario
currant la pasa (de Corinto)
currency la moneda
current la corriente
curtain la cortina
cushion el cojín
custom (tradition) la costumbre
customer el/la cliente
customs (control) la aduana
customs declaration la declaración aduanera
cut el corte
to cut cortar
cutlery los cubiertos
to cycle ir en bicicleta
cycle track el carril bici
cycling el ciclismo
cyst el quiste
cystitis la cistitis

D

daily (each day) cada día; diario
dairy produce los productos lácteos
dam la presa
damage el/los daño(s)
damp húmedo(a)
dance el baile
to dance bailar
danger el peligro
dangerous peligroso(a)

dark oscuro(a)
after dark por la noche
date la fecha
date of birth la fecha de nacimiento
daughter la hija
daughter-in-law la cuñada
dawn el amanecer
day el día
every day todos los días
per day al día
dead muerto(a)
deaf sordo(a)
dear (on letter) querido(a)
(expensive) caro(a)
debt la deuda
debit card la tarjéta de débito
decaffeinated coffee el descafeinado
have you decaff? ¿tiene descafeinado?
December diciembre
deck chair la tumbona
to declare declarar
nothing to declare nada que declarar
deep profundo(a)
deep freeze el ultracongelador
deer el ciervo
to defrost descongelar
to de-ice descongelar
delay el retraso
how long is the delay? ¿cuánto lleva de retraso?
delayed retrasado(a)
delicatessen la charcutería
delicious delicioso(a)
demonstration la manifestación
dental floss el hilo dental
dentist el/la dentista
dentures la dentadura postiza
deodorant el desodorante
department (gen) el departamento
(in shop) la sección
department store los grandes almacenes
departure lounge la sala de embarque
departures las salidas
deposit la fianza

to describe describir
description la descripción
desk (in hotel, airport) el mostrador
dessert el postre
details los detalles
(personal) los datos personales
detergent el detergente
detour el desvío
to develop (photos) revelar
diabetes la diabetes
diabetic diabético(a)
I'm diabetic soy diabético(a)
to dial marcar
dialling code el prefijo
dialling tone el tono de marcar/
marcado
diamond el diamante
diapers los pañales
diaphragm el diafragma
diarrhoea la diarrea
diary la agenda
dice los dados
dictionary el diccionario
to die morir
diesel el diesel; el gasóleo
diet la dieta
I'm on a diet estoy a dieta
special diet la dieta especial
different distinto(a)
difficult difícil
digital camera la cámara digital
digital radio la radio digital
to dilute diluir
dinghy el bote
dining room el comedor
dinner (evening meal) la cena
to have dinner cenar
diplomat el/la diplomático(a)
direct (train, etc) directo(a)
directions (instructions) las
instrucciones
to ask for directions preguntar
el camino
directory (phone) la guía telefónica
directory enquiries la información
telefónica
dirty sucio(a)
disability la discapacidad

130

disabled el/la discapacitado(a);
el/la minusválido(a)
to disagree no estar de acuerdo
to disappear desaparecer
disaster el desastre
disco la discoteca
discount el descuento
to discover descubrir
disease la enfermedad
dish el plato
dishtowel el paño de cocina
dishwasher el lavavajillas
dishwasher powder el detergente
para lavavajillas
disinfectant el desinfectante
disk (floppy) el disquete
to dislocate (joint) dislocarse
disposable desechable
distance la distancia
distant distante; lejano(a)
distilled water el agua destilada
district el barrio
to disturb molestar
ditch la cuneta
to dive tirarse al agua
diversion el desvío
divorced divorciado(a)
DIY shop la tienda de bricolaje
dizzy mareado(a)
to do hacer
doctor el/la médico(a)
documents los documentos
dog el perro
dog food la comida para perros
dog lead la correa del perro
doll la muñeca
dollar el dólar
domestic (flight) nacional
donor card la tarjeta de donante
door la puerta
doorbell el timbre
double doble
double bed la cama de matrimonio
double room la habitación doble
doughnut el donut
down: to go down bajar
to download descargar
downstairs abajo

Down's syndrome síndrome (de) Down
he/she has Down's syndrome
  tiene síndrome (de) Down
dozen la docena
drain el desagüe
draught (of air) la corriente
there's a draught hay corriente
draught lager la cerveza de barril
to draw dibujar
drawer el cajón
drawing el dibujo
dress el vestido
to dress (to get dressed) vestirse
dressing (for food) el aliño
  (for wound) el vendaje
dressing gown la bata
drill (tool) la taladradora
drink la bebida
to drink beber
drinking water el agua potable
to drive conducir
driver el/la conductor(a)
driving licence el carné de conducir
drought la sequía
to drown ahogarse
drug la droga
  (medicine) la medicina
drunk borracho(a)
dry seco(a)
to dry secar
dry-cleaner's la tintorería; la limpieza
  en seco
due: *when is it due?* ¿para cuándo
  está previsto?
dummy (for baby) el chupete
during durante
dust el polvo
duster el trapo del polvo
dustpan and brush el cepillo y
  (el) recogedor
duty-free libre de impuestos
duvet el edredón nórdico
duvet cover la funda nórdica
DVD el DVD
DVD drive (la) unidad *or* (el) lector
  de DVD
DVD player el reproductor de DVD
DVD writer (el) grabador de DVD

dye el tinte
dynamo la dinamo

E

each cada
ear (outside) la oreja
  (inside) el oído
earache el dolor de oído(s)
I have earache me duele el oído
earlier antes
early temprano
to earn ganar
earphones los auriculares
earplugs los tapones para los oídos
earrings los pendientes
earth la tierra
earthquake el terremoto
east el este
Easter la Pascua; la Semana Santa
easy fácil
to eat comer
ecological ecológico(a)
eco-tourism ecoturismo
egg el huevo
fried egg el huevo frito
hard-boiled egg el huevo duro
scrambled eggs los huevos revueltos
soft-boiled egg el huevo pasado por
  agua
eggplant la berenjena
either... or... o... o...
elastic band la goma
elastoplast® la tirita
elbow el codo
electric eléctrico(a)
electric blanket la manta eléctrica
electric razor la maquinilla de afeitar
electric toothbrush el cepillo de
  dientes eléctrico
electrician el/la electricista
electricity la electricidad
electricity meter el contador de
  electricidad
electric point el enchufe
electric shock la descarga eléctrica
electronic electrónico(a)
electronic organizer el agenda
  electrónica *f*

elevator el ascensor
e-mail el email
to e-mail s.o. mandar un email a algn
e-mail address el email
embassy la embajada
emergency la emergencia
emergency exit la salida de emergencia
empty vacío(a)
end el fin
engaged (to marry) prometido(a)
(toilet, phone) ocupado(a)
engine el motor
England Inglaterra
English inglés/inglesa
(language) el inglés
Englishman/-woman el inglés/la inglesa
to enjoy (to like) gustar
enjoy your meal! ¡qué aproveche!
I enjoy dancing me gusta bailar
I enjoy swimming me gusta nadar
to enjoy oneself divertirse
enough bastante
that's enough ya basta
enquiry desk la información
to enter entrar en
entertainment el entretenimiento
entrance la entrada
entrance fee el precio de entrada
envelope el sobre
epileptic epiléptico(a)
epileptic fit el ataque epiléptico
equal igual
equipment el equipo
eraser la goma (de borrar)
error el error
escalator la escalera mecánica
to escape escapar
espadrilles las alpargatas
essential imprescindible
estate agent's la agencia inmobiliaria
estate car la furgoneta; la camioneta
euro el euro
euro cent el céntimo
Europe Europa
European el/la europeo(a)
European Union la Unión Europea

even (not odd) par
evening la tarde
in the evening por la tarde
this evening esta tarde
tomorrow evening mañana por la tarde
evening dress (man's) el traje de etiqueta
(woman's) el traje de noche
evening meal la cena
every cada
everyone todo el mundo; todos
everything todo
everywhere en todas partes
examination el examen
example: *for example* por ejemplo
excellent excelente
except excepto
excess baggage el exceso de equipaje
exchange el cambio
to exchange cambiar
exchange rate el tipo de cambio
exciting emocionante
excursion la excursión
excuse: *excuse me!* perdón
exercise el ejercicio
exhaust pipe el tubo de escape
exhibition la exposición
exit la salida
expenses los gastos
expensive caro(a)
expert el/la experto(a)
to expire (ticket, etc) caducar
to explain explicar
explosion la explosión
to export exportar
express (train) el expreso
express: *to send a letter express* enviar una carta por correo urgente
extension (electrical) el alargador
extra (in addition) de más
(more) extra; adicional
eye el ojo
eyebrows las cejas
eye drops el colirio
eyelashes las pestañas
eyeliner el lápiz/perfilador de ojos
eye shadow la sombra de ojos

F

fabric la tela
face la cara
face cloth la toallita
facial la limpieza de cutis
facilities las instalaciones
fact el hecho
factor (sunblock) factor
factor 25 factor 25
factory la fábrica
to fade desteñir
to faint desmayarse
fainted desmayado(a)
fair (hair) rubio(a)
(just) justo(a)
fair (funfair) la feria
fake falso(a)
fall (autumn) el otoño
to fall caer; caerse
he/she has fallen se ha caído
false teeth la dentadura postiza
family la familia
famous famoso(a)
fan (electric) el ventilador
(hand-held) el abanico
(football, etc) el/la hincha
(jazz, etc) el/la aficionado(a)
fan belt la correa del ventilador
fancy dress el disfraz
far lejos
how far is it? ¿a cuánto está?
is it far? ¿está lejos?
farm la granja
farmer el/la granjero(a)
farmers' market el mercado agrícola
farmhouse la granja
fashionable de moda
fast rápido(a)
too fast demasiado rápido
to fasten (seatbelt, etc) abrocharse
fat (plump) gordo(a)
(in food, on person) la grasa
saturated fats las grasas saturadas
unsaturated fats las grasas
  insaturadas/no saturadas
father el padre
father-in-law el suegro
fault (defect) el defecto

it's not my fault no tengo la culpa
favour el favor
favourite favorito(a); preferido(a)
to fax mandar por fax
fax el fax
by fax por fax
fax number el número de fax
February febrero
to feed dar de comer
to feel sentir
I don't feel well no me siento bien
I feel sick estoy mareado(a)
feet los pies
felt-tip pen el rotulador
female femenino
ferry el ferry; el transbordador
festival el festival
to fetch (to bring) traer
(to go and get) ir a buscar
fever la fiebre
few pocos(as)
a few algunos(as)
fiancé(e) el/la novio(a)
field el campo
to fight luchar
file (computer) el fichero
(nail) la lima
to fill llenar
(form) rellenar
fill it up, please! (car) lleno, por favor!
fillet el filete
filling (in tooth) el empaste
film (at cinema) la película
(for camera) el carrete
Filofax® la agenda Filofax® *f*
filter el filtro
to find encontrar
fine (to be paid) la multa
finger el dedo
to finish acabar
finished terminado(a)
fire (flames) el fuego
(blaze) el incendio
fire! ¡fuego!
fire alarm la alarma de incendios
fire brigade los bomberos
fire engine el coche de bomberos
fire escape la salida de incendios

fire exit la salida de incendios
fire extinguisher el extintor
fireplace la chimenea
fireworks los fuegos artificiales
firm (company) la empresa
first primero(a)
first aid los primeros auxilios
first aid kit el botiquín de primeros auxilios
first class de primera clase
first name el nombre de pila
fish (food) el pescado
(alive) el pez
to fish pescar
fisherman el pescador
fishing permit la licencia de pesca
fishing rod la caña de pescar
fishmonger's la pescadería
fit (seizure) el ataque
to fit (clothes) quedar bien
it doesn't fit no queda bien
to fix arreglar
can you fix it? ¿puede arreglarlo?
fizzy con gas
flag la bandera
flames las llamas
flash (for camera) el flash
flashlight la linterna
flask (thermos) el termo
flat (apartment) el piso
(battery) descargado(a)
(beer) sin gas
flat llano(a)
it's flat no tiene gas
flat tyre la rueda pinchada
flavour el sabor
which flavour? ¿qué sabor?
flaw el defecto
fleas las pulgas
fleece el vellón
flesh la carne
flex el cable eléctrico
flight el vuelo
flip flops las chanclas/chancletas
flippers las aletas
flood la inundación
flash flood la riada
floor (of building) el piso

(of room) el suelo
which floor? ¿qué piso?
on the ground floor en la planta baja
on the first floor en el primer piso; en la primera planta
on the second floor en el segundo piso; en la segunda planta
floorcloth la bayeta
floppy disk el disquete
florist's shop la floristería
flour la harina
flower la flor
flu la gripe
fly la mosca
to fly volar
fly sheet el toldo impermeable
fog la niebla
foggy: *it's foggy* hay niebla
foil (tinfoil) el papel de estaño
to fold doblar
to follow seguir
food la comida
food poisoning la intoxicación por alimentos
foot el pie
on foot a pie
football el fútbol
football match el partido de fútbol
football pitch el campo de fútbol
football player el/la futbolista
footpath (in country) el sendero
for para; por
for me para mí
for you para usted/ti
for him/her/us para él/ella/nosotros
forbidden prohibido(a)
forehead la frente
foreign extranjero(a)
foreign currency la moneda extranjera
foreigner el/la extranjero(a)
forest el bosque
forever para siempre
to forget olvidar
fork (for eating) el tenedor
(in road) la bifurcación
form (document) el impreso
formal dress el traje de etiqueta

fortnight quince días
forward adelante
foul (football) la falta
fountain la fuente
four-wheel drive la tracción
a las cuatro ruedas
fox el zorro
fracture la fractura
fragile frágil
fragrance el perfume
frame (picture) el marco
France Francia
free (not occupied) libre
(costing nothing) gratis
free-range de granja
freezer el congelador
French francés/francesa
(language) el francés
French bean la judía verde
French fries las patatas fritas
frequent frecuente
fresh fresco(a)
fresh water el agua dulce
Friday el viernes
fridge el frigorífico
fried frito(a)
friend el/la amigo(a)
frisbee® el frisbee®
frog la rana
from de; desde
from England de Inglaterra
from Scotland de Escocia
front la parte delantera
in front of delante de
front door la puerta principal
frost la helada
frozen congelado(a)
fruit la fruta
dried fruit la fruta seca
fruit juice el zumo (de fruta)
fruit salad la macedonia
to fry freír
frying pan la sartén
fuel (petrol) la gasolina
fuel gauge el indicador de la
gasolina
fuel pump (in car) el surtidor de
gasolina

fuel tank el depósito de gasolina
full lleno(a)
(occupied) ocupado(a)
full board la pensión completa
fumes (of car) los gases
fun la diversión
funeral el funeral
funfair la feria
funny (amusing) divertido(a)
fur la piel
furnished amueblado(a)
furniture los muebles
fuse el fusible
fuse box la caja de fusibles
future el futuro

G

gallery la galería
game el juego
(animal) la caza
garage el garaje
(for repairs) el taller
(for petrol) la gasolinera
garden el jardín
garlic el ajo
gas el gas
gas cooker la cocina de gas
gas cylinder la bombona de gas
gastritis la gastritis
gate (airport) la puerta
gay (person) gay
gear la marcha
first gear la primera
second gear la segunda
third gear la tercera
fourth gear la cuarta
neutral el punto muerto
reverse la marcha atrás
gearbox la caja de cambios
gear cable el cable de cambio
gear lever la palanca de cambio
generous generoso(a)
gents (toilet) el servicio de caballeros
genuine auténtico(a)
German alemán/alemana
(language) el alemán
German measles la rubeola
Germany Alemania

to get (to obtain) conseguir
(to receive) recibir
(to bring) traer
to get in (vehicle) subir (al)
to get out (of vehicle) bajarse de
gift el regalo
gift shop la tienda de regalos
gigabyte el gigabyte
gigahertz el gigaherzio
girl la chica
girlfriend la novia
to give dar
to give back devolver
glacier el glaciar
glass (for drinking) el vaso
(substance) el cristal
a glass of water un vaso de agua
a glass of wine un vaso de vino
glasses (spectacles) las gafas
glasses case la funda de gafas
gloves los guantes
glue el pegamento
gluten el gluten
GM-free no transgénico(a)
to go ir
I'm going to... voy a...
we're going to... vamos a...
to go home irse a casa
to go back volver
to go in entrar (en)
to go out salir
goat la cabra
God Dios
goggles (for swimming) las gafas
de natación
(for skiing) las gafas de esquí
(for diving) las gafas de buceo
gold el oro
golf el golf
golf ball la pelota de golf
golf clubs los palos de golf
golf course el campo de golf
good bueno(a)
very good muy bueno
good afternoon buenas tardes
goodbye adiós
good day buenos días
good evening buenas tardes

(when dark) buenas noches
good morning buenos días
good night buenas noches
goose el ganso
gram(me) el gramo
grandchild el/la nieto(a)
granddaughter la nieta
grandfather el abuelo
grandmother la abuela
grandparents los abuelos
grandson el nieto
grapefruit el pomelo
grapes las uvas
grass la hierba
grated (cheese, etc) rallado(a)
grater (for cheese, etc) el rallador
greasy grasiento(a)
great (big) grande
(wonderful) estupendo(a)
Great Britain Gran Bretaña
green verde
green card la carta verde
greengrocer's la frutería
greetings card la tarjeta de felicitación
grey gris
grill el grill
(barbecue) la parrilla
to grill gratinar
(on barbecue) asar a la parrilla
grilled gratinado(a)
(on barbecue) a la parrilla
grocer's la tienda de alimentación
ground el suelo
ground floor la planta baja
on the ground floor en la planta baja
groundsheet el suelo (de tela)
impermeable
group el grupo
guarantee la garantía
guard (on train) el/la jefe(a) de tren
guava la guayaba
guest el/la invitado(a)
(in hotel) el/la huésped
guesthouse la pensión
guide (tour guide) el/la guía
to guide guiar
guidebook la guía turística
guided tour la visita con guía

guitar la guitarra
gun la pistola
gym el gimnasio
gym shoes las zapatillas de deporte
gynaecologist el/la ginecólogo(a)

H

haemorrhoids las hemorroides
hail el granizo
hair el pelo
hairbrush el cepillo del pelo
haircut el corte de pelo
hairdresser el/la peluquero(a)
hairdryer el secador de pelo
hair dye el tinte del pelo
hair gel la gomina
hairgrip la horquilla
hair mousse la espuma del pelo
hair spray la laca
half medio(a)
half an hour media hora
half board la media pensión
half fare el billete reducido para niños
half-price a mitad de precio
ham el jamón
(cooked) el jamón de York
(cured) el jamón serrano
hamburger la hamburguesa
hammer el martillo
hand la mano
handbag el bolso
handbreak el freno de mano
hand luggage el equipaje de mano
hand-made hecho(a) a mano
handicapped minusválido(a);
  discapacitado(a)
handkerchief el pañuelo
handle (of cup) el asa
(of door) el pomo
handlebars el manillar
hands-free kit (for phone) el equipo
  manos libres
hands-free phone el teléfono de
  manos libres
handsome guapo(a)
hang gliding el vuelo con ala delta
hangover la resaca
to hang up (phone) colgar

to happen pasar
what happened? ¿qué ha pasado?
happy feliz
happy birthday! ¡feliz cumpleaños!;
  ¡felicidades!
harbour el puerto
hard duro(a)
(difficult) difícil
hard disk el disco duro
Hard drive (el) disco duro *or* (la) unidad
  de disco duro
hardware shop la ferretería
to harm (person) hacer daño a
(crops, etc) dañar
harvest la cosecha
hat el sombrero
to have tener
I have... tengo
I don't have... no tengo...
we have... tenemos...
we don't have... no tenemos...
do you have...? ¿tiene...?
to have to tener que
hay fever la alergia al polen
he él
head la cabeza
headache el dolor de cabeza
I have a headache me duele la cabeza
headlights los faros
headphones los auriculares
head waiter el maître
health la salud
health food shop la tienda de
  dietética
healthy sano(a)
to hear oír
hearing aid el audífono
heart el corazón
heart attack el infarto
heartburn el ardor de estómago
heater la estufa
heating la calefacción
to heat up (food) calentar
heavy pesado(a)
heel (of foot) el talón
(of shoe) el tacón
heel bar la tienda de reparación
  de calzado en el acto

height la altura
helicopter el helicóptero
hello hola
(on phone) ¿diga?
helmet (for bike, etc) el casco
help! ¡socorro!
to help ayudar
can you help me? ¿puede ayudarme?
hem el dobladillo
hepatitis la hepatitis
her su
herb la hierba
herbal tea la infusión
here aquí
here is... aquí tiene...
here is my passport aquí tiene mi
pasaporte
hernia la hernia
hi! ¡hola!
to hide (something) esconder
(oneself) esconderse
high alto(a)
high blood pressure la tensión alta
high chair la trona
high tide la marea alta
hill la colina
hill-walking el montañismo
him él
hip la cadera
hip replacement la prótesis de cadera
hire (bike, boat, etc) el alquiler
bike hire el alquiler de bicicletas
boat hire el alquiler de barcas
car hire el alquiler de coches
to hire alquilar
hired car el coche de alquiler
his su
historic histórico(a)
history la historia
to hit pegar
to hitchhike hacer autostop; hacer
dedo
HIV positive seropositivo(a)
hobby el hobby; el pasatiempo
to hold tener
(to contain) contener
hold-up (traffic jam) el atasco
hole el agujero

holiday las vacaciones
(public) la fiesta
on holiday de vacaciones
holiday rep el/la guía turístico(a)
home la casa
at home en casa
homesick: to be homesick tener
morriña
I'm homesick tengo morriña
homeopathic homeopático(a)
homeopathy la homeopatía
homosexual homosexual
honest sincero(a)
honey la miel
honeymoon la luna de miel
hood (jacket) la capucha
hook (fishing) el anzuelo
to hope esperar
I hope so/not espero que sí/no
horn (car) el claxon
hors d'oeuvre los entremeses
horse el caballo
horse racing la hípica
horse riding la equitación
hosepipe la manguera
hospital el hospital
hostel el hostal
hot caliente
hot water el agua caliente
I'm hot tengo calor
it's hot (weather) hace calor
hot-water bottle la bolsa de agua
caliente
hotel el hotel
hour la hora
half an hour media hora
house la casa
housewife/husband la/el ama(o)
de casa
house wine el vino de la casa
housework las tareas domésticas
how (in what way) cómo
how are you? ¿cómo está?
how many? ¿cuántos?
how much? ¿cuánto?
hungry: to be hungry tener hambre
to hunt cazar
hunting permit el permiso de caza

hurry: *I'm in a hurry* tengo prisa
to hurt (injure) hacer daño
my back hurts me duele la espalda
that hurts eso duele
husband el marido
hut (bathing/beach) la caseta
(mountain) el refugio
hydrofoil el hidrodeslizador
hypodermic needle la aguja
hipodérmica

I

I yo
ice el hielo
(cube) el cubito
with/without ice con/sin hielo
ice box la nevera
icecream el helado
ice lolly el polo
ice rink la pista de patinaje
to ice skate patinar sobre hielo
ice skates los patines de hielo
iced tea el té helado
idea la idea
identity card el carné de identidad
if si
ignition el encendido
ignition key la llave de contacto
ill enfermo(a)
illness la enfermedad
immediately inmediatamente;
en seguida
immersion heater el calentador
eléctrico
immigration la inmigración
immobilizer (on car) el inmobilizador
immunisation la inmunización
to import importar
important importante
impossible imposible
to improve mejorar
in dentro de; en
in 10 minutes dentro de diez minutos
in London en Londres
in front of delante de
inch la pulgada = approx. 2.5 cm
included incluido(a)
inconvenient inoportuno(a)

to increase aumentar
indicator (in car) el intermitente
indigestion la indigestión
indigestion tablets las pastillas
para la indigestión
indoors dentro
infection la infección
infectious contagioso(a)
information la información
information desk la información
ingredients los ingredientes
inhaler (for medication) el inhalador
injection la inyección
to injure herir
injured herido(a)
injury la herida
ink la tinta
inn la pensión
inner tube la cámara
inquiries información
inquiry desk la información
insect el insecto
insect bite la picadura de insecto
insect repellent el repelente contra
insectos
inside dentro de
instant coffee el café instantáneo
instead of en lugar de
instructor el/la instructor(a)
insulin la insulina
insurance el seguro
insurance certificate la póliza
de seguros
to insure asegurar
insured asegurado(a)
iPod® el iPod®
to intend to pensar
internet access:
do you have internet access?
¿tiene acceso a Internet?
interesting interesante
international internacional
internet el/la Internet
internet café el cibercafé
interpreter el/la intérprete
interval (theatre, etc) el descanso;
el intermedio
interview la entrevista

into en
into town al centro
to introduce to presentar a
invitation la invitación
to invite invitar
invoice la factura
Ireland Irlanda
Irish irlandés/irlandesa
iron (for clothes) la plancha
(metal) el hierro
to iron planchar
ironing board la tabla de planchar
ironmonger's la ferretería
island la isla
it lo/la
Italian italiano(a)
(language) el italiano
Italy Italia
itch el picor
to itch picar
it itches pica
item el artículo
itemized bill la factura detallada
IUD el DIU

J

jack (for car) el gato
jacket la chaqueta
jam (food) la mermelada
jammed (stuck) atascado(a)
January enero
jar (honey, jam, etc) el tarro
jaundice la ictericia
jaw la mandíbula
jealous celoso(a)
jeans los vaqueros
jelly (dessert) la gelatina
jellyfish la medusa
jet ski la moto acuática
jetty el embarcadero
Jewish judío(a)
jeweller's la joyería
jewellery las joyas
job el empleo
to jog hacer footing
to join (club, etc) hacerse socio de
to join in participar en
joint (body) la articulación

to joke bromear
joke la broma
journalist el/la periodista
journey el viaje
judge el/la juez(a)
jug la jarra
juice el zumo
a carton of juice un brik de zumo
July julio
to jump saltar
jumper el jersey
jump leads (for car) los cables
de arranque
junction (road) la bifurcación
June junio
jungle la jungla
just: *just two* sólo dos
I've just arrived acabo de llegar

K

to keep (to retain) guardar
kennel la caseta (del perro)
kettle el hervidor (de agua)
key la llave
card key (used in hotel) la llave tarjeta
keyboard el teclado
keycard (electronic key eg in hotel)
la tarjeta-llave
keyring el llavero
to kick dar una patada a
kid (child) el/la crío(a)
kidneys los riñones
to kill matar
kilo(gram) el kilo(gramo)
kilometre el kilómetro
kind (person) amable
(sort) la clase
what kind? ¿qué clase?
king el rey
kiosk el quiosco
kiss el beso
to kiss besar
kitchen la cocina
kitchen paper el papel de cocina
kite la cometa
kiwi fruit el kiwi
knee la rodilla
knee highs las medias cortas

knickers las bragas
knife el cuchillo
to knit hacer punto
to knock (on door) llamar
to knock down (car) atropellar
to knock over (vase, glass) tirar
knot el nudo
to know (have knowledge of) saber
(person, place) conocer
I don't know no sé
to know how to saber
to know how to swim saber nadar
kosher kosher

L

label la etiqueta
lace (fabric) el encaje
laces (for shoes) los cordones
ladder la escalera (de mano)
ladies (toilet) el servicio de señoras
lady la señora
lager la cerveza (rubia)
bottled lager la cerveza (rubia) de botella
draught lager la cerveza (rubia) de barril
lake el lago
lamb el cordero
lamp la lámpara
lamppost la farola
lampshade la pantalla (de lámpara)
land el terreno
to land aterrizar
landlady la dueña (de la casa)
landline phone el teléfono fijo
landlord el dueño (de la casa)
landslide el desprendimiento de tierras
lane el carril
language el idioma; la lengua
language school la escuela/academia de idiomas
laptop el ordenador portátil
laptop bag el maletín de ordenador portátil
large grande
last último(a)
last night anoche
last time la última vez

last week la semana pasada
last year el año pasado
the last bus el último autobús
the last train el último tren
late tarde
sorry I'm late siento llegar tarde
the train is late el tren viene con retraso
later más tarde
to laugh reírse
launderette la lavandería automática
laundry service el servicio de lavandería
lavatory (in house) el wáter
(in public place) los servicios
law la ley
lawn el césped
lawyer el/la abogado(a)
laxative el laxante
layby la zona de descanso
lead (electric) el cable
lead (metal) el plomo
lead-free sin plomo
leaf la hoja
leak (of gas, liquid) la fuga
(in roof) la gotera
to leak: *it's leaking* (radiator, etc) está goteando
to learn aprender
learning disability:
he/she has a learning disability tiene problemas de aprendizaje
lease (rental) el alquiler
leather el cuero
to leave (a place) irse de
(leave behind) dejar
when does the train leave? ¿a qué hora sale el tren?
leek el puerro
left: *on/to the left* a la izquierda
left-handed (person) zurdo(a)
left-luggage (office) la consigna
left-luggage locker la consigna automática
leg la pierna
legal legal
leisure centre el polideportivo
lemon el limón

lemonade la gaseosa
lemongrass la limonaria
to lend prestar
length la longitud
lens (photographic) el objetivo
(contact lens) la lentilla
lesbian lesbiana
less menos
less than menos de que
lesson la clase
to let (to allow) permitir
(to hire out) alquilar
letter la carta
(of alphabet) la letra
letterbox el buzón
lettuce la lechuga
level crossing el paso a nivel
library la biblioteca
licence el permiso
(driving) el carné de conducir
lid la tapa
lie (untruth) la mentira
to lie down acostarse
lifebelt el salvavidas
lifeboat el bote salvavidas
lifeguard el/la socorrista
life insurance el seguro de vida
life jacket el chaleco salvavidas
life raft la balsa salvavidas
lift (elevator) el ascensor
can you give me a lift? ¿me lleva?
lift pass (on ski slopes) el forfait
light (not heavy) ligero(a)
light la luz
have you a light? ¿tiene fuego?
light bulb la bombilla
lighter el encendedor; el mechero
lighthouse el faro
lightning el relámpago
like (similar to) como
to like gustar
I like coffee me gusta el café
I don't like... no me gusta...
I'd like to... me gustaría...
we'd like to... nos gustaría...
lilo® la colchoneta hinchable
lime (fruit) la lima
line (row, queue) la fila

(telephone) la línea
linen el lino
lingerie la lencería
lips los labios
lip-reading la lectura de labios
lip salve el cacao para los labios
lipstick la barra de labios
liqueur el licor
list la lista
to listen to escuchar
litre el litro
litter (rubbish) la basura
little pequeño(a)
a little... un poco...
to live vivir
he lives in a flat vive en un piso
I live in Edinburgh vivo en Edimburgo
liver el hígado
living room el salón
loaf el pan de molde
local de la región; del país
lock (on door, box) la cerradura
the lock is broken la cerradura
  está rota
to lock cerrar con llave
locker (luggage) la consigna
locksmith el/la cerrajero(a)
log (for fire) el leño
log book (car) los papeles del coche
lollipop la piruleta; el chupón
London Londres
in London en Londres
to London a Londres
long largo(a)
for a long time (por) mucho tiempo
long-sighted hipermétrope
to look after cuidar
to look at mirar
to look for buscar
loose suelto(a)
it's come loose se ha soltado
lorry el camión
to lose perder
lost perdido(a)
I've lost... he perdido...
I'm lost me he perdido
lost property office la oficina
  de objetos perdidos

lot: *a lot of* mucho
lotion la loción
lottery la lotería
loud (sound, voice) fuerte
(volume) alto(a)
loudspeaker el altavoz
lounge el salón
love el amor
to love (person) querer
I love swimming me encanta nadar
I love you te quiero
lovely precioso(a)
low bajo(a)
low-alcohol con baja graduación
low-fat bajo(a) en calorías
low tide la marea baja
luck la suerte
lucky: *to be lucky* tener suerte
luggage el equipaje
luggage allowance el equipaje
  permitido
luggage rack el portaequipajes
luggage tag la etiqueta
luggage trolley el carrito
lump (swelling) el bulto
(on head) el chichón
lunch la comida
lunch break la hora de la comida
lung el pulmón
luxury de lujo

M

machine la máquina
mad loco(a)
magazine la revista
maggot el gusano
magnet el imán
magnifying glass la lupa
maid (in hotel) la camarera
maiden name el apellido de soltera
mail el correo
by mail por correo
main principal
main course (of meal) el plato
  principal
main road la carretera principal
Majorca Mallorca
make (brand) la marca

to make hacer
make-up el maquillaje
male masculino(a)
mallet el mazo
man el hombre
to manage (be in charge of) dirigir
manager el/la gerente
mango el mango
manicure la manicura
manual (gear change) manual
many muchos(as)
map (of region, country) el mapa
(of town) el plano
marble el mármol
March marzo
margarine la margarina
marina el puerto deportivo
mark (stain) la mancha
market el mercado
when is the market? ¿cuándo hay
  mercado?
where is the market? ¿dónde está
  el mercado?
market place la plaza (del mercado)
marmalade la mermelada de naranja
married casado(a)
are you married? ¿está casado(a)?
I'm married estoy casado(a)
to marry casarse con
marsh la marisma
mascara el rímel®
masher (potato) el pasapurés
mass (in church) la misa
massage el masaje
mast el mástil
masterpiece la obra maestra
match (game) el partido
matches las cerillas
material (cloth) la tela
to matter importar
it doesn't matter no importa
what's the matter? ¿qué pasa?
mattress el colchón
May mayo
mayonnaise la mayonesa
maximum máximo(a)
Mb (megabyte) Mb
meal la comida

to mean querer decir
what does this mean? ¿qué quiere decir esto?
measles el sarampión
to measure medir
meat la carne
mechanic el/la mecánico(a)
medical insurance el seguro médico
medical treatment el tratamiento médico
medicine la medicina
medieval medieval
Mediterranean el Mediterráneo
medium rare (meat) medio(a) hecho(a)
to meet (by chance) encontrarse con (by arrangement) ver
I'm meeting her tomorrow he quedado con ella mañana
meeting la reunión
meeting point el punto de reunión
megabyte el megabyte
megahertz el megaherzio
melon el melón
to melt derretir
member (of club, etc) el/la socio(a)
membership fee la cuota de socio
memory el recuerdo
memory card *or* **stick** la tarjeta de memoria
men los hombres
to mend arreglar
meningitis la meningitis
menu la carta
set menu el menú del día
message el mensaje
metal el metal
meter el contador
metre el metro
metro (underground) el metro
metro station la estación de metro
microphone el micrófono
microwave oven el microondas
midday las doce del mediodía
middle el medio
middle-aged de mediana edad
midge el mosquito enano
midnight la medianoche

at midnight a medianoche
migraine la jaqueca; la migraña
I've a migraine tengo jaqueca
mile la milla
milk la leche
fresh milk la leche fresca
hot milk la leche caliente
long-life milk la leche de larga duración (UHT)
powdered milk la leche en polvo
semi-skimmed milk la leche semidesnatada
skimmed milk la leche desnatada
soya milk la leche de soja
with milk con leche
milkshake el batido
millimetre el milímetro
mince (meat) la carne picada
mind: *do you mind if...?* ¿le importa que...?
I don't mind no me importa
mineral water el agua mineral
minibar el minibar
minidisc el minidisc
minimum el mínimo
minister (political) el/la ministro(a) (church) el/la pastor(a)
minor road la carretera secundaria
mint (herb) la menta (sweet) la pastilla de menta
minute el minuto
mirror el espejo
miscarriage el aborto natural/espontáneo
to miss (train, etc) perder
Miss la señorita
missing (lost) perdido(a)
my son is missing se ha perdido mi hijo
mistake el error
misty: *it's misty* hay neblina
misunderstanding la equivocación
to mix mezclar
mixer (food processor) el robot (de cocina) (hand-held) la batidora
mobile (phone) el teléfono móvil
mobile number el número de móvil

mobile phone charger el cargador del (teléfono) móvil
modem el módem
modern moderno(a)
moisturizer la leche/crema hidratante
mole (on skin) el lunar
moment el momento
just a moment un momento
monastery el monasterio
Monday el lunes
money el dinero
I've no money no tengo dinero
moneybelt la riñonera
money order el giro postal
month el mes
last month el mes pasado
next month el mes que viene
this month este mes
monthly mensualmente; mensual
monument el monumento
moon la luna
mooring el atracadero; el amarradero
mop la fregona
moped el ciclomotor
more más
more than más que
more wine más vino
morning la mañana
in the morning por la mañana
this morning esta mañana
tomorrow morning mañana por la mañana
morning-after pill la píldora (anticonceptiva) del día después
mosque la mezquita
mosquito el mosquito
mosquito bite la picadura de mosquito
mosquito net la mosquitera
mosquito repellent el repelente contra mosquitos
most: *most of* la mayor parte de; la mayoría de
MOT el ITV
moth (clothes) la polilla
mother la madre
mother-in-law la suegra
motor el motor

motorbike la moto
motorboat la lancha motora
motorway la autopista
mountain la montaña
mountain bike la bicicleta de montaña
mountain biking el ciclismo de montaña
mountain rescue el rescate de montaña
mountaineering el montañismo
mouse (animal, computer) el ratón
moustache el bigote
mouth la boca
mouthwash el enjuague bucal
to move mover
it isn't moving no se mueve
movie la película
MP3 player el reproductor MP3
Mr el señor (Sr.)
Mrs la señora (Sra.)
Ms la señora (Sra.)
much mucho(a)
too much demasiado(a)
muddy embarrado(a)
mugging el atraco
mumps las paperas
muscle el músculo
museum el museo
mushrooms los champiñones
music la música
musical musical
must (to have to) deber
I must debo
we must debemos
I musn't no debo
we musn't no debemos
mustard la mostaza
my mi

N

nail (fingernail) la uña
(metal) el clavo
nailbrush el cepillo de uñas
nail clippers el cortauñas
nail file la lima (de uñas)
nail polish el esmalte de uñas
nail polish remover el quitaesmalte
nail scissors las tijeras de uñas

name el nombre
my name is... me llamo...
what's your name? ¿cómo se llama?
nanny la niñera
napkin la servilleta
nappies los pañales
narrow estrecho(a)
national nacional
national park el parque nacional
nationality la nacionalidad
natural natural
nature la naturaleza
nature reserve la reserva natural
navy blue azul marino
near to cerca de
near to the bank cerca del banco
is it near? ¿está cerca?
necessary necesario(a)
neck el cuello
necklace el collar
nectarine la nectarina
to need necesitar
I need... necesito...
we need... necesitamos...
I need to go tengo que ir
needle la aguja
a needle and thread una aguja e hilo
negative (photo) el negativo
neighbour el/la vecino(a)
nephew el sobrino
net la red
the Net (internet) la Red
neutral *(in neutral, car)* (en) punto muerto
never nunca
I never drink wine nunca bebo vino
new nuevo(a)
news (TV, radio, etc) las noticias
newsagent's la tienda de prensa
newspaper el periódico
newsstand el kiosko de prensa
New Year el Año Nuevo
Happy New Year! ¡Feliz Año Nuevo!
New Year's Eve la Nochevieja
New Zealand Nueva Zelanda
next próximo(a)
next to al lado de
next week la próxima semana

the next stop la próxima parada
the next train el próximo tren
nice (person) simpático(a)
(place, holiday) bonito(a)
niece la sobrina
night la noche
at night por la noche
last night anoche
per night por noche
tomorrow night mañana por la noche
tonight esta noche
night club el club nocturno
nightdress el camisón
night porter el guarda nocturno
no no
no entry prohibida la entrada
no ice sin hielo
no problem ¡por supuesto!
no smoking prohibido fumar
(without) sin
no sugar sin azúcar
nobody nadie
noise el ruido
it's very noisy hay mucho ruido
non-alcoholic sin alcohol
none ninguno(a)
non-smoker el/la no fumador(a)
non-smoking no fumador
normal normal
north el norte
Northern Ireland Irlanda del Norte
nose la nariz
nosebleed la hemorragia nasal
not no
I am not... no estoy...; no soy...
note (banknote) el billete
(written) la nota
note pad el bloc
nothing nada
nothing else nada más
notice (sign) el anuncio
(warning) el aviso
notice board el tablón de anuncios
novel la novela
November noviembre
now ahora
nowhere en ninguna parte
nuclear nuclear

nudist beach la playa nudista
number el número
numberplate (car) la matrícula
nurse la/el enfermera(o)
nursery school la guardería/escuela infantil
nursery slope la pista para principiantes
nut (for bolt) la tuerca
nuts (to eat) los frutos secos

O

oar el remo
oats los copos de avena
to obtain obtener
occupation (work) la profesión
ocean el océano
October octubre
odd (strange) raro(a)
(not even) impar
of de
a glass of wine un vaso de vino
made of... hecho(a) de...
off (light, etc) apagado(a)
(rotten) pasado(a)
office la oficina
often a menudo
how often? ¿cada cuánto?
oil el aceite
oil filter el filtro de aceite
oil gauge el indicador del aceite
ointment la pomada
OK ¡vale!
old viejo(a)
how old are you? ¿cuántos años tiene?
I'm ... years old tengo ... años
old age pensioner el/la pensionista
olive la aceituna
olive oil el aceite de oliva
olive tree el olivo
on (light, TV, engine) encendido(a)
on sobre; encima
on the table sobre la mesa
on time a la hora
once una vez
at once en seguida
one-way dirección única

onion la cebolla
only sólo
open abierto(a)
to open abrir
opera la ópera
operation la operación
operator (phone) el/la telefonista
opposite (to) enfrente (de)
opposite the bank enfrente del banco
quite the opposite! ¡todo lo contrario!
optician's la óptica
or o
orange (fruit) la naranja
(colour) naranja
orange juice el zumo de naranja
orchestra la orquesta
order: *out of order* averiado(a)
to order (in restaurant) pedir
can I order? ¿puedo pedir?
organic biológico(a); ecológico(a)
to organize organizar
ornament el adorno
other: *the other one* el/la otro(a)
have you any others? ¿tiene otros(as)?
our nuestro(a)
out (light) apagado(a)
he's (gone) out ha salido
outdoor (pool, etc) al aire libre
outside: *it's outside* está fuera
oven el horno
ovenproof dish resistente al horno
over (on top of) (por) encima de
to be overbooked tener overbooking
to overcharge cobrar de más
overdone (food) demasiado hecho(a)
overdose la sobredosis
to overheat recalentar
to overload sobrecargar
to oversleep quedarse dormido(a)
to overtake (in car) adelantar
to owe deber
I owe you... le debo...
you owe me... me debe...
owner el/la propietario(a)
oxygen el oxígeno

P

pace el ritmo
pacemaker el marcapasos
to pack (luggage) hacer las maletas
package el paquete
package tour el viaje organizado
packet el paquete
padded envelope el sobre acolchado
paddling pool la piscina hinchable
padlock el candado
page la página
paid pagado(a)
I've paid he pagado
pain el dolor
painful doloroso(a)
painkiller el analgésico; el calmante
to paint pintar
paintbrush el pincel
painting (picture) el cuadro
pair el par
palace el palacio
pale pálido(a)
palmtop computer el ordenador
  de bolsillo
pan (saucepan) la cacerola
(frying) la sartén
pancake el crep(e)
panniers (for bike) las alforjas
panties las bragas
pants (men's underwear) los
  calzoncillos
panty liner el salvaslip
paper el papel
paper hankies los pañuelos de papel
paper napkins las servilletas de papel
papoose (for carrying baby) la mochila
  portabebés
paragliding el parapente
paralysed paralizado(a)
paramedic el/la paramédico(a)
parcel el paquete
pardon? ¿cómo?
I beg your pardon! ¿perdón?
parents los padres
park el parque
to park aparcar
parking disc el tique de aparcamiento
parking meter el parquímetro

parking ticket (fine) la multa por
  aparcamiento indebido
partner (business) el/la socio(a)
(boy/girlfriend) el/la compañero(a)
party (group) el grupo
(celebration) la fiesta
(political) el partido
pass (mountain) el puerto
(train) el abono
(bus) el bonobús
passenger el/la pasajero(a)
passionfruit la fruta de la pasión
passport el pasaporte
passport control el control de
  pasaportes
password la contraseña
pasta la pasta
pastry (dough) la masa
(cake) el pastel
path el camino
patient (in hospital) el/la paciente
pavement la acera
to pay pagar
I'd like to pay quisiera pagar
where do I pay ¿dónde se paga?
payment el pago
payphone el teléfono público
PDA el/la PDA
peace la paz
peach el melocotón
peak rate la tarifa máxima
pear la pera
pearls las perlas
peas los guisantes
pedal el pedal
pedalo el hidropedal
pedestrian el peatón
pedestrian crossing el paso
  de peatones
to pee hacer pipí
to peel (fruit) pelar
peg (for clothes) la pinza
(for tent) la estaca
pen el bolígrafo; el boli
pencil el lápiz
penfriend el/la amigo(a) por
  correspondencia
penicillin la penicilina

penis el pene
penknife la navaja
pensioner el/la jubilado(a); el/la pensionista
people la gente
people carrier el monovolumen
pepper (spice) la pimienta
(vegetable) el pimiento
per por
per day al día
per hour por hora
per person por persona
per week a la semana
50 km per hour 50 Km. por hora
perfect perfecto(a)
performance la función
perfume el perfume
perhaps quizá(s)
period (menstruation) la regla; el periodo
perm la permanente
permit el permiso
person la persona
personal organizer la agenda
personal stereo el walkman®
pet el animal doméstico
pet food la comida para animales
pet shop la pajarería
petrol la gasolina
4-star petrol la gasolina súper
unleaded petrol la gasolina sin plomo
petrol cap el tapón del depósito
petrol pump el surtidor
petrol station la gasolinera
petrol tank el depósito
pharmacy la farmacia
pharmacist farmacéutico(a)
phone el teléfono
(mobile) el móvil
(hands free) el teléfono 'manos libres'
by phone por teléfono
to phone llamar por teléfono
phonebook la guía (telefónica)
phonebox la cabina (telefónica)
phone call la llamada (telefónica)
phonecard la tarjeta telefónica
photocopier la fotocopiadora
photocopy la fotocopia

to photocopy fotocopiar
photograph la fotografía
to take a photograph hacer una fotografía
phrase book la guía de conversación
piano el piano
to pick (choose) elegir
(pluck) coger
pickled en vinagre
pickpocket el/la carterista
picnic el picnic
to have a picnic ir de picnic
picnic area el merendero
picnic hamper la cesta de la merienda
picnic rug la mantita
picture (painting) el cuadro
(photo) la foto
pie (fruit) la tarta
(meat) el pastel de carne
(and/or vegetable) la empanada
piece el trozo
pier el embarcadero; el muelle
pig el cerdo
pill la píldora
to be on the pill tomar la píldora
pillow la almohada
pillowcase la funda de almohada
pilot el/la piloto
pin el alfiler
PIN number el (número) PIN
pineapple la piña
pink rosa
pipe (smoker's) la pipa
(drain, etc) la tubería
pitch (place for tent/caravan) la parcela
pity: *what a pity* iqué pena!
pizza la pizza
place el lugar
place of birth el lugar de nacimiento
plain (yoghurt) natural
plait la trenza
plan (of town) el plano
plane (airplane) el avión
plant la planta
plaster (sticking) la tirita®
(for broken limb) la escayola
plastic (made of) de plástico

plastic bag la bolsa de plástico
plate el plato
platform el andén
which platform? ¿qué andén?
play (theatre) la obra
to play (games) jugar
play area la zona recreativa
play park el parque infantil
playroom el cuarto de juegos
pleasant agradable
please por favor
pleased contento(a)
pleased to meet you encantado(a) de conocerle(la)
pliers los alicates
plug (electrical) el enchufe
(for sink) el tapón
to plug in enchufar
plum la ciruela
plumber el/la fontanero(a)
plumbing (pipes) las cañerías
(craft) la fontanería
plunger (for sink) el desatascador
p.m. de la tarde
poached (egg, fish) escalfado(a)
pocket el bolsillo
point el punto
points (in car) los platinos
poison el veneno
poisonous venenoso(a)
police (force) la policía
policeman/woman el/la policía
police station la comisaría
polish (for shoes) el betún
(for furniture) el limpiamuebles
pollen el polen
polluted contaminado(a)
pony el poni
pony-trekking la excursión a caballo
pool la piscina
pool attendant el/la encargado(a) de la piscina
poor pobre
pop socks los calcetines cortos
popular popular
pork el cerdo
port (seaport) el puerto
(wine) el oporto

porter (hotel) el portero
(at station) el mozo
portion la porción; la ración
Portugal Portugal
Portuguese portugués/portuguesa
(language) el portugués
possible posible
post: *by post* por correo
to post echar al correo
postbox el buzón
postcard la postal
postcode el código postal
poster el póster
postman/woman el/la cartero(a)
post office la oficina de Correos
to postpone aplazar
pot (for cooking) la olla
potato la patata
baked potato la patata asada
boiled potatoes las patatas hervidas
fried potatoes las patatas fritas
mashed potatoes el puré de patatas
roast potatoes las patatas asadas
sautéed potatoes las patatas salteadas
potato masher el pasapurés
potato peeler el pelador
potato salad la ensalada de patatas
pothole el bache
pottery la cerámica
pound (money) la libra
to pour echar; servir
powder el polvo
in powder form en polvo
powdered milk la leche en polvo
power (electicity) la electricidad
power cut el apagón
pram el cochecito (de bebé)
to pray rezar
to prefer preferir
pregnant embarazada
I'm pregnant estoy embarazada
to prepare preparar
to prescribe prescribir
prescription la receta médica
present (gift) el regalo
preservative el conservante
president el/la presidente(a)

pressure la presión
pretty bonito(a)
price el precio
price list la lista de precios
priest el sacerdote; el cura
prime minister el/la primer(a) ministro(a)
print (photo) la copia
to print imprimir
printer la impresora
printout el listado
prison la cárcel
private privado(a)
prize el premio
probably probablemente
problem el problema
professor el/la catedrático(a)
programme (TV, radio) el programa
prohibited prohibido(a)
promise la promesa
to promise prometer
to pronounce pronunciar
how's it pronounced? ¿cómo se pronuncia?
Protestant protestante
to provide proporcionar
public público(a)
public holiday la fiesta (oficial)
pudding el postre
to pull tirar
I've pulled a muscle me ha dado un tirón en el músculo
to pull over (car) hacerse a un lado
pullover el jersey
pump (bike, etc) la bomba
(petrol) el surtidor
puncture el pinchazo
puncture repair kit el kit para reparar pinchazos
puppet la marioneta
puppet show el espectáculo de marionetas
purple morado(a)
purpose el propósito
on purpose a propósito
purse el monedero
to push empujar
pushchair la sillita de paseo

to put (place) poner
pyjamas el pijama
Pyrenees los Pirineos

Q
quality la calidad
quantity la cantidad
quarantine la cuarentena
to quarrel discutir; pelearse
quarter el cuarto
quay el muelle
queen la reina
query la pregunta
question la pregunta
queue la cola
to queue hacer cola
quick rápido(a)
quickly de prisa
quiet (place) tranquilo(a)
quilt el edredón
quite bastante
it's quite good es bastante bueno
quite expensive bastante caro
quiz el concurso

R
rabbit el conejo
rabies la rabia
race (sport) la carrera
race course (horses) el hipódromo
racket (tennis, etc) la raqueta
radiator (car, heater) el radiador
radio la radio
(digital) la radio digital
(car) la radio del coche
raft la balsa
railcard el carné de descuento para el tren
railway el ferrocarril
railway station la estación de tren
rain la lluvia
to rain: it's raining está lloviendo
raincoat el impermeable
rake el rastrillo
rape la violación
to rape violar
rare (unique) excepcional
(steak) poco hecho(a)

rash (skin) el sarpullido
raspberry la frambuesa
rat la rata
rate (price) la tarifa
rate of exchange el tipo de cambio
raw crudo(a)
razor la maquinilla de afeitar
razor blades las hojas de afeitar
to read leer
ready listo(a)
to get ready prepararse
real verdadero(a)
to realize darse cuenta de
rearview mirror el (espejo) retrovisor
receipt el recibo
receiver (phone) el auricular
reception desk la recepción
receptionist el/la recepcionista
to recharge (battery, etc) recargar
recharger el cargador
recipe la receta
to recognize reconocer
to recommend recomendar
to record (on tape, etc) grabar
(facts) registrar
to recover (from illness) recuperarse
to recycle reciclar
red rojo(a)
to reduce reducir
reduction el descuento
to refer to referirse a
refill el recambio
refund el reembolso
to refuse negarse
regarding con respecto a
region la región
register el registro
to register (at hotel) registrarse
registered (letter) certificado(a)
registration form la hoja de
  inscripción
to reimburse reembolsar
relation (family) el/la pariente
relationship la relación
to remain (stay) quedarse
to remember acordarse (de)
I don't remember no me acuerdo
remote control el mando a distancia

removal firm la empresa de mudanzas
to remove quitar
rent el alquiler
to rent alquilar
rental el alquiler
repair la reparación
to repair reparar
to repeat repetir
to reply contestar
report el informe
to report informar
request la solicitud
to request solicitar
to require necesitar
to rescue rescatar
reservation la reserva
to reserve reservar
reserved reservado(a)
resident el/la residente
resort el centro turístico
rest (repose) el descanso
(remainder) el resto
to rest descansar
restaurant el restaurante
restaurant car el coche restaurante
retired jubilado(a)
to return (to go back) volver
(to give back something) devolver
return (ticket) de ida y vuelta
to reverse dar marcha atrás
to reverse the charges llamar
  a cobro revertido
reverse charge call la llamada
  a cobro revertido
reverse gear la marcha atrás
rheumatism el reumatismo
rib la costilla
rice el arroz
rich (person) rico(a)
(food) pesado(a)
to ride a horse montar a caballo
right (correct) correcto(a)
to be right tener razón
right: on/to the right a la derecha
right of way el derecho de paso
to ring (bell, to phone) llamar
it's ringing está sonando
ring el anillo

ring road la carretera de circunvalación
ripe maduro(a)
river el río
road la carretera
road sign la señal de tráfico
roadworks las obras
roast asado(a)
roll (bread) el panecillo
rollerblades los patines en línea
romantic romántico(a)
roof el tejado
roof-rack la baca
room (in house, hotel) la habitación
(space) sitio
double room la habitación doble
family room la habitación familiar
single room la habitación individual
room number el número de
habitación
room service el servicio de
habitaciones
root la raíz
rope la cuerda
rose la rosa
rosé wine el (vino) rosado
rotten (fruit, etc) podrido(a)
rough (sea) picado(a)
round (shape) redondo(a)
roundabout (traffic) la rotonda
row (line, theatre) la fila
to row (boat) remar
rowing (sport) el remo
rowing boat el bote de remos
royal real
rubber (material) la goma
(eraser) la goma de borrar
rubber band la goma
rubber gloves los guantes de goma
rubbish la basura
rubella la rubeola
rucksack la mochila
rug la alfombra
ruins las ruinas
ruler (for measuring) la regla
to run correr
rush hour la hora punta
rusty oxidado(a)
rye el centeno

S

sad triste
saddle (bike) el sillín
(horse) la silla de montar
safe seguro(a)
is it safe? ¿es seguro(a)?
safe (for valuables) la caja fuerte
safety belt el cinturón de seguridad
safety pin el imperdible
to sail (sport, leisure) navegar
sailboard la tabla de windsurf
sailing (sport) la vela
sailing boat el velero
saint el/la santo(a)
salad la ensalada
green salad la ensalada verde
mixed salad la ensalada mixta
potato salad la ensalada de patatas
tomato salad la ensalada de tomate
salad dressing el aliño
salami el salchichón; el salami
salary el sueldo
sale(s) las rebajas
salesman/woman el/la vendedor(a)
sales rep el/la representante
salt la sal
salt water el agua salada
salty salado(a)
same mismo(a)
sample la muestra
sand la arena
sandals las sandalias
sandwich el bocadillo; el sándwich
toasted sandwich el sándwich tostado
sanitary towels las compresas
satellite dish la antena parabólica
satellite TV la televisión por satélite
satnav el sistema de navegación por
satélite
Saturday el sábado
sauce la salsa
tomato sauce la salsa de tomate
saucepan la cacerola
saucer el platillo
sauna la sauna
sausage la salchicha
to save (life) salvar
(money) ahorrar

savoury salado(a)
saw la sierra
to say decir
scales (weighing) el peso
to scan escanear
scan el escáner
scarf (woollen) la bufanda
(headscarf) el pañuelo
scenery el paisaje
schedule el programa
school la escuela
primary school la escuela primaria
secondary school el instituto de
enseñanza secundaria
scissors las tijeras
score (of match) la puntuación
to score a goal marcar un gol
Scot el escocés/la escocesa
Scotland Escocia
Scottish escocés/escocesa
scouring pad el estropajo
screen (computer, TV) la pantalla
screenwash el limpiacristales
screw el tornillo
screwdriver el destornillador
phillips screwdriver® el
destornillador de estrella
scuba diving el submarinismo
sculpture la escultura
sea el mar
seafood el/los marisco(s)
seam (of dress) la costura
to search buscar
search engine el buscador
seasick mareado(a)
seaside la playa
at the seaside en la playa
season (of year) la estación
(holiday) la temporada
in season del tiempo
seasonal estacional; de temporada
season ticket el abono
seasoning el condimento
seat (chair) la silla
(in bus, train) el asiento
seatbelt el cinturón de seguridad
seaweed las algas
second segundo(a)

second (time) el segundo
second class de segunda clase
second-hand de segunda mano
secretary el/la secretario(a)
security la seguridad
security check el control de seguridad
security guard el/la guarda de
seguridad
sedative el sedante
to see ver
self-catering sin servicio de comidas
self-employed autónomo(a)
self-service el self-service;
el autoservicio
to sell vender
do you sell...? ¿tiene...?
sell-by date la fecha de límite de venta
Sellotape® el celo
to send enviar
senior citizen el/la jubilado(a)
sensible sensato(a)
separated (couple) separado(a)
separately: *to pay separately* pagar
por separado
September septiembre
septic tank el pozo séptico; la fosa
séptica
serious (accident, etc) grave
to serve servir
service (in church) la misa
(in restaurant) el servicio
is service included? ¿está incluido
el servicio?
service charge el servicio
service station la estación de servicio
serviette la servilleta
set menu el menú del día
settee el sofá
several varios(as)
to sew coser
sex el sexo
shade la sombra
into the shade a la sombra
to shake (bottle) agitar
shallow poco profundo(a)
shampoo el champú
shampoo and set lavar y marcar
to share compartir; dividir

sharp (razor, knife) afilado(a)
to shave afeitarse
shaver la maquinilla de afeitar
shaving cream la crema de afeitar
shawl el chal
she ella
sheep la oveja
sheet (bed) la sábana
shelf el estante
shell (seashell) la concha
(egg, nut) la cáscara
sheltered protegido(a)
shepherd el/la pastor(a)
sherry el jerez
to shine brillar
shingles el herpes zóster; la culebrilla
ship el barco
shirt la camisa
shock el susto
(electric) la descarga
shock absorber el amortiguador
shoe el zapato
shoelaces los cordones (de los zapatos)
shoe polish el betún
shoe shop la zapatería
shop la tienda
to shop hacer las compras; comprar
shop assistant el/la dependiente(a)
shopping las compras
to go shopping ir de compras/tiendas
shopping centre el centro comercial
shore la orilla
short corto(a)
shortage la escasez
short circuit el cortocircuito
short cut el atajo
shorts los pantalones cortos
short-sighted miope
shoulder el hombro
to shout gritar
show (theatrical) el espectáculo
to show enseñar
shower (bath) la ducha
(rain) el chubasco
to take a shower ducharse
shower cap el gorro de ducha
shower gel el gel de ducha
to shrink encoger

shut (closed) cerrado(a)
to shut cerrar
shutters (outside) las persianas
shuttle service el servicio regular
 de enlace
sick (ill) enfermo(a)
I feel sick tengo ganas de vomitar
side el lado
side dish la guarnición
sidelight la luz de posición
sidewalk la acera
sieve (for liquids) el colador
(for flour, etc) el tamiz
sightseeing: to go sightseeing
 hacer turismo
sightseeing tour el recorrido turístico
sign la señal
to sign firmar
signal la señal; el tono
there's no signal no hay señal/tono
signature la firma
signpost la señal
silk la seda
silver la plata
SIM card la tarjeta SIM
similar to parecido(a) a
since desde; puesto que
since 1974 desde 1974
since you're not Spanish puesto que
 no es español(a)
to sing cantar
single (unmarried) soltero(a)
(bed, room) individual
single ticket el billete de ida
sink (in kitchen) el fregadero
sir señor
sister la hermana
sister-in-law la cuñada
to sit sentarse
sit down, please siéntese, por favor
site (website) el sitio
size (clothes) la talla
(shoes) el número
to skate patinar
skateboard el monopatín
skates los patines
skating rink la pista de patinaje
ski el esquí

to ski esquiar
ski boots las botas de esquí
skiing el esquí
ski instructor el/la monitor(a) de esquí
ski jump el salto de esquí
ski lift el telesquí
ski pants los pantalones de esquí
ski pass el forfait
ski pole/stick el bastón de esquí
ski run/piste la pista de esquí
ski suit el traje de esquí
to skid patinar
skin la piel
skirt la falda
sky el cielo
sledge el trineo
to sleep dormir
to sleep in quedarse dormido(a)
sleeper (on train) la litera
sleeping bag el saco de dormir
sleeping car el coche cama
sleeping mat la esterilla; la colchoneta
sleeping pill el somnífero
slice (of bread) la rebanada
(of ham) la loncha
sliced bread el pan de molde
slide (photo) la diapositiva
to slip resbalarse
slippers las zapatillas
slow lento(a)
to slow down reducir la velocidad
slowly despacio
small pequeño(a)
smaller than más pequeño(a) que
smell el olor
a bad smell un mal olor
a nice smell un buen olor
smile la sonrisa
to smile sonreír
to smoke fumar
can I smoke? ¿puedo fumar?
I don't smoke no fumo
smoke el humo
smoke alarm la alarma contra incendios
smoked ahumado(a)
smokers (sign) fumadores
smooth liso(a)
SMS message el mensaje SMS

snack el tentempié
to have a snack tomar algo
snack bar la cafetería
snake la serpiente
snake bite la mordedura de serpiente
to sneeze estornudar
to snore roncar
snorkel el esnórkel
snorkelling buceo con tubo (de respiración); buceo de superficie
snow la nieve
to snow nevar
it's snowing está nevando
snow board el snowboard
snowboarding: to go snowboarding ir a hacer snowboard
snow chains las cadenas (para la nieve)
snow tyres los neumáticos antideslizantes
snowed up aislado(a) por la nieve
soap el jabón
soap powder el detergente
sober sobrio(a)
socket (for plug) el enchufe
socks los calcetines
soda water la soda
sofa el sofá
sofa bed el sofá-cama
soft blando
soft drink el refresco
software el software
soldier el soldado
sole (of foot, shoe) la suela
soluble soluble
some algunos(as)
someone alguien
something algo
sometimes a veces
son el hijo
son-in-law el yerno
song la canción
soon pronto
as soon as possible lo antes posible
sore throat el dolor de garganta
sorry: sorry! ¡perdón!
I'm sorry! ¡lo siento!
sort el tipo

what sort? ¿qué tipo?
soup la sopa
sour amargo(a)
soured cream la nata agria
south el sur
souvenir el souvenir
spa el spa; el balneario
space el espacio
spade la pala
Spain España
Spaniard el/la español(a)
Spanish español(a)
spam (email) el spam; el correo basura
spanner la llave inglesa
spare parts los repuestos
spare room el cuarto de invitados
spare tyre la rueda de repuesto
spare wheel la rueda de repuesto
sparkling espumoso(a)
sparkling water el agua con gas
sparkling wine el vino espumoso
spark plug la bujía
to speak hablar
do you speak English? ¿habla inglés?
speaker (loudspeaker) el altavoz
special especial
specialist el/la especialista
speciality la especialidad
speed la velocidad
speedboat la lancha motora
speeding el exceso de velocidad
speeding ticket la multa por exceso
  de velocidad
speed limit la velocidad máxima
to exceed the speed limit exceder
  la velocidad máxima
speedometer el velocímetro
spell: *how is it spelt?* ¿cómo se
  escribe?
to spend (money) gastar
spice la especia
spicy picante
spider la araña
SPF (sun protection factor) el FPS
  (factor de protección solar)
to spill derramar
spinach las espinacas
spine la columna (vertebral)

spin-dryer la secadora-centrifugadora
spirits el alcohol
splinter la astilla
spoke (wheel) el radio
sponge la esponja
spoon la cuchara
sport el deporte
sports centre el polideportivo
sports shop la tienda de deportes
spot (pimple) la espinilla
sprain el esguince
spring (season) la primavera
(metal) el muelle
square (in town) la plaza
squash (game) el squash
to squeeze apretar
(lemon) exprimir
squid el calamar
stadium el estadio
stage el escenario
stain la mancha
stained glass la vidriera
stairs las escaleras
stale (bread) duro(a)
stalls (theatre) las butacas (de patio)
stamp (postage) el sello
to stand estar de pie
star la estrella
to start (car) poner en marcha
starter (in meal) entrante
(in car) la puesta en marcha
station la estación
stationer's la papelería
statue la estatua
stay la estancia
enjoy your stay! ¡que lo pase bien!
to stay (remain) quedarse
I'm staying at the hotel... estoy
  alojado(a) en el hotel...
steak el filete
to steal robar
steamed al vapor
steel el acero
steep: *is it steep?* ¿hay mucha
  pendiente?
steeple la aguja
steering wheel el volante
step el peldaño

stepdaughter la hijastra
stepfather el padrastro
stepmother la madrastra
stepson el hijastro
stereo el estéreo
sterling (pounds) las libras esterlinas
steward (on plane) el auxiliar de vuelo
stewardess (on plane) la azafata
to stick (with glue) pegar
sticking plaster la tirita®
still (not fizzy) sin gas
sting la picadura
to sting picar
stitches (surgical) los puntos
stockings las medias
stomach el estómago
stomach upset el trastorno estomacal
stone la piedra
to stop parar
store (shop) la tienda
storey el piso
storm la tormenta
(at sea) el temporal
story la historia
straightaway inmediatamente
straight on todo recto
strange extraño(a)
straw (for drinking) la pajita
strawberry la fresa
stream el arroyo
street la calle
street map el plano de la ciudad
strength la fuerza
stress el estrés
strike (of workers) la huelga
string la cuerda
striped a rayas
stroke (medical) la trombosis
strong fuerte
stuck: *it's stuck* está atascado(a)
student el/la estudiante
student discount el descuento
 para estudiantes
stuffed relleno(a)
stung picado(a)
stupid tonto(a)
subscription la suscripción
subtitles los subtítulos

subway (train) el metro
(passage) el paso subterráneo
suddenly de repente
suede el ante
sugar el azúcar
sugar-free sin azúcar
to suggest sugerir
suit (men's and women's) el traje
suitcase la maleta
sum la suma
summer el verano
summer holidays las vacaciones
 de verano
summit la cumbre
sun el sol
to sunbathe tomar el sol
sunblock la protección solar
sunburn la quemadura del sol
suncream el protector solar;
 la crema solar
Sunday el domingo
sunglasses las gafas de sol
sunny: *it's sunny* hace sol
sunrise la salida del sol
sunroof el techo solar
sunscreen el filtro solar
sunset la puesta de sol
sunshade la sombrilla
sunstroke la insolación
suntan el bronceado
suntan lotion el bronceador
supermarket el supermercado
supper la cena
supplement el suplemento
to supply suministrar
to surf hacer surf
to surf the net navegar por Internet
surfboard la tabla de surf
surgery (operation) la operación
surname el apellido
surprise la sorpresa
surrounded by rodeado(a) de
to survive sobrevivir
suspension (of car) la suspensión
to swallow tragar
to sweat sudar
sweater el jersey
sweatshirt la sudadera

sweet (not savoury) dulce
(dessert) el dulce
sweetener el edulcorante; la sacarina®
sweets los caramelos
to swell (injury, etc) hincharse
to swim nadar
swimming pool la piscina
swimsuit el bañador
swing (for children) el columpio
swipecard la tarjeta magnética
Swiss suizo(a)
switch el interruptor
to switch off apagar
to switch on encender
Switzerland Suiza
swollen hinchado(a)
synagogue la sinagoga
syringe la jeringuilla

T

table la mesa
tablecloth el mantel
tablespoon la cuchara de servir
table tennis el ping-pong
tablet (pill) la pastilla
tailor's la sastrería
to take (medicine, etc) tomar
how long does it take? ¿cuánto
 tiempo se tarda?
take-away (food) para llevar
to take off despegar
to take out (of bag, etc) sacar
talc los polvos de talco
to talk to hablar con
tall alto(a)
tampons los tampones
tangerine la mandarina
tank (petrol) el depósito
 (fish) la pecera
tap el grifo
tap water el agua corriente
tape (video) la cinta
tape measure el metro
tape recorder el casete
tart la tarta
taste el sabor
to taste probar
can I taste it? ¿puedo probarlo?

tax el impuesto
taxi el taxi
taxi driver el/la taxista
taxi rank la parada de taxis
tea el té
herbal tea la infusión
lemon tea el té con limón
strong tea el té cargado
teabag la bolsita de té
teapot la tetera
teaspoon la cucharilla
tea towel el paño de cocina
to teach enseñar
teacher el/la profesor(a)
team el equipo
tear (in material) el rasgón
teat (on baby's bottle) la tetina
teenager el/la adolescente
teeth los dientes
telegram el telegrama
telephone el teléfono
to telephone llamar por teléfono
telephone box la cabina (telefónica)
telephone call la llamada (telefónica)
telephone card la tarjeta telefónica
telephone directory la guía
 (telefónica)
telephone number el número
 de teléfono
television la televisión
to tell decir
temperature la temperatura
to have a temperature tener fiebre
temporary provisional
tenant el/la inquilino(a)
tendon el tendón
tennis el tenis
tennis ball la pelota de tenis
tennis court la pista de tenis
tennis racket la raqueta de tenis
tent la tienda de campaña
tent peg la estaca
terminal (airport) la terminal
terrace la terraza
to test (try out) probar
testicles los testículos
tetanus el tétanos
to text mandar un mensaje de texto a

text message el mensaje de texto
to text mandar un mensaje de texto a
I'll text you te mandaré un mensaje
than que
more than five más de cinco
more than you más que tú
to thank agradecer
thank you gracias
thank you very much muchas gracias
that ese/esa
(more remote) aquel/aquella
that one ése/ésa/eso
(more remote) aquél/ aquélla/aquello
the el/la/los/las
theatre el teatro
theft el robo
their su/sus
them ellos/ellas
(direct) los/las
there (over there) allí
there is/there are hay
thermometer el termómetro
these estos/estas
these ones éstos/éstas
they ellos/ellas
thick (not thin) grueso(a)
thief el ladrón/la ladrona
thigh el muslo
thin (person) delgado(a)
thing la cosa
my things mis cosas
to think pensar
(to be of opinion) creer
thirsty: *I'm thirsty* tengo sed
this este/esta/esto
this one éste/ésta
thorn la espina
those esos/esas
(more remote) aquellos/aquellas
those ones ésos/ésas
(more remote) aquéllos/aquéllas
thread el hilo
throat la garganta
throat lozenges las pastillas para
  la garganta
through por
thumb el pulgar
thunder el trueno

thunderstorm la tormenta
Thursday el jueves
thyme el tomillo
ticket (bus, train, etc) el billete
(entrance fee) la entrada
a book of tickets un abono
a return ticket un billete de ida y
  vuelta
a single ticket un billete de ida
a tourist ticket un billete turístico
ticket collector el/la revisor(a)
ticket office el despacho de billetes
tide (sea) la marea
high tide la marea alta
low tide la marea baja
tidy arreglado(a)
to tidy up ordenar
tie la corbata
tight (fitting) ajustado(a)
tights las medias
tile (roof) la teja
(floor) la baldosa
till (cash desk) la caja
(until) hasta
till 2 o'clock hasta las 2
time el tiempo
(clock) la hora
what time is it? ¿qué hora es?
timer (on cooker) el temporizador
timetable el horario
tin (can) la lata
tinfoil el papel de estaño
tin-opener el abrelatas
tip la propina
to tip dar propina
tipped (cigarette) con filtro
tired cansado(a)
tissues los kleenex®
to a
to London a Londres
to the airport al aeropuerto
toadstool el hongo venenoso
toast (to eat) la tostada
(raising glass) el brindis
tobacco el tabaco
tobacconist's el estanco
today hoy
toddler el/la niño(a) pequeño(a)

toe el dedo del pie
together juntos(as)
toilet los aseos; los servicios
toilet for disabled los servicios para minusválidos
toilet brush la escobilla del wáter
toilet paper el papel higiénico
toiletries los artículos de baño
token (for bus) el vale
toll (motorway) el peaje
tomato el tomate
tinned tomatoes los tomates en lata
tomato juice el zumo de tomate
tomato soup la sopa de tomate
tomorrow mañana
tomorrow morning mañana por la mañana
tomorrow afternoon mañana por la tarde
tomorrow evening mañana por la tarde/noche
tongue la lengua
tonic water la tónica
tonight esta noche
tonsillitis la amigdalitis
too (also) también
too big demasiado grande
too small demasiado pequeño(a)
too hot (food) demasiado caliente
too noisy demasiado ruidoso(a)
tool la herramienta
toolkit el juego de herramientas
tooth el diente
toothache el dolor de muelas
toothbrush el cepillo de dientes
toothpaste la pasta de dientes
toothpick el palillo
top: *the top floor* el último piso
top (of hill) la cima
(shirt) el top
(t-shirt) la camiseta
on top of... sobre...
topless: *to go topless* hacer topless
torch (flashlight) la linterna
torn rasgado(a)
total (amount) el total
to touch tocar
tough (meat) duro(a)

tour (trip) el viaje
(of museum, etc) la visita
guided tour la visita con guía
tour guide el/la guía turístico(a)
tour operator el/la tour operador(a)
tourist el/la turista
tourist office la oficina de turismo
tourist route la ruta turística
tourist ticket el billete turístico
to tow remolcar
towbar la barra de remolque
tow rope el cable de remolque
towel la toalla
tower la torre
town la ciudad
town centre el centro de la ciudad
town hall el ayuntamiento
town plan el plano de la ciudad
toxic tóxico(a)
toy el juguete
toy shop la juguetería
tracksuit el chándal
traditional tradicional
traffic el tráfico
traffic jam el atasco
traffic lights el semáforo
traffic warden el/la guardia de tráfico
trailer el remolque
train el tren
by train en tren
the first train el primer tren
the last train el último tren
the next train el próximo tren
trainers las zapatillas de deporte
tram el tranvía
tranquillizer el tranquilizante
to translate traducir
translation la traducción
to travel viajar
travel agent's la agencia de viajes
travel guide la guía de viajes
travel insurance el seguro de viaje
travel sickness el mareo
traveller's cheque el cheque de viaje
tray la bandeja
treatment el tratamiento
tree el árbol

trekking poles los bastones
  de trekking
trip la excursión
trolley (luggage, shopping) el carrito
trouble el apuro
to be in trouble estar en apuros
trousers los pantalones
truck el camión
true verdadero(a)
trunk (luggage) el baúl
trunks (swimming) el bañador
truth la verdad
to try (attempt) probar
to try on (clothes) probarse
t-shirt la camiseta
Tuesday el martes
tumble-dryer la secadora
tunnel el túnel
to turn girar
to turn around girar
to turn off (light, etc) apagar
(tap) cerrar
to turn on (light, etc) encender
(tap) abrir
turquoise (colour) turquesa
tweezers las pinzas
twice dos veces
twin-bedded room la habitación
  con dos camas
twins los/las mellizos(as)
identical twins los/las gemelos(as)
twisted torcido(a)
to type escribir a máquina
typical típico(a)
tyre el neumático
tyre pressure la presión
  de los neumáticos

U

ugly feo(a)
ulcer la úlcera
umbrella el paraguas
(sunshade) la sombrilla
uncle el tío
uncomfortable incómodo(a)
unconscious inconsciente
under debajo de
undercooked medio crudo

underground (metro) el metro
underpants los calzoncillos
underpass el paso subterráneo
to understand entender
do you understand? ¿entiende?
I don't understand no entiendo
underwear la ropa interior
underwater debajo del agua
to undress desvestirse
unemployed desempleado(a)
United Kingdom el Reino Unido
United States (los) Estados Unidos
university la universidad
unleaded petrol la gasolina sin plomo
unlikely poco probable
to unlock abrir (con llave)
to unpack (suitcases) deshacer
  las maletas
unpleasant desagradable
to unplug desenchufar
to unscrew destornillar
up: *to get up* levantarse
upstairs arriba
urgent urgente
urine la orina
us nosotros(as)
USA EE.UU.
USB flash drive (key drive) el lápiz
  USB; el USB flash drive
USB port el puerto USB
to use usar
useful útil
username el nombre de usuario
usual habitual
usually por lo general
U-turn el cambio de sentido

V

vacancy (in hotel) la habitación libre
vacant libre
vacation las vacaciones
vaccination la vacuna
vacuum cleaner la aspiradora
vagina la vagina
valid válido(a)
valley el valle
valuable de valor
valuables los objetos de valor

value el valor
valve la válvula
van la furgoneta
vase el florero
VAT el IVA
vegan vegetariano(a) estricto(a)
I'm vegan soy vegetariano(a) estricto(a)
vegetables las verduras
vegetarian vegetariano(a)
I'm vegetarian soy vegetariano(a)
vehicle el vehículo
vein la vena
velvet el terciopelo
vending machine la máquina
  expendedora
venereal disease la enfermedad
  venérea
ventilator el ventilador
very muy
vest la camiseta
vet el/la veterinario(a)
via por
to video (from TV) grabar (en vídeo)
video el vídeo
video camera la videocámara
video cassette la cinta de vídeo
video game el videojuego
video recorder el vídeo
video tape la cinta de vídeo
view la vista
village el pueblo
vinegar el vinagre
vineyard la viña
viper la víbora
virus el virus
visa el visado
visit la visita
to visit visitar
visiting hours (hospital) las horas
  de visita
visitor el/la visitante
vitamin la vitamina
voice la voz
voicemail el buzón de voz
volcano el volcán
volleyball el voleibol
voltage el voltaje
volts los vóltios

to vomit vomitar
voucher el vale; el bono

W
wage el sueldo
waist la cintura
waistcoat el chaleco
to wait for esperar
waiter/waitress el/la camarero(a)
waiting room la sala de espera
to wake up despertarse
Wales Gales
walk un paseo
to go for a walk dar un paseo
to walk andar
walking boots las botas de montaña
walking stick el bastón
wall (inside) la pared
(outside) el muro
wallet la cartera
to want querer
I want quiero
we want queremos
war la guerra
ward (hospital) la sala
wardrobe el armario
warehouse el almacén
warm caliente
it's warm (weather) hace calor
to warm up (milk, etc) calentar
warning triangle el triángulo
  señalizador
to wash (oneself) lavar(se)
wash and blow dry lavado y
  secado a mano
washbasin el lavabo
washing machine la lavadora
washing powder el detergente
washing-up bowl el barreño
washing-up liquid el líquido
  lavavajillas
wasp la avispa
wasp sting la picadura de avispa
waste bin el cubo de la basura
to watch (look at) mirar
watch el reloj
watchstrap la correa de reloj
water el agua

bottled water el agua mineral
drinking water el agua potable
hot/cold water el agua caliente/fría
mineral water el agua mineral
sparkling water el agua con gas
still water el agua sin gas
waterfall la cascada
water heater el calentador de agua
watermelon la sandía
waterproof impermeable
(watch) sumergible
to waterski hacer esquí acuático
watersports los deportes acuáticos
waterwings los manguitos
waves (on sea) las olas
waxing (hair removal) la depilación (con cera)
way (manner) la manera
(route) el camino
way in (entrance) la entrada
way out (exit) la salida
we nosotros(as)
weak (coffee, tea) poco cargado(a)
to wear llevar
weather el tiempo
weather forecast el pronóstico del tiempo
web (internet) el/la Internet
website la página web
wedding la boda
wedding anniversary el aniversario de boda
wedding present el regalo de boda
wedding ring la alianza
Wednesday el miércoles
week la semana
during the week durante la semana
last week la semana pasada
next week la semana que viene
per week por semana
this week esta semana
weekday el día laborable
weekend el fin de semana
next weekend el próximo fin de semana
this weekend este fin de semana
weekly semanal
weekly ticket el billete semanal
to weigh pesar

weight el peso
welcome! ¡bienvenido(a)!
well (water) el pozo
well bien
he's not well no se encuentra bien
well done (steak) muy hecho(a)
wellington boots las botas de agua
Welsh galés/galesa
(language) el galés
west el oeste
wet mojado(a)
(weather) lluvioso(a)
wetsuit el traje de bucear
what? ¿qué?
wheel la rueda
wheelchair la silla de ruedas
wheel clamp el cepo
when? ¿cuándo?
where? ¿dónde?
which? ¿cuál?
which one? ¿cuál?
which ones? ¿cuáles?
while: *in a while* dentro de un rato
whisky el whisky
white blanco(a)
who? ¿quién?
whole entero(a)
wholemeal bread el pan integral
whose? ¿de quién?
why? ¿por qué?
wide ancho(a)
widow la viuda
widower el viudo
width el ancho
wife la mujer
wi-fi la red inalámbrica; el WiFi
wig la peluca
wild salvaje
to win ganar
wind el viento
windbreak el cortavientos
windmill el molino de viento
window la ventana
(shop) el escaparate
(in car, train) la ventanilla
windscreen el parabrisas
windscreen wipers los limpiaparabrisas

to windsurf hacer windsurf
windy: *it's windy* hace viento
wine el vino
red wine el (vino) tinto
white wine el vino blanco
dry wine el vino seco
rosé wine el (vino) rosado
sparkling wine el (vino) espumoso
house wine el vino de la casa
wine list la carta de vinos
wing el ala
wing mirror el retrovisor exterior
winter el invierno
wire el alambre
wireless inalámbrico
wireless internet el/la Internet WiFi
with con
with ice con hielo
with milk con leche
with sugar con azúcar
without sin
without ice sin hielo
without milk sin leche
without sugar sin azúcar
woman la mujer
wonderful maravilloso(a)
wood (material) la madera
(forest) el bosque
wooden de madera
wool la lana
word la palabra
work el trabajo
to work (person) trabajar
(machine, car) funcionar
it doesn't work no funciona
work permit el permiso de trabajo
world el mundo
world-wide mundial
worried preocupado(a)
worse peor
worth: *it's worth...* vale...
to wrap (parcel) envolver
wrapping paper el papel de envolver
wrinkles las arrugas
wrist la muñeca
to write escribir
please write it down escríbalo,
por favor

writing paper el papel de escribir
wrong: *what's wrong* ¿qué pasa?
wrought iron el hierro forjado

X

X-ray la radiografía
to x-ray hacer una radiografía

Y

yacht el yate
year el año
last year el año pasado
next year el año que viene
this year este año
yearly anual; anualmente
yellow amarillo(a)
Yellow Pages las páginas amarillas
yes sí
yesterday ayer
yet: *not yet* todavía no
yoghurt el yogur
plain yoghurt el yogur natural
yolk la yema
you (polite singular) usted
(polite plural) ustedes
(singular with friends) tú
(plural with friends) vosotros
young joven
your (polite) su/sus
(familiar) tu/tus
youth hostel el albergue juvenil

Z

zebra crossing el paso de peatones
zero el cero
zip la cremallera
zone la zona
zoo el zoo
zoom lens el zoom
zucchini el calabacín

Dictionary

A

a to; at
a la estación to the station
a las 4 at 4 o'clock
a 30 kilómetros 30 km away
abadejo *m* haddock
abadía *f* abbey
abajo below; downstairs
abanico *m* fan *(hand-held)*
abeja *f* bee
abierto(a) open
abogado(a) *m/f* lawyer
abonado(a) *m/f* season-ticket holder
abonado a canal/a la televisión digital subscriber
abonar to pay; to credit
abono *m* season ticket
aborto *m* abortion
aborto natural miscarriage
abrebotellas *m* bottle opener
abrelatas *m* tin-opener
abrigo *m* coat
abril *m* April
abrir to open; to turn on *(tap)*
abrocharse to fasten *(seatbelt, etc)*
absceso *m* abscess
abuela *f* grandmother
abuelo *m* grandfather
aburrido(a) boring
acá *esp Lat. Am.* here
acabar to finish
acampar to camp
acceso *m* access
acceso andenes to the platforms
acceso prohibido no access
acceso vías to the platforms
¿tiene acceso a Internet? do you have internet access?
accidente *m* accident
aceite *m* oil
aceite bronceador suntan oil
aceite de girasol sunflower oil
aceite de oliva olive oil
aceituna *f* olive

aceitunas aliñadas marinated olives
aceitunas rellenas stuffed olives
acelerador *m* accelerator
acento *m* accent
aceptar to accept
acera *f* pavement; sidewalk
acero *m* steel
ácido *m* acid
acompañar to accompany
aconsejar to advise
acto *m* act
en el acto while you wait *(repairs)*
actor *m* actor
actriz *f* actress
acuerdo *m* agreement
¡de acuerdo! OK; alright
alojamiento y desayuno accommodation and breakfast
adaptador *m* adaptor
adelantar to overtake *(in car)*
adelante forward
adicional extra; additional
adiós goodbye; bye
administración *f* management
admitir to accept; to permit
no se admiten... ...not permitted
adolescente *m/f* teenager
aduana *f* customs
adulto(a) *m/f* adult
advertir to warn
aerodeslizador *m* hovercraft
aerolínea *f* airline
aeropuerto *m* airport
aerosol *m* aerosol
afeitarse to shave
aficionado(a) *m/f* fan *(cinema, jazz, etc)*
afilado(a) sharp *(razor, knife)*
afiliado(a) affiliated, member
afta *f* thrush
agencia *f* agency
agencia inmobiliaria state agent's
agencia de seguros insurance company
agencia de viajes travel agency
agenda *f* diary; personal organizer

agenda electrónica electronic organizer
agente *m/f* agent
agente de policía policeman/woman
agitar to shake *(bottle)*
agosto *m* August
agotado(a) sold out; out of stock
agradable pleasant
agradecer to thank
agridulce sweet and sour
agua *f* water
agua caliente/fría hot/cold water
agua destilada distilled water
agua dulce fresh water
agua mineral mineral water
agua potable drinking water
agua salada salt water
agudo(a) sharp; pointed
águila *f* eagle
aguja *f* needle; hand *(on watch)*
aguja hipodérmica hypodermic needle
aguja de coser needle
agujero *m* hole
ahogarse to drown
ahora now
ahorrar to save *(money)*
ahumado(a) smoked
aire *m* air
aire acondicionado air-conditioning
al aire libre open-air; outdoor
ajo *m* garlic
ala *f* wing
alargador *m* extension lead
alarma *f* alarm
albahaca *f* basil
albarán *m* delivery note
albaricoque *m* apricot
albergue *m* hostel
albergue juvenil youth hostel
alcanzar to reach; to get
alcohol *m* alcohol; spirits
alcohólico(a) alcoholic
alemán(mana) German
Alemania *f* Germany
alergia *f* allergy
alergia al polen hay fever
alérgico(a) a allergic to
aletas *fpl* flippers
alfarería *f* pottery

alfiler *m* pin
alfombra *f* carpet; rug
alforjas *fpl* panniers *(for bike)*
algas *fpl* seaweed
algo something
algodón *m* cotton
algodón hidrófilo cotton wool
alguien someone
alguno(a) some; any
algunos(as) some; a few
alicates *mpl* pliers
alimentación *f* grocer's; food
alimento *m* food
aliño *m* dressing *(for food)*
allí there *(over there)*
almacén *m* store; warehouse
grandes almacenes department stores
almendra *f* almond
almohada *f* pillow
almuerzo *m* lunch
alojamiento *m* accommodation
alpargatas *fpl* espadrilles
alquilar to rent; to hire
se alquila for hire
alquiler *m* rent; rental
alquiler de coches car hire
alrededor about; around
altavoz *m* loudspeaker
alto(a) high; tall
alta tensión high voltage
altura *f* altitude; height
alubia *f* bean
alubias blancas butter beans
alubias pintas red kidney beans
amable pleasant; kind
amapola *f* poppy
amargo(a) bitter; sour
amarillo(a) yellow; amber *(traffic light)*
ambientador *m* air freshener
ambos(as) both
ambulancia *f* ambulance
ambulancia aérea air ambulance
ambulatorio *m* health centre
América del Norte *f* North America
amigo(a) *m/f* friend
amigo(a) por correspondencia
  penfriend
amor *m* love

amortiguador *m* shock absorber
ampolla *f* blister
analgésico *m* painkiller
análisis *m* analysis
análisis de sangre blood test
ananá(s) *m* pineapple
ancho *m* width
ancho(a) wide
anchoa *f* anchovy *(salted)*
anchura *f* width
ancla *f* anchor
Andalucía *f* Andalusia
andaluz(a) Andalusian
andar to walk
andén *m* platform
añejo(a) mature; vintage
anestesia *f* anaesthetic
anestesia general general anaesthetic
anestesia local local anaesthetic
anfiteatro *m* circle *(theatre)*
angina (de pecho) *f* angina
anillo *m* ring
animal *m* animal
animal doméstico pet
anís *m* aniseed liqueur; anisette
aniversario *m* anniversary
aniversario de boda wedding anniversary
año *m* year
Año Nuevo New Year
ante *m* suede
antena *f* aerial; antenna
antena parabólica satellite dish
anteojos *mpl (Lat. Am.)* binoculars
antes (de) before
antiácido *m* antacid
antibiótico *m* antibiotic
anticonceptivo *m* contraceptive
anticongelante *m* antifreeze
anticuario *m* antique shop
anticuario(a) m/f antique dealer
anticuario *adj* antiquarian
antigüedades *fpl* antiques
tienda de antigüedades antique shop
antiguo(a) old; ancient
antihistamínico *m* antihistamine
antiséptico *m* antiseptic
anual annual
anular to cancel

anunciar to announce; to advertise
anuncio *m* advertisement; notice
anzuelo *m* hook *(fishing)*
apagado(a) off *(light, etc)*
apagar to switch off; to turn off
aparato *m* appliance
aparato de aire acondicionado
  air-conditioning unit
aparcamiento *m* car park
aparcar to park
apartado de Correos *m* PO Box
apartamento *m* flat; apartment
apellido *m* surname
apendicitis *f* appendicitis
aperitivo *m* aperitif *(drink)*; appetizer;
  snack *(food)*
apertura *f* opening
apio *m* celery
aplazar to postpone
apostar por to bet on
aprender to learn
apretar to squeeze
apto(a) suitable
aquí here
aquí tiene... here is...
araña *f* spider
árbitro *m* referee
árbol *m* tree
arco iris *m* rainbow
ardor de estómago *m* heartburn
arena *f* sand
armario *m* wardrobe; cupboard
arquitecto(a) *m/f* architect
arquitectura *f* architecture
arrancar to start
arreglar to fix; to mend
arriba upstairs; above
hacia arriba upward(s)
arroyo *m* stream
arroz *m* rice
arruga *f* wrinkle
arte *m* art
artesanía *f* crafts
artesano(a) *m/f* craftsman/woman
articulación *f* joint *(body)*
artículo *m* article
artículos de ocasión bargains
artículos de regalo gifts

artículos de tocador/baño toiletries
artista *m/f* artist
artritis *f* arthritis
asado(a) roast
asar a la parrilla/brasa to barbecue
ascensor *m* lift
asegurado(a) insured
asegurar to insure
aseos *mpl* toilets
asiento *m* seat
asiento de niños child safety seat
asiento elevador m booster seat
asistencia *f* help; assistance
asistencia técnica repairs
asma *m* asthma
aspiradora *f* vacuum cleaner
aspirina *f* aspirin
astilla *f* splinter
atacar to attack
atajo *m* short cut
ataque *m* fit *(seizure)*
ataque al corazón heart attack
ataque de asma asthma attack
ataque epiléptico epileptic fit
atascado(a) jammed *(stuck)*
atasco *m* hold-up *(traffic jam)*
atención *f* attention
atención al cliente customer service
aterrizar to land
ático *m* attic; loft
atracadero *m* mooring
atraco *m* mugging *(person)*
atrás behind
atropellar to knock down *(car)*
ATS *m/f* nurse
atún *m* tuna fish
audífono *m* hearing aid
aumentar to increase
auricular *m* receiver *(phone)*
auriculares *mpl* headphones
auténtico(a) genuine; real
autobús *m* bus
autocar *m* coach *(bus)*
autoestop *m* hitch-hiking
automático(a) automatic
autónomo(a) self-employed
autónomo freelancer
autopista *f* motorway

autor(a) *m/f* author
autoservicio *m* self-service
autovía dual carriageway
auxiliar de vuelo *m/f* air steward/
 stewardess
Av./Avda. *abbrev. for* **avenida**
avalancha *f* avalanche
ave *f* bird
aves de corral poultry
avellana *f* hazelnut
avena *f* oats
avenida *f* avenue
avería *f* breakdown *(car)*
averiado(a) out of order; broken down
avión *m* airplane; aeroplane
avión sanitario; ambulancia aérea
 air ambulance
aviso *m* notice; warning
avispa *f* wasp
ayer yesterday
ayudar to help
ayuntamiento *m* town/city hall
azafata *f* air hostess; stewardess
azafrán *m* saffron
azúcar *m* sugar
azúcar glas(é) icing sugar
azul blue
azul claro light blue
azul marino dark/navy blue
día azul cheap day for train travel
zona azul controlled parking area

B
babero *m* baby's bib
baca *f* roof rack
bahía *f* bay *(along coast)*
bailar to dance
baile *m* dance
bajar to go down(stairs); to drop
 (temperature)
bajarse (del) to get off *(bus, etc)*
bajo(a) low; short; soft *(sound)*
bajo en calorías low-fat
más bajo lower
balcón *m* balcony
balneario *m* spa
balón *m* ball
baloncesto *m* basketball

balsa f raft
balsa salvavidas f life raft
bañador m swimming costume/trunks
banana f banana
bañarse to go swimming; to bathe; to have a bath
banca f banking; bank
banco m bank; bench
banda f band *(musical)*
banda ancha broadband
bandeja f tray
bandera f flag
bañista m/f bather
baño m bath; bathroom
con baño with bath
bar m bar
bar de cóctel cocktail bar
barato(a) cheap
barba f beard
barbacoa f barbecue
barbería f barber's
barbilla f chin
barca f small boat
barco m ship; boat
barco de vela sailing boat
barra f bar; counter; bread stick
barra de labios lipstick
barra de pan French bread
barreño (de plástico) m washing-up bowl
barrera f barrier; crash barrier
barrio m district; suburb
barrio chino red light district
barro m mud
bastante enough; quite
bastón m walking stick
bastón de esquí ski pole/stick
bastones de trekking mpl trekking poles
basura f rubbish; litter
bata f dressing gown
bate m bat *(baseball, cricket)*
batería f battery *(in car)*; musical instrument *(drums)*
batería de cocina set of kitchen equipment
batido m milkshake
batidora f blender *(hand-held)*
baúl m trunk *(luggage)*

bautizo m christening
to be ser; estar
bebé m baby
beber to drink
bebida f drink
bebida sin alcohol soft drink
beicon m bacon
béisbol m baseball
berenjena f aubergine/eggplant
berro m watercress
berza f cabbage
besar to kiss
beso m kiss
betún m shoe polish
biberón m baby's bottle
biblioteca f library
bici f bicycle
bicicleta f bicycle
bicicleta de cross f BMX
bicicleta de montaña mountain bike
bien well
bienvenido(a) welcome
bifurcación f fork *(in road)*
bigote m moustache
billete m ticket
billete de ida single ticket
billete de ida y vuelta return ticket
billetera f wallet
bistec m steak
bisutería f costume jewellery
blanco(a) white
dejar en blanco leave blank *(on form)*
blando(a) soft
bloc m note pad
blusa f blouse
boca f mouth
bocadillo m sandwich *(made with French bread)*
boda f wedding
bodega f wine cellar; restaurant
bolígrafo m biro; pen
bollo m roll; bun
bolsa f bag; stock exchange
bolsa de basura rubbish/bin bag
bolsa de plástico plastic bag
bolsa de playa beach bag
bolsillo m pocket
bolsita de té f teabag

bolso *m* handbag
bomba *f* pump *(bike, etc)*; bomb
bomba de bicicleta bicycle pump
bombero(a) *m/f* fireman/woman;
firefighter
bomberos *mpl* fire brigade
bombilla *f* light bulb
bombona de gas *f* gas cylinder
bombonería *f* confectioner's
bombones *mpl* chocolates
bonito(a) pretty; nice-looking
bono *m* voucher
bonobús *m* bus pass
borracho(a) drunk
bosque *m* forest; wood
bota *f* boot
bote *m* boat; tin; can
bote neumático rubber dinghy
bote salvavidas lifeboat
botella *f* bottle
botón *m* button
bragas *fpl* knickers
brazo *m* arm
brécol *m* broccoli
bricolaje *m* do-it-yourself; DIY
brillar to shine
brindis *m* toast *(raising glass)*
británico(a) British
broma *f* joke
bromear to joke
bronceado *m* suntan
bronceado(a) sun-tanned
bronceador *m* suntan lotion
broncearse to tan
bronquitis *f* bronchitis
brújula *f* compass
bucear to dive
buceo con tubo (de respiración)
snorkelling
bueno(a) good; fine
¡buenos días! good morning!
¡buenas tardes! good afternoon/evening!
¡buenas noches! good evening/night!
bufanda *f* scarf *(woollen)*
bufé *m* buffet
búho *m* owl
bujía *f* spark plug
bulto *m* lump *(swelling)*

buñuelo *m* fritter; doughnut
bunyi *m* bungee jumping
buscador *m* search engine
buscar to look for
butacas *fpl* stalls *(theatre)*
butano *m* Calor gas®
butifarra *f* Catalan sausage
buzón *m* postbox; letterbox
buzón de voz voicemail

C

caballeros *mpl* gents
caballo *m* horse
montar a caballo to go riding
cabello *m* hair
cabeza *f* head
cabina *f* cabin
cabina (telefónica) phone box
cable *m* wire; cable
cable de cambio gear cable
cable de freno brake cable
cable de remolque tow rope
cables de arranque jump leads
cabra *f* goat
cacahuete *m* peanut
cacao *m* cocoa
cacao para los labios lip salve
cacerola *f* saucepan
cachemira *f* cashmere
cada every; each
cada día daily *(each day)*
cada uno each (one)
cadena chain; channel *(TV)*; WC cistern
cadena de música music centre;
music radio station
cadera *f* hip
caducado(a) out-of-date
caducar to expire *(ticket, passport)*
caer(se) to fall
café *m* café; coffee; coffee-shop
(café) cortado espresso with a dash of
milk
(café) descafeinado decaff coffee
(café) exprés/expreso espresso coffee
café con hielo iced coffee
café con leche white coffee
café en grano coffee beans
café instantáneo instant coffee

café molido ground coffee
café solo black coffee
corto de café milky coffee
cafetera *f* cafetière
cafetería *f* snack bar; café
caja *f* cashdesk; box
caja de ahorros savings bank
caja de cambios gearbox
caja de fusibles fuse box
caja fuerte safe
cajero(a) *m/f* teller; cashier
cajero automático cash dispenser;
  auto-teller
cajón *m* drawer
calabacín *m* courgette/zucchini
calabaza *f* pumpkin
calamares *mpl* squid
calambre *m* cramp
calcetines *mpl* socks
calculadora *f* calculator
caldereta *f* stew *(fish, lamb)*
caldo *m* stock; consommé
calefacción *f* heating
calendario *m* calendar
calentador *m* heater
calentador de agua water heater
calentar to heat up *(milk, etc)*
calentura *f* cold sore
calidad *f* quality
caliente hot
calle *f* street; fairway *(golf)*
callejón sin salida *m* cul-de-sac
calmante *m* painkiller
calvo(a) bald
calzada *f* roadway
calzada deteriorada uneven road surface
calzado *m* footwear
calzados shoe shop
calzoncillos *mpl* underpants
cama *f* bed
dos camas twin beds
cama individual single bed
cama de matrimonio double bed
cámara *f* camera; inner tube
cámara digital *f* digital camera
camarera *f* waitress; chambermaid
camarero *m* barman; waiter
camarote *m* cabin

cambiar to change; to exchange
cambiarse to get changed
cambio *m* change; exchange; gear
caminar to walk
camino *m* path; road; route
camino particular private road
camión *m* lorry
camioneta *f* estate car
camisa *f* shirt
camisería *f* shirt shop
camiseta *f* t-shirt; vest
camisón *m* nightdress
campana *f* bell
camping *m* campsite
campo *m* countryside; field; pitch
campo de fútbol football pitch
campo de golf golf course
caña *f* cane; rod
caña (de cerveza) glass of beer
caña de pescar fishing rod
Canadá *m* Canada
canadiense Canadian
Canal de la Mancha *m* English Channel
canasto *m* large basket
cancelación *f* cancellation
cancelar to cancel
cáncer *m* cancer
cancha court
cancha de baloncesto basketball court
cancha de tenis *f* tennis court
canción *f* song
candado *m* padlock
candado de bicicleta bike lock
candela *f* candle; fire
canela *f* cinnamon
canguro *m* kangaroo
canguro *m/f* babysitter
canoa *f* canoe
cansado(a) tired
cantante *m/f* singer
cantar to sing
cantidad *f* quantity
capilla *f* chapel
capital *f* capital *(city)*
capitán *m* captain
capó *m* bonnet; hood *(of car)*
capucha *f* hood *(jacket)*
capuchino *m* cappuccino

cara *f* face
caramelo *m* sweet; caramel
caravana *f* caravan
carbón *m* coal
carbón vegetal charcoal
carbón dulce symbolic sweet resembling a piece of charcoal given to children for Christmas and for *día de Reyes* (6th of January) when they haven't behaved well during the year.
carburador *m* carburettor
carburante *m* fuel
cárcel *f* prison
carga *f* charge
no tengo batería I've run out of charge
necesito cargar el teléfono I need to charge my phone
cargador *m* recharger
cargador de móvil mobile phone charger
cargar to load; charge
cargar en cuenta to charge to account
cargo *m* charge
a cargo del cliente at the customer's expense
Caribe *m* Caribbean
carnaval *m* carnival
carne *f* meat
carne asada roast meat
carne picada mince *(meat)*
carné de conducir *m* driving licence
carné de identidad *m* identity card *(DNI)*
carnicería *f* butcher's
caro(a) dear; expensive
carpintería *f* carpenter's shop
carrera *f* career; race *(sport)*
carrete *m* film *(for camera)*; fishing reel
carretera *f* road
carretera comarcal secondary road, B-road
carretera nacional A-road
carretera de circunvalación ring road
carril *m* lane *(on road)*
carrito *m* trolley
carta *f* letter; playing card; menu
carta aérea air mail letter
carta certificada registered letter
carta de vinos wine list
carta verde green card

cartel *m* poster
cartelera *f* entertainments guide
cartera *f* wallet; briefcase
carterista *m/f* pickpocket
cartero(a) *m/f* postman/woman
cartón *m* cardboard
casa *f* house; home; household
casa de socorro first-aid post
casado(a) married
casarse (con) to marry
cascada *f* waterfall
cáscara *f* shell *(egg, nut)*
casco *m* helmet
casero(a) home-made
comida casera home cooking
caseta *f* beach hut; kennel
casete *m* cassette; tape recorder
casi almost
caso: *en caso de* in case of
caspa *f* dandruff
castaña *f* chestnut
castañuelas *fpl* castanets
castellano(a) Spanish; Castilian
castillo *m* castle
catalán/catalana Catalonian
catalizador *m* catalytic converter
catálogo *m* catalogue
catedral *f* cathedral
católico(a) Catholic
causa *f* cause
a causa de because of
causar to cause
cava *m* cava; sparkling white wine
caza *f* hunting; game
cazar to hunt
CD-ROM *m* CD ROM
cebo *m* bait *(for fishing)*
cebolla *f* onion
ceder to give way
ceda el paso give way
celeste light blue
celo *m* Sellotape®
celoso(a) jealous
cementerio *m* cemetery
cena *f* dinner; supper
cenar to have dinner
cenicero *m* ashtray
centímetro *m* centimetre

céntimo m euro cent
centralita f switchboard
centro m centre
centro de negocios business centre
Centroamérica f Central America
cepillo m brush
cepillo de dientes toothbrush
cepillo del pelo hairbrush
cepillo de uñas nailbrush
cepillo de barrer/para el suelo scrubbing brush
cera f wax
hacerse la cera to wax one's legs or arms, etc.
cera facial facial wax
cera corporal body wax
cerámica f ceramics; pottery
cerca (de) near; close to
cercanías fpl outskirts
tren de cercanías suburban train
cerdo m pig; pork
cereza f cherry
cerillas fpl matches
cero m zero
cerrado(a) closed
cerrado por reforma closed for repairs
cerradura f lock
cerrar con llave to lock
cerro m hill
certificado m certificate
certificado(a) registered
certificar to register
cervecería f pub
cerveza f beer; lager
cesta f basket
cestería f basketwork (shop)
chalet (sing); **chalets** pl m villa
chaleco m waistcoat
chaleco salvavidas life jacket
champán m champagne
champiñón m mushroom
champú m shampoo
chancl(et)as fpl flip flops
chaqueta f jacket
charcutería f delicatessen
chat; sala de chat (internet) chatroom
cheque m cheque
cheque de viaje traveller's cheque

cheque al portador cheque payable to the bearer
chica f girl
chichón m lump (on head)
chico m boy
chico(a) small
chile m chilli
chimenea f fireplace; chimney
chiringuito m beach bar; stall
chocar to crash (car)
chocolate m chocolate; hot chocolate
chocolate puro/negro plain chocolate
chocolate blanco white chocolate
chocolate con leche milk chocolate
chófer m chauffeur; driver
chorizo m hard pork sausage
chubasco m shower (rain)
chuleta f cutlet; chop
chupete m dummy (for baby)
churrería f stand or stall selling **churros** with different shapes and fillings
churro m thin/thick fritter batter stick sprinkled with sugar, usually eaten with thick hot chocolate
ciclismo de montaña m mountain biking
ciclista m/f cyclist
ciego(a) blind
cielo m sky; heaven
cien hundred
CIF m tax number (for business)
cifra f number; figure
cigarra f cicada
cigarrillo m cigarette
cigarro m cigar; cigarette
cima f top; peak
cine m cinema
cine de verano open-air cinema
cinta f tape; ribbon
cinta de vídeo video cassette
cinta virgen blank tape
cinta métrica tape measure
cinta limpiadora head-cleaning tape
cinta aislante insulating tape
cinta adhesiva (also known as **celo**, **celofán** or **fixo**) sellotape
cintura f waist
cinturón m belt
cinturón de seguridad safety belt

circulación f traffic
circular to drive; to circulate
circule por la derecha keep right *(road sign)*
ciruela f plum
ciruela pasa prune
cirujano(a) m/f surgeon
cirujano plástico plastic surgeon
cisterna f cistern; tank
cistitis f cystitis
cita f appointment
ciudad f city; town
ciudadano(a) m/f citizen
clarete m light red wine
claro(a) light *(colour)*; clear
clase f class; type; lesson
clase preferente club/business class
clase turista economy class
clavícula f collar bone
clavija f peg
clavo m nail *(metal)*; clove *(spice)*
cliente m/f customer; client
climatizado(a) air-conditioned
clínica f clinic; private hospital
club nocturno m night club
cobrador m conductor *(train, bus)*
cobrar to charge; to cash
cobrar demasiado to overcharge
cobro m payment
cobro revertido (call) reverse charge
cocer to cook; to boil
coche m car; coach *(on train)*
coche cama m sleeping car
coche comedor m dining car
coche restaurante m restaurant car
cochecito (de bebé) m pram
cocido m thick stew
cocido(a) cooked; boiled
cocina f kitchen; cooker; cuisine
cocinar to cook
coco m coconut
código m code
código de barras barcode
código postal postcode
codo m elbow
coger to catch; to get; to pick up *(phone)*
cola f glue; queue; tail
colador m strainer; colander
colcha beadspread

colchón m mattress
colchoneta f sleeping mat
colega m/f colleague
colegio m school
colgante pendant
colgar to hang up
coliflor f cauliflower
colina f hill
colisionar to crash
collar m necklace
color m colour
columna vertebral f spine
columpio m swing *(for children)*
comedor m dining room
comenzar to begin
comer to eat
comercio m trade; business
comestibles mpl groceries
comida f food; meal
se sirven comidas meals served
comidas caseras home cooking
comisaría f police station
como as; like; since
¿cómo? how?; pardon?
cómodo(a) comfortable
compañero(a) m/f colleague; partner
compañía f company
compartimento m compartment
completo(a) full; no vacancies
comportarse to behave
compositor(a) m/f composer
compra f purchase
compras shopping
comprar to buy
comprender to understand
compresa f sanitary towel
comprobar to check
con with
concha f sea-shell
concierto m concert
concurrido(a) busy; crowded
concurso m competition; quiz
condón m condom
conducir to drive
conductor(a) m/f driver
conectar to connect; to plug in
conejo m rabbit
conferencia f conference

confirmación _f_ confirmation
confirmar to confirm
confitería _f_ cake shop
confitura _f_ jam
congelado(a) frozen
congelador _m_ freezer
conjunto _m_ group _(music)_; outfit
conmoción cerebral _f_ concussion
conocer to know; to be acquainted with
conseguir to obtain
conserje _m_ caretaker
conservar to keep
conservas _fpl_ tinned foods
consigna _f_ left-luggage office
construir to build
consulado _m_ consulate
consultorio _m_ doctor's surgery
consumición _f_ consumption; drink
consumir to eat; to use
consumir (preferentemente) antes de... best before...
contacto _m_ contact; ignition _(car)_
contador _m_ meter
contagioso(a) infectious
contaminado(a) polluted
contener to hold _(to contain)_
contenido _m_ contents
contento(a) pleased
contestador automático _m_ answerphone
contestar to answer; to reply
continuación _f_ sequel
continuar to continue
contra against
contrareembolso cash on delivery.
contrato _m_ contract
control _m_ inspection; check
control de seguridad security check
convento _m_ convent; monastery
copa _f_ glass; goblet
copa de helado mixed ice cream
tomar una copa to have a drink
copia _f_ copy; print _(photo)_
copiar to copy
corazón _m_ heart
corbata _f_ tie
corcho _m_ cork
cordero _m_ lamb; mutton

cordillera _f_ mountain range
coro _m_ choir
corral: de corral free-range
correa _f_ strap; belt
correa de reloj watchstrap
correa del perro dog's lead
correcto(a) right _(correct)_
correo _m_ mail
correo basura spam
correo electrónico e-mail
correo certificado registered post
correo urgente special delivery
Correos _m_ post office
correr to run
corrida de toros _f_ bullfight
corriente _f_ power; current _(electric, water)_; draught _(of air)_
cortacircuito(s) _m_ circuit breaker
cortado _m_ espresso coffee with dash of milk
cortado(a) blocked _(road)_; shy
cortar to cut
cortauñas _m_ nail clippers
corte _m_ cut
cortina _f_ curtain
corto(a) short
cortocircuito(s) short circuit
cosa _f_ thing
cosecha _f_ harvest; vintage _(wine)_
coser to sew
costa _f_ coast
costar to cost
costero(a) coastal
costumbre _f_ custom _(tradition)_
coto _m_ reserve
coto de caza/pesca hunting/fishing by licence
crédito _m_ credit
a crédito on credit
creer to think; to believe
crema _f_ cream _(lotion)_
crema bronceadora/solar suntan lotion
crema de afeitar shaving cream
cremallera _f_ zip
crisis nerviosa _f_ nervous breakdown
cruce _m_ junction; crossroads
crucero _m_ cruise
crucigrama _m_ crossword puzzle

crudo(a) raw
cruzar to cross
c/u (cada uno) each (one)
cuaderno *m* exercise book; notebook
cuadro *m* picture; painting
a/de cuadros checked *(pattern)*
cuajada *f* curd
¿cuál? which?
¿cuándo? when?
¿cuánto? how much?
¿cuántos? how many?
cuarentena *f* quarantine
Cuaresma *f* Lent
cuarto *m* room
cuarto de baño bathroom
cuarto de estar living room
cubierto *m* cover charge *(in restaurant);* menu
cubierto(a) covered; indoor
cubiertos *mpl* cutlery
cubo *m* bucket; pail; bin
cubrir to cover
cucaracha *f* cockroach
cuchara *f* spoon
cuchara de postre dessert spoon
cuchara de servir tablespoon
cucharilla *f* teaspoon
cuchillo *m* knife
cuenta *f* bill; account
cuerda *f* string; rope
cuero *m* leather
cuerpo *m* body
cuidado *m* care
¡cuidado! look out!
¡(ten) cuidado! (be) careful!
cuidado con el escalón mind the step!
cuidadoso(a) careful
cultivar to grow; to farm
cumpleaños *m* birthday
¡feliz cumpleaños! happy birthday!
cuna *f* cradle; cot
cuñado(a) *m/f* brother/sister-in-law
curva *f* bend; curve
curvas peligrosas dangerous bends

D

dado *mpl* dice
daltónico(a) colour-blind

daños *mpl* damage
dar to give
dar de comer to feed
dar marcha atrás to reverse
dar propina to tip *(waiter, etc)*
dar un paseo to go for a walk
dátil *m* date *(fruit)*
datos *mpl* data; information
dcha. abbrev. for **derecha**
de of; from
de acuerdo all right *(agreed)*
debajo (de) under; underneath
deber to owe; to have to
debido(a) a due to
decir to tell; to say
declarar to declare
dedo *m* finger
dedo anular ring finger
dedo gordo/pulgar thumb; big toe
dedo índice index finger
dedo meñique little finger
dedo del pie toe
defecto *m* fault; defect
de granja/corral free-range
degustación *f* tasting *(wine, etc)*
dejar to let; to leave
dejar libre la salida keep clear
delante de in front of
delegación *f* regional office *(government)*
delgado(a) thin; slim
delicioso(a) delicious
delito *m* crime
demasiado too much
demasiado hecho(a) overdone
demora *f* delay
denominación de origen *f* guarantee of quality of food products
dentadura postiza *f* dentures
dentífrico *m* toothpaste
dentista *m/f* dentist
dentro (de) inside
departamento *m* compartment; department
dependiente(a) *m/f* sales assistant
deporte *m* sport
depósito de gasolina *m* petrol tank
derecha *f* right(-hand side)
a la derecha on/to the right

derecho m right; law
derechos de aduana customs duty
derecho(a) right; straight
derramar to spill
derrapar to skid
derrape m skid
derretir to melt
desabrochar to unfasten
desafilado(a) blunt *(knife, blade)*
desaparecer to disappear
desarrollar to develop
desatascador m plunger *(for sink)*
desayuno m breakfast
descafeinado(a) decaffeinated
descansar to rest
descanso m rest; interval
descarga eléctrica f electric shock
descargado(a) flat *(battery)*
descargar to download
descargarse to run down; to go flat *(battery)*
descongelar to defrost; to de-ice
describir to describe
descubrir to discover
descuento m discount; reduction
desde since; from
desear to want; to wish
desembarcadero m quay
desempleado(a) unemployed
desenchufado(a) off; disconnected; unplugged
deseo m wish; desire
desfile m parade
deshacer to undo; to unpack
desinfectante m disinfectant
desmaquillador/desmaquillante m make-up remover
toallitas desmaquilladoras/ desmaquillantes makeup remover towels
desmayado(a) fainted
desnatado(a) skimmed
desodorante m deodorant
despacho m office
despacio slowly; quietly
despegar to take-off; to remove; to peel off
despertador m alarm (clock)

despertarse to wake up
después after; afterward(s)
desteñir: *no destiñe* colourfast
destino m destination
destornillador m screwdriver
destornillar to unscrew
desvestirse to get undressed
desvío m detour; diversion
detalle m detail; nice gesture
al detalle retail *(commercial)*
detener to arrest
detergente m detergent; washing powder
destilería de cerveza artesanal micro-brewery
detrás (de) behind
deuda f debt
devolver to give/put back
día m day
día festivo/de fiesta public holiday; holiday
día laborable/hábil working day; weekday
día lectivo school/college day
día libre day off
día azul cheap ticket day
todo el día all day
diabético(a) m/f diabetic
diamante m diamond
diario(a) daily
a diario every day
diarrea f diarrhoea
dibujo m drawing
diccionario m dictionary
diciembre m December
diente m tooth
dieta f diet
difícil difficult
dificultad f difficulty
¿diga(me)? hello? *(on phone)*
dinero m money
dinero (en) efectivo cash
(dinero) suelto change
Dios m God
diplomático(a) m/f diplomat
dirección f direction; address; (Aut) steering; steering wheel
dirección de correo electrónico e-mail address

dirección particular home address
dirección prohibida no entry
dirección única one-way
directo(a) direct *(train, etc)*
director(a) *m/f* director; manager
dirigir to manage
disco *m* record; disk
disco duro hard disk
discoteca *f* disco; nightclub
discrecional optional
discutir to quarrel; to argue
diseño *m* design; drawing
disponible available
disquete *m* floppy disk
distancia *f* distance
distinto(a) different
distribuidor automático *m* vending
  machine
distrito *m* district
DIU *m* coil *(IUD)*
diversión *f* fun
divertido(a) funny *(amusing)*
divertirse to enjoy oneself
divisa *f* foreign currency
divorciado(a) divorced
doblado(a) folded; dubbed *(film)*
doblar to fold
doble double
docena *f* dozen
documentos *mpl* documents
documentación del vehículo *f*
  log book *(for car)*
dólar *m* dollar
dolor *m* ache; pain
dolor de cabeza headache
dolor de garganta sore throat
dolor de muelas toothache
dolor de oídos earache
doloroso(a) painful
domicilio *m* home address
domingo *m* Sunday
dominó *m* dominoes
¿dónde? where?
dormir to sleep
dormitorio *m* bedroom
dorso *m* back
véase al dorso please turn over
dosis *f* dose; dosage

droga *f* drug
ducha *f* shower
ducharse to take a shower
dueño(a) *m/f* owner
dulce sweet
agua dulce fresh water
dulce *m* dessert; sweet
durante during
duro(a) hard; tough
DVD *m* DVD

E

echar to pour; to throw; to post
ecológico(a) organic; environmentally
  friendly
ecológico(a) ecological
ecoturismo *m* eco-tourism
edad *f* age *(of person)*
edad mínima age limit
edificio *m* building
edredón *m* duvet; quilt
edulcorante *m* sweetener
EE.UU. USA
efecto *m* effect
efectos personales belongings
eje *m* axle *(car)*
ejemplar *m* copy *(of book)*
el the
él he; him
electricidad *f* electricity
electricista *m/f* electrician
eléctrico(a) electric(al)
electrónico(a) electronic
elegir to choose
ella she; her
ello it
ellos(as) they; them
embajada *f* embassy
embalse *m* reservoir
embarazada pregnant
embarcadero *m* jetty; pier
embarcarse to board
embarque *m* boarding
embrague *m* clutch *(in car)*
emisión *f* broadcasting
emitido por issued by
emocionante exciting
empachado(a) upset *(stomach)*

empezar to begin
empleo *m* employment; use
empresa *f* firm; company
empujar to push
empuje push
en in; into; on
encaje *m* lace *(fabric)*
encantado(a) pleased to meet you!
encargado(a) *m/f* person in charge
encargar to order in advance
encendedor *m* (cigarette) lighter
encender to switch on; to light
encender las luces switch on headlights
encendido(a) on *(light, TV, engine)*
enchufar to plug in
enchufe *m* plug; point; socket
encima de onto; on top of
encontrar to find
encontrarse con to meet *(by chance)*
enero *m* January
enfadado(a) angry
enfermedad *f* disease
enfermera(o) *m/f* nurse
enfermería *f* infirmary; first-aid post
enfermo(a) ill
enfrente (de) opposite
¡enhorabuena! congratulations!
enjuagar to rinse
enjuague bucal *m* mouthwash
enlace *m* connection *(train, etc)*
ensalada *f* salad
enseñar to show; to teach
entender to understand
entero(a) whole
entierro *m* funeral
entrada *f* entrance; admission; ticket
entrada de abono season ticket
entrada libre admission free
entrada por delante enter at the front
entrada principal main entrance
entradas limitadas limited tickets
entradas numeradas numbered tickets
no hay entradas sold out
sacar una entrada to buy a ticket
entrar to go in; to get in; to enter
entre among; between
entreacto *m* interval
entregar to deliver

entremeses *mpl* hors d'œuvres
entrevista *f* interview
envase *m* container; packaging
enviar to send
envío *m* shipment
envolver to wrap
epiléptico(a) epileptic
equipaje *m* luggage; baggage
equipaje de mano hand-luggage
equipo *m* team; equipment
equipo manos libres hands-free kit
(for phone)
equitación *f* horseriding
equivocación *f* mistake;
misunderstanding
error *m* mistake
es he/she/it is
escala *f* stopover
escalar to climb *(mountains)*
escalera *f* stairs; ladder
escalera de incendios fire escape
escalera (de mano) ladder
escalera mecánica escalator
escaleras *fpl* stairs
escalón *m* step *(stair)*
escanear to scan
escáner *m* scan
escapar to escape
escaparate *m* shop window
escenario *m* stage *(theatre)*
escoba *f* broom *(brush)*
escocés(cesa) Scottish
Escocia *f* Scotland
escoger to choose
esconder to hide
escribir to write
escrito: *por escrito* in writing
escuchar to listen to
escuela *f* school
escultura *f* sculpture
escurrir to wring
ese/esa that
esguince *m* sprain
esmalte *m* varnish
esos/esas those
espacio *m* space
espalda *f* back *(of body)*
España *f* Spain

español(a) Spanish
espantoso(a) awful
esparadrapo *m* sticking plaster
espárrago asparagus
especia *f* spice
especialidad *f* speciality
especialista *m/f* specialist
espectáculo *m* entertainment; show
espejo *m* mirror
espejo retrovisor rear-view mirror
esperar to wait (for); to hope
espere su turno please wait your turn
espina *f* fish bone; thorn
espina dorsal spine
espinacas *fpl* spinach
espinilla *f* spot *(pimple)*; shin
esponja *f* sponge
esposa *f* wife
esposo *m* husband
espuma *f* foam; mousse *(for hair)*
espuma de afeitar shaving foam
espumoso(a) frothy; sparkling
esq. *abbrev. for* **esquina**
esquí *m* skiing; ski
esquí acuático water-skiing
esquí de fondo cross-country skiing
esquiar to ski
esquina *f* street corner
está you *(formal)*/he/she/it is
estación *f* railway station; season
estación de autobuses bus/coach
 station
estación de servicio petrol/service
 station
estacionamiento *m* parking space
estacionar to park
estadio *m* stadium
Estados Unidos *mpl* United States
estanco *m* tobacconist's
estante *m* shelf
estantería bookcase; shelving
estar to be
estatua *f* statue
este *m* east
éste/esta this
estéreo *m* stereo
esterilla *f* sleeping mat
estómago *m* stomach

estornudar to sneeze
estos/éstas these
estragón *m* tarragon
estrecho(a) narrow
estrella *f* star
estreñimiento *m* constipation
estreno *m* premiere; new release
estropeado(a) out of order; broken;
 damaged
estudiante *m/f* student
etiqueta *f* label; ticket; tag
de etiqueta formal dress
euro *m* euro
Europa *f* Europe
evidente obvious
evitar to avoid
examen *m* examination
excelente excellent
excepcional rare *(unique)*
excepto except
exceso *m* excess
excursión *f* tour; excursion
éxito *m* success
expedido(a) issued
experto(a) expert
explicar to explain
exportación *f* export
exportar to export
exposición *f* exhibition
expreso *m* express train
exprimir to squeeze
extintor *m* fire extinguisher
extranjero(a) *m/f* foreigner
en el extranjero abroad

F

FC/f.c. *abbrev. for* **ferrocarril**
fabada *f* pork and bean stew
fábrica *f* factory
fácil easy
factor factor
factura *f* receipt; bill; account
factura detallada itemized bill
facturación *f* check-in
falda *f* skirt
falso(a) fake; false
falta *f* foul *(football)*; lack
familia *f* family

famoso(a) famous
farmacia *f* chemist's; pharmacy
farmacia de guardia duty chemist
farmacéutico(a) *m/f* pharmacist
faro *m* headlamp; lighthouse
faro antiniebla fog-lamp
farola *f* lamppost
faros *mpl* headlights
favor *m* favour
por favor please
favorito(a) favourite
fax *m* fax
febrero *m* February
fecha *f* date
fecha de adquisición date of purchase
fecha de caducidad/vencimiento
  expiry date
fecha de expedición date of issue
fecha de nacimiento date of birth
feliz happy
¡Feliz Año Nuevo! Happy New Year!
¡Feliz Navidad! Merry Christmas!
femenino(a) feminine
feo(a) ugly
feria *f* trade fair; funfair
feria de artesanía(s) craft fair
ferrocarril *m* railway
festivos *mpl* public holidays
fiambre *m* cold meat
fianza *f* bail bond; deposit
fibra sintética *f* man-made fibre
ficha *f* token; counter *(in games)*
fichero *m* file *(computer)*
fiebre *f* fever
fiesta *f* party; public holiday
fila *f* row; line *(row, queue)*
filete *m* fillet; steak
filial *f* branch
filtro *m* filter
filtro de aceite oil filter
filtro solar sunscreen
fin *m* end
fin de semana weekend
fin de curso end of school year
finalizar to end; to finish
finca *f* farm; country house
fino fine; thin
fino *m* light, dry, very pale sherry

firma *f* signature
firmar to sign
firme aquí sign here
flojo(a) weak *(coffee, tea)*
flor *f* flower
florero *m* vase
floristería *f* florist's shop
foca *f* seal
foco *m* spotlight; headlamp
folleto *m* leaflet; brochure
fonda *f* inn; small restaurant
fondo *m* bottom *(of pool, etc)*
fontanero *m* plumber
forfait *m* lift pass *(skiing)*
formulario *m* form
fósforo *m* match
foto *f* picture; photo
fotocopia *f* photocopy
fotocopiar to photocopy
fotocopiadora *f* photocopier
fotografía *f* photograph
fotógrafo(a) *m/f* photographer
FPS (factor de protección solar) *m*
  SPF (sun protection factor)
fractura *f* fracture
frágil fragile
frambuesa *f* raspberry
francés(cesa) French
Francia *f* France
frecuente frequent
fregadero *m* sink *(in kitchen)*
fregona *f* mop *(for floor)*
freír to fry
frenar to brake
freno *m* brake
freno de mano handbrake
frente a opposite
frente *f* forehead
fresa *f* strawberry
fresco(a) fresh; crisp; cool
frigorífico *m* fridge
frío(a) cold
frito(a) fried
frontera *f* border; frontier
frotar to rub
fruta *f* fruit
fruta del tiempo fruit in season
fruta de la pasión passionfruit

fruteria f fruit shop
frutos secos mpl nuts (to eat)
fuego m fire
fuente f fountain
fuera outdoors; out
fuerte strong; loud
fuga f leak (of gas, liquid)
fumadores mpl smokers
fumar to smoke
prohibido fumar no smoking
función f show
funcionar to work; to function
no funciona out of order
funcionario(a) m/f civil servant
funda f case; cover; crown (for tooth); pillowcase
funda de gafas glasses case
funda nórdica duvet cover
furgoneta f estate car
fusible m fuse
fútbol m football
futbolista m/f football player

G

gafas fpl glasses
gafas de sol sunglasses
galería f gallery
galería de arte art gallery
galés(lesa) Welsh
Gales m Wales
gallego(a) Galician
galleta f biscuit
ganar to earn; to win (sports, etc)
garaje m garage
garantía f guarantee
garganta f throat
gas m gas
con gas fizzy
gas butano Calor gas®
gas ciudad town gas
gas natural natural gas
sin gas non-fizzy; still
gasa f gauze; nappy
gaseosa f lemonade
gasoil m diesel fuel
gasóleo m diesel oil
gasolina f petrol
gasolina sin plomo unleaded petrol

gasolina súper 4-star petrol
gasolinera f petrol station
gastado(a) worn
gastar to spend (money)
gastos mpl expenses
gastritis f gastritis
gato m cat; jack (for car)
gaviota f seagull
gemelo(a) m/f identical twin
gemelos pl cufflink; binoculars
gendarme m/f policeman/woman (Lat. Am.)
gendarmería f police (Lat. Am.)
género m type; material
generoso(a) generous
gente f people
gerente m/f manager/manageress
gigabyte m gigabyte
gigaherzio m gigahertz
ginebra f gin
ginecólogo(a) m/f gynaecologist
girar to turn around
globo m balloon
glorieta f roundabout
gluten m gluten
golfo de Vizcaya m Bay of Biscay
goma f rubber; eraser
gomita f rubber band
gordo(a) fat
gorra f cap (hat)
gorro m hat
gotera f leak
gótico(a) Gothic
GPS (sistema global de navegación) GPS (global positioning system)
grabar en vídeo to video (from TV)
gracias thank you
muchas gracias thank you very much
grada f tier
gramo m gram(me)
Gran Bretaña f Great Britain
grande large; big; tall
grandes almacenes mpl department store
granja f farm
de granja free-range
granjero(a) m/f farmer
grasiento(a) greasy

gratinado(a) au gratin; grilled
gratinar to grill
gratis free *(costing nothing)*
grave serious *(accident, etc)*
grifo *m* tap
gripe *f* flu
gris grey
gritar to shout
grosella negra *f* blackcurrant
grosella roja *f* redcurrant
grúa *f* crane; breakdown van
grueso(a) thick *(not thin)*
grupo *m* group; band *(rock)*
grupo sanguíneo blood group
guacamole *m* avocado dip
guantes *mpl* gloves
guantes de goma rubber gloves
guapo(a) handsome; attractive
guardacostas *m/f* coastguard
guardar to put away; to keep
guardarropa *m* cloakroom
guardería *f* nursery; crèche
guardia infantil nursery school
guardia *f* guard
de guardia on duty
Guardia Civil Civil Guard
guarnición *f* garnish
guerra *f* war
guía *m/f* courier; guide
Guía del ocio f What's on
guía (telefónica) *f* phone directory
guiar to guide
guindilla *f* chilli pepper
guiso *m* stew; casserole
guitarra *f* guitar
gusano *m* maggot; worm
gustar to like; to enjoy
guayaba *f* guava

H

haba *f* broad bean
habano *m* Havana cigar
habitación *f* room
habitación doble double room
habitación familiar family room
habitación individual single room
habitación triple triple room
hablar (con) to speak/talk to

se habla inglés English spoken
hacer to do; to make
hacer autoestop to hitchhike
hacer cola to queue
hacer daño to hurt; to damage
hacer footing to jog
hacer las maletas to pack *(case)*
hacer punto to knit
hacer surf to surf
hacer topless to go topless
hacer transbordo de to change *(bus/train)*
hacer transbordo en to change at
hacer turismo to sightsee
hacia toward(s)
hacia arriba upwards, up
hacia abajo downwards, down
hacia adelante forwards
hacia atrás backwards
hamburguesa *f* hamburger
harina *f* flour
harina con levadura self-raising flour
harina de pescado fish-meal
harina de repostería pastry flour
harina de trigo wheat flour
hasta until; till
hay there is/there are
hecho(a) finished; done
hecho a (la) medida made-to-measure
hecho a mano handmade
hecho(a) de... made of...
helada *f* frost
heladería *f* ice-cream parlour
helado *m* ice cream
helicóptero *m* helicopter
hemorragia *f* haemorrhage
hemorroides *fpl* haemorrhoids
hepatitis *f* hepatitis
herida *f* wound; injury
herido(a) injured
herir to hurt
hermano(a) *m/f* brother/sister
hermoso(a) beautiful
hernia *f* hernia
herramienta *f* tool
hervido(a) boiled
hervidor de agua *m* kettle
hervir to boil
hidrofoil *m* hydrofoil

hidropedal m pedal boat/pedalo
hielo m ice
con/sin hielo with/without ice
hierba f grass; herb
hierbabuena f mint
hierro m iron
hierro forjado wrought iron
hígado m liver
higo m fig
higos chumbos prickly pears
hijo(a) m/f son/daughter
hilo m thread; linen
hincha m/f fan *(football, etc)*
hinchado(a) swollen
hipermercado m hypermarket
hípica f showjumping
hipódromo m racecourse *(horses)*
histórico(a) historic
hogar m home; household
hoja f sheet; leaf
hoja de registro registration form
hoja de afeitar razor blade
hola hello; hi!
hombre m man
hombro m shoulder
homeopatía homeopathy
homeopático(a) homeopathic
hora f hour; appointment
hora punta rush hour
horas de visita visiting hours
horario m timetable
horario de apertura opening hours
horario de cierre closing time
horario de visitas visiting hours
horchata de chufa f refreshing tiger nut drink
hormiga f ant
horno m oven
al horno baked; roasted
(horno) microondas microwave
horquilla f hairgrip
hospital m hospital
hostal m small hotel; hostel
hotel m hotel
hoy today
huelga f strike *(of workers)*
hueso m bone
huésped m/f guest

huevo m egg
huevo de Pascua Easter egg
huevos de corral free-range eggs
huevos duros hard-boiled eggs
huevos escalfados poached eggs
huevos revueltos scrambled eggs
humo m smoke

I

ida f outward journey
de ida y vuelta return *(ticket)*
idioma m language
iglesia f church
igual equal
imán m magnet
impar odd *(number)*
imperdible m safety pin
impermeable m raincoat; waterproof
importante important
importar to matter; to import
importe total m total *(amount)*
imprescindible essential
impreso m form
impreso de solicitud application form
impresos printed matter
impuesto m tax
inalámbrico wireless
incendio m fire
incluido(a) included
incómodo(a) uncomfortable
inconsciente unconscious
indicaciones fpl directions
índice m index
indigestión f indigestion
individual individual; single
infarto m heart attack
infección f infection
inferior inferior; lower
inflamación f inflammation
información f information
información de contacto contact details
informe m report *(medical, police)*
infracción f offence
infracción de tráfico traffic offence
ingeniero(a) m/f engineer
Inglaterra f England
inglés(lesa) English
ingredientes mpl ingredients

inhalador *m* inhaler *(for medication)*
inmediatamente immediately
inmobilizador immobilizer
inmunización *f* immunisation
inquilino(a) *m/f* tenant
insecto *m* insect
insolación *f* sunstroke
instituto *m* institute; secondary school
instrucciones *fpl* directions; instructions
instructor(a) *m/f* instructor
instrumento *m* tool
insulina *f* insulin
interesante interesting
interior inside
intermitente *m* indicator *(in car)*
internacional international
Internet *m/f* internet
Internet sin cables; Internet WiFi
  wireless internet
intérprete *m/f* interpreter
interruptor *m* switch
intoxicación por alimentos *f* food
  poisoning
introducir to introduce; to insert
introduzca monedas insert coins
inundación *f* flood
invierno *m* winter
invitación *f* invitation
invitado(a) *m/f* guest
invitar to invite
inyección *f* injection
iPod® iPod®
ir to go
ir a buscar to fetch
ir de compras/tiendas to go shopping
ir en bicicleta to cycle
irse a casa to go home
irse de to leave *(a place)*
Irlanda *f* Ireland
Irlanda del Norte *f* Northern Ireland
irlandés(desa) Irish
isla *f* island
Italia *f* Italy
italiano(a) Italian
itinerario *m* route; schedule
ITV *m* MOT
IVA *m* VAT
izq./izqda. *abbrev. for* **izquierda**

izquierda *f* left
izquierdo(a) left

J

jabón *m* soap
jamás never
jamón *m* ham
jamón serrano cured ham
jamón (de) York cooked ham
Japón *m* Japan
japonés(nesa) *m/f* Japanese
jaqueca *f* bad headache
jardín *m* garden
jarra *f* jug; mug
jefe(a) *m/f* chief; head; boss
jerez *m* sherry
jerga *f* slang
jeringuilla *f* syringe
joven young
joya *f* jewel
joyas jewellery
joyería *f* jeweller's
jubilado(a) *m/f* retired person
jubilarse to retire
judías *fpl* beans
judías verdes green beans
judío(a) Jew
juego *m* game
jueves *m* Thursday
juez(a) *m/f* judge
jugador(a) *m/f* player
jugar to play; to gamble
julio *m* July
jugo *m* juice
juguete *m* toy
juguetería *f* toy shop
junio *m* June
junto(a) together
junto a next to
juventud *f* youth

K

kikos *(snack)* salted, toasted maize,
  very popular in Spain
kilo *m* kilo(gram)
kilometraje *m* mileage
kilometraje (i)limitado (un)limited
  mileage

kilómetro *m* kilometre
kiosko (de prensa) *m* newsstand
kiwi *m* kiwi fruit
kleenex® *m* tissue

L

la the; her; it; you *(formal)*
labio *m* lip
laborable working *(day)*
laborables weekdays
laca *f* hair spray
lado *m* side
al lado de beside
ladrar to bark
ladrillo *m* brick
ladrón(ona) *m/f* thief
lago *m* lake
lámpara *f* lamp
lana *f* wool
lancha *f* launch
lancha motora motor launch
lápiz *m* pencil
lápiz de ojos eyeliner; eye pencil
lápiz de labios lipstick
lápiz USB USB flash drive
largo(a) long
largo recorrido long-distance *(train, etc)*
lata *f* can *(container)*; tin
latón *m* brass
lavable washable
lavabo *m* lavatory; washbasin
lavado de coches *m* car wash
lavado(a) washed
lavado en seco dry-cleaning
lavado y marcado shampoo and set
lavadora *f* washing machine
lavanda *f* lavender
lavandería *f* laundry; launderette
lavavajillas *m* dishwasher
lavar to wash
lavarse to wash oneself
laxante *m* laxative
leche *f* milk
leche desnatada skimmed milk
leche de soja soya milk
leche de vaca cow's milk
leche entera wholemilk
leche hidratante moisturizer

leche semidesnatada semi-skimmed milk
lechuga *f* lettuce
lectura de labios *f* lip-reading
leer to read
legumbres *fpl* pulses
lejía *f* bleach
lejos far
lencería *f* lingerie
lengua *f* language; tongue
lente *f* lens
lentes de contacto contact lenses
lentejas *fpl* lentils
lentillas *fpl* contact lenses
lento(a) slow
león *m* lion
lesbiana *f* lesbian
letra *f* letter *(of alphabet)*
levantar to lift
levantarse to get up; to rise
ley *f* law
libra *f* pound *(currency, weight)*
libra esterlina pound sterling
libre free/vacant
dejen el paso libre keep clear
libre de impuestos tax-free
librería *f* bookshop
libro *m* book
licencia *f* permit; licence
licenciarse to graduate
licor *m* liqueur
licores spirits
lidia *f* bullfight
ligero(a) light *(not heavy)*
lima *f* file *(for nails)*; lime
límite *m* limit; boundary
límite de velocidad speed limit
limón *m* lemon
limonada *f* lemonade
limonaria *f* lemongrass
limpiar to clean
limpieza en seco *f* dry-cleaning
limpio(a) clean
línea *f* line
lino *m* linen
linterna *f* torch; flashlight
liquidación *f* sales
liquidación por cierre closing-down sale

liquidación de existencias stock clearance
líquido *m* liquid
líquido de frenos brake fluid
líquido del embrague clutch fluid
liso(a) plain; smooth
lista *f* list
lista de correos poste restante
lista de espera waiting list
lista de precios price list
listo(a) ready
listo(a) para comer ready-cooked
listado *m* printout
litera *f* berth; couchette; sleeper
litoral *m* coast
litro *m* litre
llaga *f* ulcer *(mouth)*
llamada *f* call
llamada a cobro revertido reverse charge call
llamar to call; to ring; to knock *(on door)*
llano(a) flat
llanta *f* tyre
llave *f* key; tap; spanner
llave de contacto ignition key
llaves del coche car keys
llave inglesa spanner
llave tarjeta card key
llavero *m* keyring
Lleg. *abbrev. for* **llegadas**
llegada *f* arrival
llegadas arrivals
llegar to arrive; to come
llenar to fill; to fill in
lleno(a) full (up)
lleno, por favor fill it up, please
llevar to bring; to wear; to carry
para llevar to take away
llorar to cry *(weep)*
lluvia *f* rain
lobo *m* wolf
local *m* premises; bar
localidad *f* place
localidades tickets *(theatre)*
loción *f* lotion
loncha *f* slice *(ham, etc)*
Londres *m* London
longitud *f* length

lotería *f* lottery
luces *fpl* lights
luchar to fight
lugar *m* place
lugar de expedición issued in
lugar fresco/seco cool/dry place
lugar de nacimiento place of birth
lujo *m* luxury
luna *f* moon
luna de miel honeymoon
lunes *m* Monday
lupa *f* magnifying glass
luz *f* light
luz de carretera/larga full-beam headlights
luz corta/de cruce dipped headlights
luz de freno brake light
luz de posición sidelight

M

macedonia *f* fruit salad
madera *f* wood
madrastra *f* stepmother
madre *f* mother
maduro(a) ripe; mature
maíz *m* maize; corn
mal/malo(a) bad *(weather, news)*
maleta *f* case; suitcase
maletero *m* boot *(car)*
maletín de ordenador portátil *m* laptop bag
Mallorca *f* Majorca
malo(a) bad
mañana tomorrow
mañana *f* morning
mancha *f* stain; mark
mandar to send
mandar un mensaje de texto to text
te mandaré un mensaje (de texto) I'll text you
mandíbula *f* jaw
mando a distancia *m* remote control
manera *f* way; manner
manga *f* sleeve
mango *m* mango
manguera *f* hosepipe
manillar *m* handlebars
manicura *f* manicure

mano *f* hand
de segunda mano secondhand
manopla *f* mitten
manopla de horno oven glove
maquinilla de afeitar shaver
manso(a) tame *(animal)*
manta *f* blanket
mantel *m* tablecloth
mantener to maintain; to keep
mantequería *f* dairy products *(Lat. Am.)*
mantequilla *f* butter
mantequilla de cacahuete peanut butter
mantita *f* picnic rug
manzana *f* apple; block *(of houses)*
manzanilla *f* camomile tea; dry sherry
mapa *m* map
mapa de carreteras road map
maquillaje *m* make-up
máquina *f* machine
máquina de afeitar razor
máquina de fotos camera
mar *m* sea
marca *f* brand; make
marcapasos *m* pacemaker
marcar to dial
marcar un gol to score a goal
marcha *f* gear
marcha atrás reverse gear
marco *m* picture frame
marea *f* tide
marea alta/baja high/low tide
mareado(a) sick *(car, sea)*; dizzy
margarina *f* margarine
marido *m* husband
marioneta *f* puppet
mariposa *f* butterfly
marisco *m* seafood; shellfish
marisquería *f* seafood restaurant
mármol *m* marble
marrón brown
marroquí Moroccan
marroquinería *f* leather goods
martes *m* Tuesday
martillo *m* hammer
marzo *m* March
más more; plus
más que more than
más tarde later

masa *f* pastry *(dough)*
masaje *m* massage
masculino(a) male
matar to kill
matrícula *f* number plate
matrimonio *m* marriage
máximo *m* maximum
mayo *m* May
mayonesa *f* mayonnaise
mayor bigger; biggest
la mayor parte de most of
mayor de edad adult
mayor que bigger than
mayores de 18 años over-18s
mayúscula *f* capital letter
mazapán *m* marzipan
mazo *m* mallet
mecánico *m* mechanic
mechero *m* lighter
medianoche *f* midnight
medias *fpl* tights; stockings
medicina *f* medicine; drug
médico(a) *m/f* doctor
medida *f* measurement; size
medio *m* the middle
medio(a) half
media hora half an hour
media pensión half board
medio hecho(a) medium rare
mediodía: las doce del mediodía midday; noon
medir to measure
Mediterráneo *m* Mediterranean
medusa *f* jellyfish
megabyte *m* megabyte
megahercio *m* megahertz
mejicano(a) *m/f* Mexican
Méjico *m* Mexico
mejilla *f* cheek
mejor best; better
mejor que better than
mejorana *f* marjoram
melocotón *m* peach
melón *m* melon
menaje *m* kitchen utensils
menaje de hogar household goods
mendigo(a) *m/f* beggar
menestra *f* vegetable stew

meningitis *f* meningitis
menor smaller/smallest; least
Menorca *f* Minorca
menos minus; less; except
menos que less than
mensaje *m* message
mensaje de texto text message
mensual monthly
menta *f* mint; peppermint
mentira *f* lie *(untruth)*
menú *m* menu
menú del día set menu
mercado *m* market
mercado agrícola farmers' market
mercadillo *m* flea market
mercancías *fpl* goods
mercería *f* haberdasher's
merendero *m* open-air snack bar; picnic area
merienda *f* afternoon snack; picnic
mermelada *f* jam
mermelada de naranja orange marmalade
mes *m* month
mesa *f* table
mesón *m* traditional restaurant
metal *m* metal
metro *m* metre; underground; tape measure
México *m* Mexico
mezclar to mix
mi my
mí me
micrófono *m* microphone
miel *f* honey
mientras while
miércoles *m* Wednesday
miga *f* crumb
migraña *f* migraine
mil thousand
mil millones billion
milímetro *m* millimetre
millón *m* million
minidisc *m* minidisk
mínimo *m* minimum
minusválido(a) *m/f* disabled person
minuto *m* minute
miope short-sighted

mirar to look at; to watch
misa *f* mass *(in church)*
mismo(a) same
mitad *f* half
mixto(a) mixed
mochila *f* backpack; rucksack
mochila portabebés baby sling
moda *f* fashion
moderno(a) modern
modo *m* way; manner
modo de empleo instructions for use
mojado(a) wet
mole *m* black chilli sauce
molestar to disturb
molestia *f* nuisance; discomfort
molido(a) ground *(coffee beans, etc)*
molino *m* mill
molino de viento windmill
monasterio *m* monastery
moneda *f* currency; coin
introduzca monedas insert coins
monedero *m* purse
monitor(a) de esquí *m/f* ski instructor
monovolumen *m* people carrier
montaña *f* mountain
montañismo *m* mountaineering
montar to ride
montar a caballo to horse ride
montilla *m* a sherry-type wine
monumento *m* monument
moqueta *f* fitted carpet
mora *f* mulberry; blackberry
morado(a) purple
mordedura *f* bite
morder to bite
moratón *m* bruise
morir to die
mosca *f* fly
mosquitera *f* mosquito net
mostrador *m* counter; desk
mostrar to show
moto *f* (motor)bike; moped
moto acuática jet ski
motocicleta *f* motorbike
motor *m* engine; motor
móvil *m* mobile phone
mozo *m* luggage porter
media pensión (MP) half board

mucho a lot; much
mucho(a) a lot (of); much
muchos(as) many
muela f tooth
muelle m quay; pier
muerto(a) dead
muestra f exhibition; sample
mujer f woman; wife
multa f fine *(to be paid)*
mundo m world
muñeca f wrist; doll
muro m wall
músculo m muscle
museo m museum; art gallery
música f music
muy very
muy hecho(a) well done *(steak)*

N

nacer to be born
nacimiento m birth
nación f nation
nacional national; domestic *(flight)*
nacionalidad f nationality
nada nothing
de nada don't mention it
nada más nothing else
nadador(a) m/f swimmer
nadar to swim
nadie nobody
naipes mpl playing cards
naranja f orange
naranjada f orangeade
nariz f nose
nata f cream
nata agria soured cream
nata montada whipped cream
natación f swimming
natural natural; fresh; plain
naturista m/f naturist
navaja f pocketknife; penknife
Navidad f Christmas
neblina f mist
necesario(a) necessary
necesidades especiales:
 personas con necesidades
 especiales people with special needs
necesitar to need; to require

nectarina f nectarine
negarse to refuse
negativo m negative *(photo)*
negocios mpl business
negro(a) black
neumático m tyre
neumáticos antideslizantes snow tyres
nevar to snow
nevera f refrigerator
nevera portátil cool-box
nido m nest
niebla f fog
nieto(a) m/f grandson/daughter
nieve f snow
niña f girl; baby girl
niñera f nanny
ningún/ninguno(a) none
niño m boy; baby; child
niños children *(infants)*
nivel m level; standard
No. *abbrev. for* **número**
noche f night
esta noche tonight
Nochebuena f Christmas Eve
Nochevieja f New Year's Eve
nocivo(a) harmful
nombre m name
nombre de pila first name
nombre de usuario username
norte m north
Norteamérica f America; USA
norteamericano(a) American
nosotros(as) we
notaría f solicitor's office
notario(a) m/f notary; solicitor
noticias fpl news
novela f novel
novia f girlfriend; fiancée; bride
noviembre m November
novio m boyfriend; fiancé; bridegroom
nube f cloud
nublado(a) cloudy
nudo m knot
nuestro(a) our; ours
Nueva Zelanda f New Zealand
nuevo(a) new
nuez f walnut
número m number; size; issue

número de móvil mobile mumber
número par/impar even/odd *(number)*
número PIN PIN number
nunca never

O

o or
o... o... either... or...
obispo *m* bishop
objetivo *m* lens *(on camera)*
objeto *m* object
objetos de valor valuables
obligatorio(a) compulsory
obra *f* work; play *(theatre)*
obra maestra masterpiece
obras road works
observar to watch
obstruido(a) blocked *(pipe)*
obtener to get *(to obtain)*
océano *m* ocean
ocio *m* spare time
octubre *m* October
ocupado engaged
oeste *m* west
oferta *f* special offer
oficina *f* office
oficina de Correos Post Office
oficio *m* church service; profession
ofrecer to offer
oído *m* ear
oír to hear
ojo *m* eye
¡ojo! look out!
ola *f* wave *(on sea)*
olivo *m* olive tree
olor *m* smell
oloroso *m* cream sherry
olvidar to forget
onda *f* wave
ópera *f* opera
operación *f* operation
operador(a) *m/f* operator
oportunidades *fpl* bargains
orden *f* command
orden *m* order
ordenador *m* computer
ordenador portátil laptop
ordenador de bolsillo palmtop

oreja *f* ear
organizar to arrange; to organize
orilla *f* shore
orina *f* urine
oro *m* gold
oscuro(a) dark; dim
oso *m* bear *(animal)*
ostra *f* oyster
otoño *m* autumn; fall
otro(a) other; another
otra vez again
oxígeno *m* oxygen

P

paciente *m/f* patient *(in hospital)*
padrastro *m* stepfather
padre *m* father
padres parents
paella *f* paella *(rice dish)*
pagado(a) paid
pagar to pay for; to pay
pagar al contado to pay cash
pagar a plazos to pay for something
in instalments
pagar por separado to pay separately
pagaré *m* IOU
página *f* page
página web website
Páginas Amarillas *fpl* Yellow Pages
pago *m* payment
pago por adelantado payment in advance
pago al contado cash payment
pague en caja please pay at cash desk
país *m* country
paisaje *m* landscape; countryside
pájaro *m* bird
pajita *f* straw *(for drinking)*
palabra *f* word
palacio *m* palace
palanca de cambio *f* gear lever
palco *m* box *(in theatre)*
pálido(a) pale
palillo *m* toothpick
palo *m* stick; mast
palo de golf golf club
paloma *f* pigeon; dove
pan *m* bread; loaf of bread
pan de centeno rye bread

pan de molde sliced bread
pan integral wholemeal bread
pan tostado toast
panadería *f* bakery
pañal *m* nappy
panecillo *m* bread roll
paño *m* flannel; cloth
pantalla *f* screen
pantalones *mpl* trousers
pantalones cortos shorts
pantalones de montar riding breeches
pantalones pirata pirate trousers
pantys *mpl* tights
pañuelo *m* handkerchief; scarf
pañuelo de papel tissue
papa *m* pope
papel *m* paper
papel de cocina/absorbente kitchen roll
papeles del coche log book *(car)*
papel higiénico toilet paper
papelería *f* stationer's
paquete *m* packet; parcel
par even *(number)*
par *m* pair
para for; towards
parabrisas *m* windscreen
parachoques *m* bumper *(car)*
parada *f* stop
parado(a) unemployed
parador *m* state-run hotel
parafarmacia shop selling pharmaceutical
  supplies, such as baby foods, suntan
  lotions, etc., but not prescriptions
parafina *f* paraffin
paraguas *m* umbrella
paraguas plegable small foldable
  umbrella
paramédico(a) *f* paramedic
parar to stop
parcela *f* pitch *(for tent/caravan)*
parecido(a) a similar to
pared *f* wall *(inside)*
pareja *f* couple *(2 people)*
parque *m* park
parque de atracciones funfair
parque nacional national park
parquímetro *m* parking meter
parrilla *f* grill; barbecue

a la parrilla grilled
particular private
partida *f* game; departure
partida de nacimiento birth certificate
partido *m* match *(sport)*; party *(political)*
partir to depart
pasa *f* raisin; currant
pasado(a) stale *(bread)*; rotten
pasaje *m* ticket; fare; alleyway
pasajero(a) *m/f* passenger
pasaporte *m* passport
pasar to happen
pasatiempo *m* hobby; pastime
Pascua *f* Easter
¡Felices Pascuas! Happy Easter!
paseo *m* walk; avenue; promenade
pasillo *m* corridor; aisle
paso *m* step; pace
paso a nivel level crossing
paso de ganado cattle crossing
paso de peatones pedestrian crossing
paso inferior subway
paso subterráneo subway
pasta *f* pastry; pasta
pasta de dientes toothpaste
pastel *m* cake; pie
pasteles pastries
pastelería *f* cakes and pastries; cake shop
pastilla *f* tablet; pill
pastilla de jabón bar of soap
pastor(a) *m/f* shepherd; minister
patata *f* potato
patatas fritas french fries; crisps
patinaje *m* skating
patinar to skate; skid
patinazo *m* skid
patines *mpl* skates
patines en línea rollerblades
pato *m* duck
pavo *m* turkey
paz *f* peace
PDA PDA
pensión completa (PC) full board
p. ej. *abbrev. for* por ejemplo
peaje *m* toll
peatón(ona) *m/f* pedestrian
peces *mpl* fish
pecho *m* chest; breast

pechuga *f* breast *(poultry)*
pedir to ask for; to order
pedir prestado to borrow
podólogo(a); callista chiropodist
pegamento *m* gum; glue
pegar to stick (on); to hit
peine *m* comb
pelar to peel *(fruit)*
película *f* film
peligro *m* danger
peligro de incendio fire hazard
peligroso(a) dangerous
pelo *m* hair
pelota *f* ball
pelota vasca Basque ball game
pelota de golf golf ball
pelota de tenis tennis ball
peluca *f* wig
peluquería *f* hairdresser's
pendientes *mpl* earrings
pene *m* penis
penicilina *f* penicillin
pensar to think
pensión *f* guesthouse
media pensión half board
pensión completa full board
pensionista *m/f* senior citizen
peor worse; worst
pequeño(a) little; small
pera *f* pear
percha *f* coat hanger
perder to lose; to miss *(train, etc)*
perdido(a) missing *(lost)*
perdiz *f* partridge
perdón *m* pardon; sorry
perdonar to forgive
perejil *m* parsley
perezoso(a) lazy
perfecto(a) perfect
perforar: *no perforar* do not pierce
perfumería *f* perfume shop
periódico *m* newspaper
periodista *m/f* journalist
perla *f* pearl
permiso *m* permission; pass; permit;
  licence
permiso de caza hunting permit
permiso de residencia residence permit

permiso de trabajo work permit
permitido(a) permitted; allowed
permitir to allow; to let
pero but
perro *m* dog
persiana *f* blind *(for window)*
persona *f* person
personal *m* staff
pesado(a) heavy; boring
pesar to weigh
pesca *f* fishing
pescadería *f* fishmonger's
pescado *m* fish
pescador(a) *m/f* fisherman/woman
pescar to fish
peso *m* weight; scales
petirrojo *m* robin
pez *m* fish
picado(a) chopped; minced; rough
  (sea); stung *(by insect)*
picadura *f* insect bite; sting
picante peppery; hot; spicy
picar to itch; to sting
pie *m* foot
piedra *f* stone
piel *f* fur; skin; leather
pierna *f* leg
pieza *f* part; room
piezas del coche car parts
pijama *m* pyjamas
pila *f* battery *(radio, etc)*
píldora *f* pill
pileta *f* sink; *(Lat. Am.)* washbasin
pimienta *f* pepper *(spice)*
a la pimienta au poivre
pimiento *m* pepper *(vegetable)*
piña *f* pineapple
pinacoteca *f* art gallery
pinchar to have a puncture
pinchazo *m* puncture
pinchitos kebabs
pinchos *mpl* savoury titbits
pinchos morunos kebabs
pintar to paint
pintura *f* paint; painting
pinza *f* clothes peg
pinzas tweezers
pipa *f* pipe *(smoker's)*

pipas sunflower seeds
pipirrana f salad with tomato, pepper, onion, egg and fish
Pirineos mpl Pyrenees
piruleta f lollipop
pisar to step on; to tread on
no pisar el césped keep off grass
piscina f swimming pool
piso m floor; storey; flat
piso deslizante slippery road
pista f track; court
pistacho m pistachio
pisto m sautéed vegetables
pistola f gun
placa f licence plate
plancha f iron *(for clothes)*
a la plancha grilled
planchar to iron
plano m plan; town map
planta f plant; floor; sole *(of foot)*
planta baja/alta ground/top floor
plata f silver; *(Lat. Am.)* money
plata de ley sterling silver
plátano m banana; plane tree
platea f stalls *(theatre)*
platería f jeweller's
platillo m saucer
platinos mpl points *(in car)*
plato m plate; dish *(food)*; course
plato del día dish of the day
plato principal main course
playa f beach; seaside
plaza f square *(in town)*
plaza de toros bull ring
plazas libres vacancies
plazo m period; expiry date
plomo m lead *(metal)*
pluma f feather
pobre poor
poco(a) little
poco hecho(a) rare *(steak)*
pocos(as) (a) few
un poco de a bit of
poder to be able
podólogo(a) m/f chiropodist
podrido(a) rotten *(fruit, etc)*
policía f police
Policía Municipal/Local local police

Policía Nacional national police
policía m/f policeman/woman
polideportivo m leisure centre
póliza f policy; certificate
póliza de seguros insurance policy
pollería f poultry shop
pollo m chicken
polo m ice lolly
poltrona f armchair
polvo m powder; dust
polvos de talco talcum powder
pomada f ointment
pomelo m grapefruit
ponche m punch
poner to put
poner en marcha to start *(car)*
ponerse en contacto to contact
por by; per; through; about
por adelantado in advance
por correo by mail
por ejemplo for example
por favor please
porción f portion
porque because
portaequipajes m luggage rack
portero m caretaker; doorman
portugués/portuguesa Portuguese
posible possible
posología f dosage
postal f postcard
postigos mpl shutters
postre m dessert; pudding
potable drinkable
potaje m stew; thick soup
pote m stew
potito m baby food
pozo m well *(water)*
pozo séptico septic tank
prado m meadow
precio m price; cost
precioso(a) lovely
precipicio m cliff; precipice
preciso(a) precise; necessary
preferir to prefer
prefijo m dialling code
pregunta f question
preguntar to ask
premio m prize

prensa *f* press
preocupado(a) worried
preparado(a) cooked
preparar to prepare; to cook
presa *f* dam
prescribir to prescribe
presentar to introduce
preservativo *m* condom
presión *f* pressure
presión arterial blood pressure
prestar to lend
primavera *f* spring *(season)*
primero(a) first
primeros auxilios mpl first aid
primo(a) *m/f* cousin
princesa *f* princess
principal main
príncipe *m* prince
principiante *m/f* beginner
prioridad (de paso) *f* right of way
prismáticos *mpl* binoculars
privado(a) private
probador *m* changing room
probar to try; to taste
probarse to try on *(clothes)*
problema *m* problem
problemas de aprendizaje:
tiene dificultades/problemas de aprendizaje he/she has a learning disability
procedente de... coming from...
productos *mpl* produce; products
productos lácteos dairy products
profesión *f* profession; job
profesor(a) *m/f* teacher; lecturer
profundo(a) deep
programa *m* programme
programa de ordenador computer program
prohibido(a) prohibited/no...
prohibido aparcar/estacionar no parking
prohibido bañarse no bathing
prohibido el paso no entry
prometer to promise
prometido(a) engaged *(to be married)*
pronóstico *m* forecast
pronóstico del tiempo weather forecast

pronto soon
pronunciar to pronounce
propiedad *f* property
propietario(a) *m/f* owner
propina *f* tip
propio(a) own
protector solar *m* suncream
protegido(a) sheltered
provisional temporary
próximo(a) next
público *m* audience
público(a) public
puchero *m* cooking pot; stew
pueblo *m* village; country
puente *m* bridge
puerro *m* leek
puerta *f* door; gate
cierren la puerta close the door
puerta de embarque boarding gate
puerta principal front door
puerto *m* port
puerto de montaña mountain pass
puerto del coche car port
puerto USB USB port
puesta de sol *f* sunset
puesta en marcha *f* starter *(of car)*
puesto de socorro first-aid post
puesto que since
pulgar *m* thumb
pulgas *fpl* fleas
pulmón *m* lung
pulpo *m* octopus
pulsera *f* bracelet
punto *m* stitch
punto muerto neutral *(car)*
puntuación *f* score *(of match)*
puré *m* purée
puro *m* cigar
puro(a) pure

Q

que than; that; which
¿qué? what?; which?
¿qué tal? how are you?
quedar to remain; to be left
quedar bien to fit *(clothes)*
queja *f* complaint
quemado(a) burnt

quemadura _f_ burn
**quemadura del sol/solar** sunburn
quemar to burn
querer to want; to love
**querer decir** to mean
querido(a) dear _(on letter)_
queroseno _m_ paraffin
queso _m_ cheese
**queso curado** cured cheese
**queso fresco** green cheese
¿quién? who?
quincena _f_ fortnight
quinientos(as) five hundred
quiosco _m_ kiosk
quiste _m_ cyst
quitaesmalte _m_ nail polish remover
quitamanchas _m_ stain remover
quitar to remove
quizá(s) perhaps

R

rabia _f_ rabies
ración _f_ portion
**raciones** snacks; tapas
radiador _m_ radiator
radio _f_ radio
radio _m_ spoke _(wheel)_
radiocasete _m_ cassette player
radiografía _f_ X-ray
rallador _m_ grater
rama _f_ branch _(of tree)_
ramo _m_ bunch _(of flowers)_
rápido _m_ express train
rápido(a) quick; fast
raqueta _f_ racket
rasgar to tear; to rip
rastrillo _m_ rake
rastro _m_ flea market
rata _f_ rat
ratero _m_ pickpocket
rato _m_ a while
ratón _m_ mouse
razón _f_ reason
real royal
rebajas _fpl_ sale(s)
recalentar to overheat; to reheat
recambio _m_ spare; refill
recargar to recharge _(battery, etc)_

recepción _f_ reception
recepcionista _m/f_ receptionist
receta _f_ prescription; recipe
recibir to receive
recibo _m_ receipt
recientemente recently
reclamación _f_ claim; complaint
reclamar to claim
recoger to collect
recogida _f_ collection
**recogida de billetes** ticket collection
  point _(at the airport, railway station...)_
**recogida de equipajes** baggage reclaim
recomendar to recommend
reconocer to recognize
recordar to remember
recorrido _m_ journey; route
**de largo recorrido** long-distance
recuerdo _m_ souvenir
recuperarse to recover _(from illness)_
red _f_ net
red inalámbrica _f_ wi-fi
redondo(a) round _(shape)_
reducción _f_ reduction
reducir to reduce
reembolsar to reimburse; to refund
reembolso _m_ refund
refresco _m_ refreshment; drink
refugio _m_ shelter; mountain hut
regadera _f_ watering can
regalo _m_ gift; present
régimen _m_ diet
región _f_ district; area; region
registrarse to register _(at hotel)_
regla _f_ period _(menstruation)_; ruler
  (for measuring)
reina _f_ queen
Reino Unido _m_ United Kingdom
reintegro _m_ withdrawal _(from bank account)_
reírse to laugh
rejilla _f_ rack _(luggage)_
relámpago _m_ lightning
rellenar to fill in
reloj _m_ clock; watch
remar to row _(boat)_
remitente _m/f_ sender
remolcar to tow
remolque _m_ tow rope; trailer

RENFE *f* Spanish National Railways
reparación *f* repair
reparar to repair
repetir to repeat
repollo *m* cabbage
representante *m/f* sales rep
reproductor de CD *m* CD player
reproductor de DVD *m* DVD player
reproductor MP3 *m* MP3 player
repuestos *mpl* spare parts
resaca *f* hangover
resbaladizo(a) slippery
resbalarse to slip
rescatar to rescue
reserva *f* booking(s); reservation
reservado(a) reserved
reservar to reserve; to book
resfriado *m* cold *(illness)*
residente *m/f* resident
resistente a resistant to
resistente al agua waterproof
resistente al calor resistant to heat
respirar to breathe
responder to answer; to reply
responsabilidad *f* responsibility
respuesta *f* answer
restaurante *m* restaurant
resto *m* the rest
retrasado(a) delayed
retraso *m* delay
sin retraso on schedule
retrato *m* portrait
retrovisor exterior *m* wing mirror
reumatismo *m* rheumatism
reunión *f* meeting
revelar to develop *(photos)*
reventón *m* blowout *(of tyre)*
revisar to check
revisión *f* car service; inspection
revisor(a) *m/f* ticket collector
revista *f* magazine
rey *m* king
rezar to pray
riada *f* flash flood
rico(a) rich *(person)*
rincón *m* corner
riñón *m* kidney
riñonera *f* bumbag

río *m* river
robar to steal
robo *m* robbery; theft
robot (de cocina) *m* food processor
rodaballo *m* turbot
rodeado(a) de surrounded by
rodilla *f* knee
rodillo *m* rolling pin
rojo(a) red
románico(a) Romanesque
romántico(a) romantic
romería *f* procession
romper to break; to tear
ron *m* rum
roncar to snore
ropa *f* clothes
ropa de cama bedclothes
ropa interior underwear
ropero *m* wardrobe
rosa *f* rose
rosa pink
rosado *m* rosé
roto(a) broken
rotonda *f* roundabout *(traffic)*
rotulador *m* felt-tip pen
rubeola *f* rubella; German measles
rubio(a) blond; fair haired
rueda *f* wheel
rueda de repuesto spare tyre
rueda pinchada flat tyre
ruido *m* noise
ruinas *fpl* ruins
ruta *f* route
ruta turística tourist route

S

S.A. *abbrev. for* **Sociedad Anónima**
sábado *m* Saturday
sábana *f* sheet *(bed)*
saber to know *(facts)*; to know how
sabor *m* taste; flavour
sacacorchos *m* corkscrew
sacar to take out *(of bag, etc)*
sacarina *f* saccharin
saco *m* sack
saco de dormir sleeping bag
sagrado(a) holy
sal *f* salt

sin sal unsalted
sala *f* hall; hospital ward
sala de chat chatroom
sala de conciertos concert hall
sala de embarque departure lounge
sala de espera waiting room
salado(a) savoury; salty
salario *m* wage
salchicha *f* sausage
saldo *m* balance *(of account)*; credit *(on mobile phone)*
saldos *mpl* sales
salida *f* exit/departure
salida de incendios fire exit
salida del sol sunrise
salir to go out; to come out
salmón *m* salmon
salmón ahumado smoked salmon
salsa *f* gravy; sauce; dressing
saltar to jump
salteado(a) sauté; sautéed
salud *f* health
¡salud! cheers!
salvar to save *(life)*
salvaslip *m* panty liner
salvavidas *m* lifebelt
salvia *f* sage *(herb)*
sandalias *fpl* sandals
sandía *f* watermelon
sangrar to bleed
sangría *f* sangria *(red wine and fruit punch)*
santo(a) saint; holy; saint's day
sarampión *m* measles
sarpullido *m* skin rash
sartén *f* frying pan
sastrería *f* tailor's
secado a mano *m* blow-dry
secador (de pelo) *m* hairdryer
secadora *f* dryer *(spin, tumble)*
secar to dry
seco(a) dry; dried *(fruit, beans)*
secretario(a) *m/f* secretary
seda *f* silk
seda dental dental floss
seguida: en seguida straight away
seguido(a) continuous
todo seguido straight on
seguir to continue; to follow

según according to
segundo *m* second *(time)*
segundo(a) second
de segunda mano secondhand
seguramente probably
seguridad *f* reliability; safety; security
seguro *m* insurance
seguro del coche car insurance
seguro de vida life insurance
seguro médico medical insurance
seguro(a) safe; certain
sello *m* stamp *(postage)*
semáforo *m* traffic lights
semana *f* week
Semana Santa Holy Week; Easter
semanal weekly
semilla *f* seed; pip
señal *f* sign; signal; road sign
no hay señal there's no signal
sencillo(a) simple; single *(ticket)*
señor *m* gentleman
Señor (Sr.) Mr; Sir
señora *f* lady
Señora (Sra.) Mrs; Ms; Madam
señorita *f* Miss
Señorita (Srta.)... Miss...
sentarse to sit
sentir to feel
separado(a) separated
septentrional northern
septiembre *m* September
sequía *f* drought
ser to be
seropositivo(a) HIV positive
serpiente *f* snake
servicio *m* service; service charge
área de servicios service area
servicio incluido service included
servicios toilets
servicios de urgencia emergency services
servilleta *f* serviette; napkin
servir to serve
sesión *f* performance; screening
sesión de noche late night performance
sesión de tarde eve performance
sesión numerada seats bookable in advance
sesos *mpl* brains

seta *f* mushroom
sexo *m* sex; gender
si if
sí yes
sida *m* AIDS
sidra *f* cider
siempre always
siento: lo siento I'm sorry
sierra *f* mountain range; saw
siga follow
siga adelante carry on
siga recto keep straight on
siglo *m* century
siguiente following; next
silencio *m* silence
silla *f* chair; seat
silla de paseo pushchair
silla de ruedas wheelchair
sillón *m* armchair
simpático(a) nice; kind
sin without
sin plomo unleaded
síndrome (de) Down *m* Down's
 syndrome
síntoma *m* symptom
sírvase vd./ud. mismo serve/
 help yourself
sistema *m* system
sistema de navegación por satélite
 satellite navigation system
sitio *m* place; space; position; site
slip *m* pants; briefs
SMS *m* SMS message
sobre on; upon; about; on top of
sobre *m* envelope
sobre acolchado padded envelope
sobrecarga *f* surcharge
sobrecargar to overload
sobredosis *f* overdose
sobrino(a) *m/f* nephew/niece
sobrio(a) sober
sociedad *f* society
Sociedad Anónima Ltd; plc
socio(a) *m/f* member; partner
socorrista *m/f* lifeguard
¡socorro! help!
soja *f* soya
sol *m* sun; sunshine

solamente only
soldado *m/f* soldier
solicitar to request
solitario *m* patience *(card game)*
solo(a) alone; lonely
sólo only
solomillo *m* sirloin
soltero(a) *m/f* bachelor/spinster
soltero(a) single *(unmarried)*
sombra *f* shade; shadow
sombra de ojos eye shadow
sombrero *m* hat
sombrilla *f* sunshade; parasol
somnífero *m* sleeping pill
sonido *m* sound
sonreír to smile
sonrisa *f* smile
sopa *f* soup
sordo(a) deaf
sorpresa *f* surprise
sótano *m* basement
soya *f* soya
spam *m* spam *(email)*
squash *m* squash *(game)*
Sr. *abbrev. for* **señor**
Sra. *abbrev. for* **señora**
Srta. *abbrev. for* **señorita**
stop *m* stop *(sign)*
su his/her/its/their/your
suavizante *m* hair conditioner;
 fabric softener
submarinismo *m* scuba diving
subterráneo(a) underground
subtítulo *m* subtitle
sucio(a) dirty
sucursal *f* branch *(of bank, etc)*
sudadera *f* sweatshirt
sudar to sweat
suegro(a) *m/f* father/mother-in-law
suela *f* sole *(of foot, shoe)*
sueldo *m* wage
suelo *m* soil; ground; floor
suelto *m* loose change *(money)*
sueño *m* dream
suerte *f* luck
¡(buena) suerte! good luck!
Suiza *f* Switzerland
suizo(a) Swiss

sujetador *m* bra
superior higher
supermercado *m* supermarket
supositorio *m* suppository
sur *m* south
surfing *m* surfing
surtidor *m* petrol pump
suspension *f* suspension (of car)
sus his/her/their/your

T

tabaco *m* tobacco; cigarettes
tabla *f* board
tabla de cortar chopping board
tabla de planchar ironing board
tabla de surf surf board
tablao (flamenco) *m* Flamenco show
tableta *f* tablet; bar (chocolate)
taco *m* stuffed tortilla
tacón *m* heel (shoe)
taladradora *f* drill (tool)
talco *m* talc
TALGO *m* Intercity express train
talla *f* size
tallarines *mpl* noodles; tagliatelle
taller *m* garage (for repairs)
talón *m* heel; counterfoil; stub
talón bancario cheque
talonario *m* cheque book
también as well; also; too
tampoco neither
tampones *mpl* tampons
tapa *f* lid
tapas *fpl* appetizers; snacks
tapón *m* cap (of bottle etc)
taquilla *f* ticket office
tarde *f* evening; afternoon
de la tarde pm
tarde late
tarifa *f* price; rate
tarifa baja cheap rate
tarifa máxima peak rate
tarjeta *f* card
tarjeta de crédito credit card
tarjéta de débito debit card
tarjeta de embarque boarding pass
tarjeta de memoria memory stick
tarjeta de visita business card

tarjeta llave keycard
tarjeta magnética swipecard
tarjeta SIM SIM card
tarjeta telefónica phonecard
tarro *m* jar; pot
tarta *f* cake; tart
tasca *f* bar; cheap restaurant
taxista *m/f* taxi driver
taza *f* cup
tazón *m* bowl (for soup, etc)
té *m* tea
teatro *m* theatre
techo *m* ceiling
techo solar sunroof
tejado *m* roof
tela *f* material; fabric
tela impermeable groundsheet
telaraña *f* web (spider)
teleférico *m* cablecar
telefonear to phone
telefonista *m/f* telephonist
teléfono *m* phone
teléfono fijo landline phone
teléfono inalámbrico cordless phone
teléfono "manos libres" hands free
   phone
teléfono móvil mobile phone
teléfono público payphone
telegrama *m* telegram
telesilla *m* ski lift; chairlift
telesquí *m* ski lift
televisión *f* television
televisor *m* television set
télex *m* telex
temperatura *f* temperature
templo *m* temple
temporada *f* season
temporada alta/baja high/low season
temporal *m* storm
temporizador *m* timer (on cooker)
temprano(a) early
tendedero *m* clothes line
tenedor *m* fork (for eating)
tener to have
tener fiebre to have a temperature
tener miedo de to be afraid of
tener morriña to be homesick
tener "overbooking" to be overbooked

tener que to have to
tener razón to be right
tener suerte to be lucky
tentempié *m* snack
tequila *m* tequila
tercero(a) third
terciopelo *m* velvet
termo *m* flask (thermos)
termómetro *m* thermometer
ternera *f* veal
terraza *f* terrace; balcony
terremoto *m* earthquake
terreno *m* land
terrorista *m/f* terrorist
testículos *mpl* testicles
tetera *f* teapot
tetina *f* teat (on baby's bottle)
ti you (sing. with friends)
tía *f* aunt
tiempo *m* time; weather
tienda *f* store; shop; tent
tienda de ropa clothes shop
tierra *f* earth
tijeras *fpl* scissors
timbre *m* doorbell; official stamp
tímido(a) shy
timón *m* rudder
tinta *f* ink
tinte *m* dye
tinte de pelo hair dye
tinto *m* red wine
tintorería *f* dry-cleaner's
tío *m* uncle
típico(a) typical
tipo *m* sort
tipo de cambio exchange rate
tique *m* ticket
tirador *m* handle
tirar to throw (away); to pull
para tirar disposable
tire pull
tirita® *f* (sticking) plaster
toalla *f* towel
tobillo *m* ankle
tocar to touch; to play (instrument)
no tocar do not touch
tocino *m* bacon; fat
todo(a) all

todo everything
todo el mundo everyone
todo incluido (TI) all inclusive
toldo awning
tomar to take; to have (food/drink)
tomar el aire/fresco to get some fresh air
tomar el sol to sunbathe
tomate *m* tomato
tomillo *m* thyme
tónica *f* tonic water
tono *m* tone
tono de llamada ringing tone
tono de marcado/marcar dialling tone
no hay tono there's no signal
tonto(a) stupid
toquen: no toquen/tocar do not touch
torcedura *f* sprain
torero *m* bullfighter
tormenta *f* thunderstorm
tornillo *m* screw
toro *m* bull
torre *f* tower
torta *f* cake
tortilla *f* omelette
tos *f* cough
toser to cough
tostada *f* toast
trabajar to work (person)
trabajo *m* work
tradicional traditional
traducción *f* translation
traducir to translate
traer to fetch; to bring
tráfico *m* traffic
tragar to swallow
traje *m* suit; outfit
traje de baño swimsuit
traje de bucear wetsuit
traje de etiqueta evening dress (man's)
traje de noche evening dress (woman's)
trampolín *m* diving board
tranquilo(a) calm; quiet
tranquilizante *m* tranquilliser
transbordador *m* car ferry
transbordo *m* transfer
transgénico(a) genetically modified
tranvía *m* tram; short-distance train
trapo *m* cloth (for cleaning, etc)

tras after; behind
trastorno estomacal *m* stomach upset
tratar con cuidado handle with care
travesía *f* crossing
tren *m* train
triángulo señalizador *m* warning triangle
triste sad
trozo *m* piece
trucha *f* trout
trueno *m* thunder
trufa *f* truffle
tú you *(singular with friends)*
tu your *(singular with friends)*
tubería *f* pipe *(drain, etc)*
tubo de escape *m* exhaust pipe
tumbarse to lie down
tumbona *f* deckchair
túnel *m* tunnel
turista *m/f* tourist
turístico(a) tourist
turno *m* turn
espere su turno wait your turn
turrón *m* nougat
TVE *abbrev. for* **Televisión Española**

U

Ud(s). *abbrev. for* **usted(es)**
úlcera *f* ulcer *(stomach)*
últimamente lately
último(a) last
ultracongelador *m* deep freeze
ultracongelado deep-frozen
ultramarinos *m* grocery shop
un(a) a/an
uña *f* nail *(finger, toe)*
ungüento *m* ointment
únicamente only
unidad *f* unit
Unión Europea *f* European Union
universidad *f* university
unos(as) some
urgencias *fpl* casualty department
urgente urgent; express
usar to use
uso *m* use; custom
uso externo/tópico for external use only
usted you *(polite singular)*

ustedes you *(polite plural)*
usuario *(nombre de)* username
útil useful
utilizar to use
uva *f* grape
uvas verdes/negras green/black grapes
UVI/UCI *f* intensive care unit

V

vaca *f* cow
vacaciones *fpl* holiday
vacaciones de verano summer holidays
vacío(a) empty
vacuna *f* vaccination
vagina *f* vagina
vagón *m* railway carriage
vale OK
vale... it's worth...
vale *m* token; voucher
válido(a) valid *(ticket, licence, etc)*
valle *m* valley
valor *m* value
válvula *f* valve
vapor *m* steam
al vapor steamed
vaqueros *mpl* jeans
variado(a) assorted; mixed
varios(as) several
vasco(a) Basque
vaso *m* glass *(for drinking)*
Vd(s). *abbrev. for* **usted(es)** *(less common)*
veces *fpl* times
vecino(a) *m/f* neighbour
vegetariano(a) *m/f* vegetarian
vehículo *m* vehicle
vela *f* candle; sail; mailing
vellón *m* fleece
velocidad *f* speed
límite de velocidad speed limit
velocidad máxima speed limit
velocímetro *m* speedometer
vena *f* vein
venda *f* bandage
vendedor(a) *m/f* salesman/woman
vender to sell
se vende for sale
veneno *m* poison
venenoso(a) poisonous

venir to come
venta *f* sale; country inn
ventana *f* window
ventanilla *f* window *(in car, train)*
ventilador *m* fan *(electric)*
ver to see; to watch
verano *m* summer
verdad *f* truth
¿de verdad? really?
verdadero(a) true; genuine
verde green
verdulería *f* greengrocer's
verduras *fpl* vegetables
vereda *f* footpath *(in the country)*
verificar to check
versión *f* version
versión original original version
vespa® *f* motor scooter
vestido *m* dress
vestir de etiqueta formal dress
vestirse to get dressed
veterinario(a) *m/f* vet
vez *f* time
vía *f* track; rails; platform
por vía oral/bucal orally
viajar to travel
viaje *m* journey; trip
viaje de negocios business trip
viaje organizado package tour
viajero *m* traveller
víbora *f* adder; viper
vida *f* life
vídeo *m* video; video recorder
videocámara *f* camcorder
videojuego *m* video game
vidriera *f* stained-glass window
vidrio *m* glass *(substance)*
vieira *f* scallop
viejo(a) old
viento *m* wind
viernes *m* Friday
Viernes Santo Good Friday
viña *f* vineyard
vinagre *m* vinegar
vinagreta *f* vinaigrette *(dressing)*
vino *m* wine
vino blanco white wine
vino rosado rosé wine

vino seco dry wine
vino tinto red wine
violación *f* rape
violar to rape
violeta *f* violet *(flower)*
virgen blank
virus *m* virus
virus del sida, VIH HIV
visa *f* visa
visita *f* visit
visitar to visit
víspera *f* eve
vista *f* view
viudo(a) *m/f* widow/widower
vivir to live
V.O. (versión original) undubbed
  version (of film)
volante *m* steering wheel
volar to fly
volcán *m* volcano
voleibol *m* volleyball
voltaje *m* voltage
voltios *mpl* volts
volumen *m* volume
volver to come/go back; to return
vomitar to vomit
vosotros you *(plural with friends)*
voz *f* voice
vuelo *m* flight
vuelta *f* turn; return; change *(money)*
vuestro(a) your *(plural with friends)*

W

Walkman® *m* Walkman®
wáter *m* lavatory; toilet
whisky *m* whisky
WiFi *m* wi-fi
windsurf *m* windsurfing

Y

y and
yate *m* yacht
yerno *m* son-in-law
yo I; me
yogur *m* yoghurt
yogur azucarado sweet yogurt
yogur desnatado low-fat yogurt
yogur natural plain yoghurt

Z

zanahoria *f* carrot
zapatería *f* shoe shop
zapatillas *fpl* slippers
zapatillas de deporte trainers
zapato *m* shoe
zarzuela *f* Spanish light opera;
  casserole
zona *f* zone
zona azul controlled parking area
zona de descanso layby
zona restringida restricted area
zorro *m* fox
zumo *m* juice
zumo de arándanos cranberry juice

Further titles in Collins' phrasebook range
Collins Gem Phrasebook

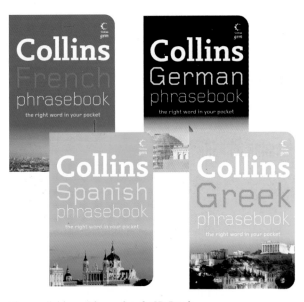

Also available as **Phrasebook CD Pack**

Other titles in the series

Afrikaans	Japanese	Russian
Arabic	Korean	Thai
Cantonese	Latin American	Turkish
Croatian	Spanish	Vietnamese
Czech	Mandarin	Xhosa
Dutch	Polish	Zulu
Italian	Portuguese	